Networks of Dissolution

NETWORKS *of* DISSOLUTION

Somalia Undone

•

ANNA SIMONS

WestviewPress
A Division of HarperCollins*Publishers*

Published in 1995 in the United States of America by Westview Press, Inc., 5500 Central Avenue, Boulder, Colorado 80301-2877, and in the United Kingdom by Westview Press, 12 Hid's Copse Road, Cumnor Hill, Oxford OX2 9JJ

Library of Congress Cataloging-in-Publication Data
Simons, Anna.
Networks of dissolution : Somalia undone / Anna Simons.
p. cm.
Includes bibliographical references and index.
ISBN 0-8133-2580-3 (HC) — ISBN 0-8133-2581-1 (PB)
1. Somalia—History—1960–1991. 2. Somalia—History—1991– 3. Somalia—Politics and government—1960– 4. Somalia—Social conditions—1960– 5. Clans—Somalia. I. Title.
DT407.S55 1995
967.7305—dc20 95-31508
CIP

The paper used in this publication meets the requirements of the American National Standard for Permanence of Paper for Printed Library Materials Z39.48-1984.

10 9 8 7 6 5 4 3 2 1

Contents

PART FIVE—FAMILY TO "FAMILY"

PART SIX—CONCLUSIONS

Acknowledgments

Funding for this research was provided by Harvard University and by the Joint Committee on African Studies of the Social Science Research Council and the American Council of Learned Societies with funds provided by the Rockefeller Foundation.

These are the people I would most like to thank: Sally Falk Moore and Leroy Vail for having taught me how, but not what, to think. For making this particular project possible, Tom Lodge, Jim Coates, and Dahir Abby. Steven Brandt was crucial to my getting a visa for Somalia and Paul Baxter first warned me that research in northern Kenya might not be possible. Paul Baxter also offered great support and guidance throughout the process and warm hospitality in Manchester.

At CRDP (Central Rangelands Development Project) Osman Sheik and Miriam Ghose continuously expedited my journey through Somali bureaucracies. Miriam especially made life much easier. Actually, it is impossible to adequately acknowledge the debt I owe everyone who congregated at CRDP. But for all the teas and meals, I must thank Abdulkadir and his wife, Fawzia, and for their patience with me: Ilkacaasi, Ambara, Bashir, Abshir, Said, Abdullahi, and others.

I am especially grateful to Farxan, his family, and friends for allowing me entry into their village and lives. Similarly, Mohamud, Ismail, and Sofia (all employed by official U.S. citizens) graciously suffered my continual questions, and Ahmed Yusuf Farah and Mohamed Hamud Sheekh at SOMAC (Somali Academy) always helped me pursue anthropology.

Veronica Culhane, Deirdre LaPin, Glenn Howze, and Jim Ellison offered moral and material support, as did Kerry Allen, Dave Scott, and Henry Williams. The late Bill Hargus was as generous an expatriate as I've ever met.

On leaving Somalia I spent six months at Ben Gurion University learning about camels from Dr. Reuven Yagil. He, his wife, Bracha, and Clara van Creveld made me feel more than at home. In London I. M. Lewis gave me critical advice at a critical moment.

I also owe a large debt to Parker Shipton, Lee Cassanelli, and two anonymous reviewers for their extensive comments on earlier drafts of this book. For her enthusiasm about a related piece of writing on Somalia, I thank Carolyn Nordstrom. I am grateful to Mary Powers for just listening.

I would be remiss if I did not acknowledge that my mother worried even more than usual during my stay in Somalia. Nor did it help her that my sister Rebecca tracked down and reported every story she could find in the aftermath of July 14th.

The one debt that I have lost the chance of ever repaying is to my father, who, for the first time ever, broke a promise to me midway through my fieldwork. He had promised he wouldn't get sick while I was away. Not only did he get sick, but worse, he succumbed to terminal cancer. To Howard Simons goes my undying thanks. None of my writing would be possible without him.

I met John Jordan in Mogadishu and he's been living with me and tolerating this project ever since. It hasn't been easy—especially knowing-but-not-really-knowing what the last few years have amounted to for Somalis.

Anna Simons

Acronyms

AC	*Africa Confidential*
ACR	*Africa Contemporary Record*
AD	*Africa Diary*
ARB	*Africa Research Bulletin*
BBC	British Broadcasting Corporation
CRDP	Central Rangelands Development Project
DFSS	Democratic Front for the Salvation of Somalia
EEC	European Economic Community
FAO	Food and Agricultural Organization of the United Nations
GTZ	Deutsche Gesellschaft für Technische Zusammenarbeit
IDA	International Development Association
IFAD	International Fund for Agricultural Development
IGADD	Inter-Governmental Authority on Drought and Development
IMF	International Monetary Fund
ION	*Indian Ocean Newsletter*
IPAL	Integrated Project in Arid Lands
LBI	Louis Berger International
NFD	Northern Frontier District
NGO	nongovernment organization
NRA	National Range Agency
NSS	National Security Service
OAU	Organization of African Unity
PVO	private voluntary organization
SNM	Somali National Movement
SOMAC	Somali Academy
SSDF	Somali Salvation Democratic Front
SUC	Somali Unity Congress
UAE	United Arab Emirates
UNESCO	United Nations Educational Scientific and Cultural Organization
UNHCR	United Nations High Commission for Refugees
USAID	United States Agency for International Development
USC	United Somali Congress
USOMC	United States Office for Military Cooperation
WFP	The World Food Program
WSLF	Western Somali Liberation Front

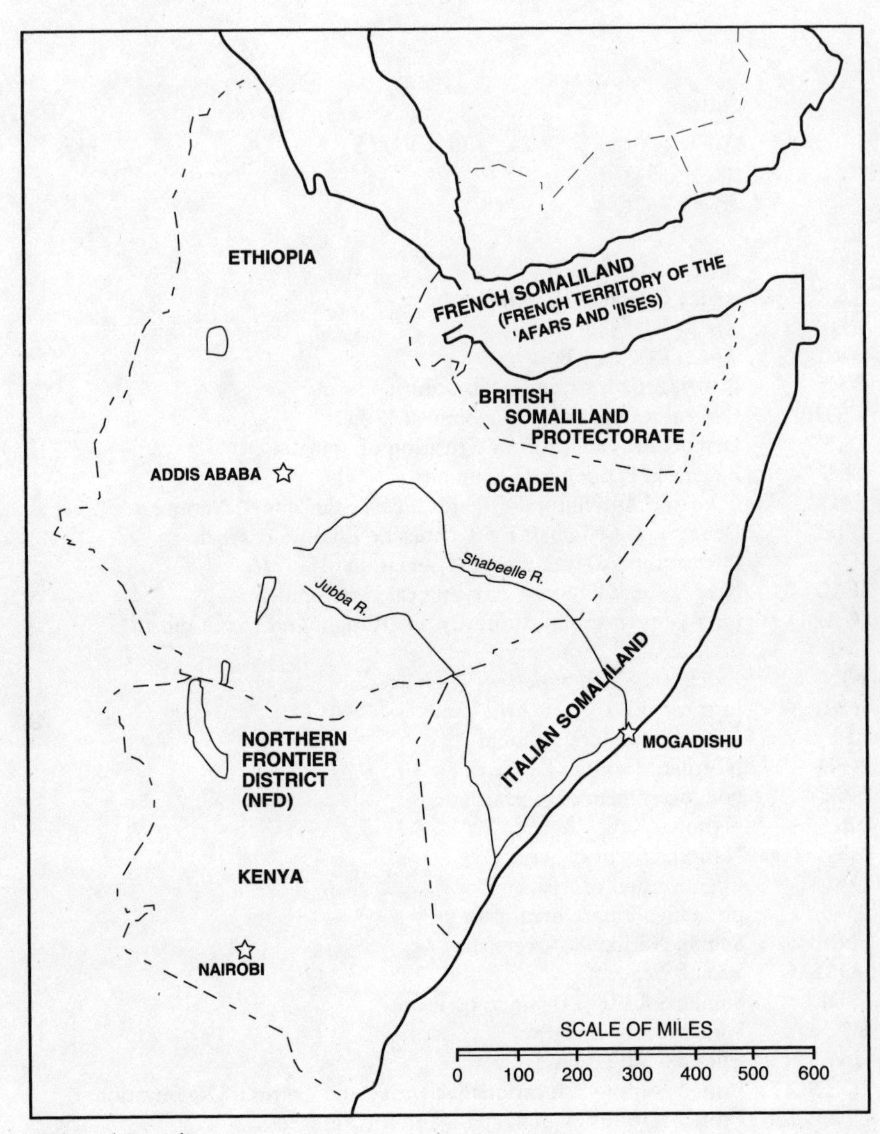

Colonial Somalia

PART ONE

Introductions

Introduction

The dissolution of Somalia has cleft the nation-state and disaggregated society. It has exposed the hollowness of nationalist rhetoric concerning the "imagined community" of one ethnicity, one culture, and one language—the definition of Somalia held up by Somalis and Somaliists alike to mark Somalia's unique place in the tribally fractured, culturally complicated landscape that is said to comprise the rest of Africa (Laitin and Samatar 1987). Consequently, Somalia's dissolution should rattle broader assumptions as well: about the content of nationalism, tribalism, and the state as defined and debated by academics, and as inhabited by individuals.

Before Somalia's dramatic emergence in 1992 as exemplar of anarchy, starvation, and famine, it was little known and hard to study. The government did not welcome journalists and it did not encourage visits by errant social scientists. Not only were there restrictions on what could be learned through conversation by any social scientist who did manage to work in the country but there were practical considerations as to where one could go and how safely. Such rules impinged on those who actually sought to learn about Somali society and also on those who remained appended to Somali society as well: the expatriates who had been sent to Somalia by their governments, aid agencies, or private nongovernmental organizations. For most of these, Somalia represented a "hardship" posting. Mogadishu, the capital, was hot, remote, and woefully underdeveloped, and the Somalis were generally felt to be difficult to deal with.

One reason that Somalis may have come across as so hard to deal with is that they were experiencing difficulties of their own. By 1989 (if not well before) the state was no longer working as many Somalis expected and would have wanted it to. It did not join them together patriotically, paternalistically, or even parenthetically. Therefore, how could Somalis have behaved in nationalistically predictable ways?

Certainly there is a great temptation to reach for analogies to help explain what has happened to Somalia and why it has disintegrated so violently. It may have been that Somalia finally became too stretched between demands radiating from the idealized supralocal (international) level downward and inward and from the local/historical (lineage) level upward and outward. Or perhaps the elasticity required to move between traditional and modern, precapitalist and capitalist, micro and macro, fluid and fixed finally turned into brittleness. Alternatively, to pretend that such dichotomies are themselves explanatory is to favor the ends of continua over the middle. It may be instead that the center of gravity shifted, or that the pivotal balance within the regime's leadership, among clans, between regions, and of socioeconomic interest groups itself gave way.

Indeed, the stance one takes depends on one's view, and there are two different sets of views that must be mentioned. The first set is intellectual. On one hand, Somaliists run a number of gamuts in terms of the manner in which they interpret their findings, either through structuralist or situational or marxist lenses (among others). On the other hand, the data on which interpretations rest come from different sources. As a geographical entity Somalia can be divided into four parts, as an ethnic entity it splits into six clan-families, and as an independent nation, Somalia joined two colonial creations into a union, which, as of May 1991, no longer exists. As a result, it is virtually impossible to consider a whole Somalia through time. Such a place has never existed for long enough; its history is swamped by the much lengthier, much more differentiated histories of its linked, but nonetheless separable, components. Consequently, where one has worked and among whom in Somalia are as much determining factors of stance as is one's ideological frame.

My own stance is at the brink of national dissolution from within the national capital—a delicate place. Dissolution is not yet a common topic for study, therefore using it for ideological argument seems premature. For now it seems more important just to grapple with describing the process. However, Somalia's dissolution is indissolubly linked to a cause or an effect (depending on one's view), which is already inescapably ideologically freighted, namely, tribalism. This proves much harder to avoid taking sides on, or issue with. However, I prefer thinking about solidarity rather than tribalism per se. Therefore my roots are in Émile Durkheim and I reject the current bromides (it is instrumental; it is primordial; it is imagined [Young 1993]), which I regard as incomplete. I tackle this issue in Chapter 12 and reconsider it in the Conclusion.

Meanwhile, how this book begins is how I believe dissolution begins—with misunderstanding. Expatriates in Somalia misunderstood Somalis, Somalis misunderstood one another, the West misperceived the "state" of Somalia, the regime in Somalia misunderstood its exact place in the world, and all sides mistook the extent to which they could or could not influence events and each other. And the compounded result of all of this misunderstanding has been singular disaster.

There are legions of reasons for "why Somalia, why now"—structural, historical, global, regional, and local. The list could, and doubtless will, continue to go on through time. I try to unravel as many threads as possible. Nevertheless, it seems unclear in which category misunderstanding best fits, even though it seems perfectly clear how it works.

If the Somali instance can be used as an example, then what leads to the creation and perpetuation of misunderstanding is not a lack of information but a surfeit of partial information. Hand in hand with this partial information is the conceit that the logic that informs one's view is accurate. Accuracy, meanwhile, is confirmed by testing this logic according to the information one gathers. But because this logic already informs one's view, of course *it* is what the information one gathers can't disconfirm. Logic also works to fill in gaps, so that no matter the quality of the information supplied, it is always made sense of. In being so powerful, logic often does a disservice, by privileging only partial or even wrong information. Worse, it can too easily make inaccurate information seem more than sufficient, particularly in hindsight.

In point of fact, the very notion that anarchy was finally on its way in Somalia convinced many expatriates that they had been right about Somalis all along. The subject of this book, then, is to determine to what extent they were, yet weren't, correct. Expatriates thus serve as our straw men for a much broader consideration of life for Somalis in Mogadishu on the cusp.

Fieldwork in Somalia was conducted between November 1988 and November 1989. My original intention was to live with camel nomads in the country's central rangelands and to study, among other things, their methods of domesticating livestock. However, due to conditions and then events beyond my control, this was not to be. Instead, I found myself confined to Mogadishu. I did spend some time in the town of Bulo Burte and one of its nearby villages. However, I was unable to return to either location because of general unrest. As a result, my research focus had to shift.

Throughout my stay in Somalia I was affiliated with the Central Rangelands Development Project (CRDP), a World Bank–funded project designed to halt desertification and improve production in the central rangelands (a land area comprising one-fifth of the country). Once it became apparent that neither I nor many of the CRDP employees would be able to return to the field, the CRDP offices provided a daily meeting point for all of us who continued to show up for nonexistent work. This afforded me an unparalleled opportunity to corner my Somali peers, since I knew talking to them would not be taking them away from any work-related duties. Indeed, things fell apart to such an extent that by July I was the only western expatriate still attached to CRDP in any way, although there were other expatriates working in the same building. This fact not only helped bring about my shift in focus but also changed people's interest in me.

Most of these people were young, male, university graduates—in their mid- to late 20s, largely unmarried, and, as young, unmarried recent students often tend to be, idealistic. Many had lived nomadic childhoods; now they were living in the capital. Some came from families well-off enough for them to not have to rely solely on civil servant salaries. In general, these tended to be the ideal citizens to not only believe but be perfectly positioned to try to practice nationalism. All through their student lives, and now in the mixed workplace, they felt they had been able to succeed without having to pay attention to clannism or clan affiliations; thus, even to themselves they represented the potential of meritocracy. However, Somalia was more and more obviously *not* a meritocracy.

In no small part this was perhaps the greatest frustration I witnessed on the part of these members of this young and educated generation of Somalis. The young civil servants I knew fiercely believed in what they had been taught in school: the value of nationalism, the merit of honest work, and the evils of nepotism. This contrasted sharply with what they saw taking place around them on a daily basis. And it was only once they themselves and their families began to suffer—from overdue salaries, rising prices, the delay of the project (and the stifling of realistic expectations for fellowships or assistance)—that they found themselves explicitly falling back on the networks they already knew how to use, and had used, although they had never had to regard these in a tribal or clannist light before.

It was the corrosive effects of this falling-back that they denounced, and as a result they condemned themselves perhaps even more harshly than they had previously condemned their elders. They recognized what they were having to succumb to and they rightfully feared what succumbing might do.

So that I could determine how some of those elders were viewing the present, one friend from CRDP provided me entrée to his "village," a neighborhood in Mogadishu adjacent to the central prison. However, entrée did not mean I could visit there alone. Rather, it simply meant that he was able to find women and men who, as long as he was there, were willing to talk with me about their lives.

I came to know and visit Somalis in other locales as well—tailors and their customers, local restaurateurs, watchmen, and others in the neighborhoods in which I lived. In all I collected life history material from sixty individuals. Interviews were conducted in Somali and English and were rarely dyadic. Not only did I generally have a friend to assist me with the language but friends or family members of the interviewees often listened in and occasionally interjected corrections or opinions.

However, despite our best attempts—mine and those of people willing to talk—the situation in Mogadishu was not particularly conducive to attempting classical ethnography. Rather, there were constraints long before the "trouble" started.

Language, as in most places, was the first and most difficult obstacle. Up until 1990 no Somali-English dictionary was available. Grammar books were either in Italian or dated back to the British colonial period. Newer books, written either for the Peace Corps or by the Mennonites concentrated on simple conversation and nothing more detailed. Thus, the only solution to trying to learn Somali was to hire a private teacher, which was relatively easy to do. The true obstacle to learning Somali well was the oft-repeated expatriate warning that if I learned Somali too quickly or too proficiently I would find myself with a one-way ticket out of the country. People knew of cases in which this had happened. Indeed, the one anthropologist who had worked for CRDP had been declared persona non grata and he apparently spoke fluent Somali, which he had learned in a mind-bogglingly short period of time. As a result, I was always careful who I said what to, and, perhaps fortunately, Somali is difficult to learn proficiently very quickly. There was, however, no difficulty in learning which topics of conversation to ignore in order to avoid appearing too clever about the lay of the land. It was illegal to discuss anything about tribe or clan and anything critical of the government was even more obviously better left unsaid. This did not mean that I did not hear various things, but I did not elicit them. In fact, often when people began to tell me about their tribe or clan I would kid them into stopping—never knowing who was baiting me and who was not—since a corollary paranoia was the widespread expatriate assumption that everyone worked for the National Security Service or NSS (the secret police).

I should also note that once I thought my ability to understand Somali was good enough to at least be able to decipher the topic of a conversation, I was often mistaken, not because I did not understand the terms being used but because they were euphemisms used purposely to throw off eavesdroppers. Consequently, perhaps due to the ease with which people could keep me in the dark, no Somali ever discouraged me from learning Somali. That remained strictly an expatriate duty. Instead, Somalis always encouraged me to learn even if I was not encouraged to always ferret out the meanings that I was, so obviously, missing.

Because of the strictly apolitical nature of what I was allowed to take verbal stabs at, my quest for knowledge was automatically constrained. However, Somalis were no less constrained in how openly and with whom they could discuss matters of a political nature, and the fact that these constraints operated on them as well as me led me to understand *that* situation, even if I could not know others.

All too clearly I could witness and see growing frustration among my friends and acquaintances even if I could not directly parse its political roots. As a result, I believe I am able to plumb for a certain depth of understanding in this work even if I cannot always reveal specific knowledge.

This is also the case in my consideration of U.S. (as well as other English-speaking people's) attitudes.

Expatriates made it clear to everyone that they were frustrated, even if they could not really say why—whether to themselves (they no longer believed in development work at all) or to one another (since, although racist views did emerge, they could never be voiced too publicly). And although I would have been much freer to ask fellow English-speakers much more pointed questions than I could ask Somalis I am not sure their responses would have been honest. As it was, I believe I was suspect; no one knew quite what to make of me since I, clearly, had a different interest in Somalis, and having any interest, let alone empathy, was unusual. Indeed, as I often tried to explain to other U.S. citizens, part of the reason why I could take such a different view was that my aim was not to goad Somalis into working, but rather to take advantage of their not working; I was happy to have them talk with me and went out of my way to talk with them. This was clearly antithetical to the aims of most expatriates. Nevertheless, because I was white, from the United States, and marginal, as long as I behaved within innocuous limits I could observe, even if it was advisable that I not fully participate in U.S. expatriate life. Full participation was also difficult because of the rigid social castes that existed within the U.S. community. Not only was I an "unofficial American," which denied me a host of privileges "official Americans" received, but the official company I did keep was low-echelon: servicemen and USAID (United States Agency for International Development) contract workers. Thus, with most expatriates I generally tried to keep my mouth shut and my ears open—the very method that could not work with Somalis.

Because my access in both communities had as much to do with my ambiguous position as it did with the political atmosphere in the country, I had a foot in both camps but no real role in either. This afforded me a certain measure of latitude, which made up for Somalia's host of constraints. Indeed, it was the dynamics of frustration in both camps that the givens in Somalia (at the time of my visit) leave me to tentatively explore.

The third element—beyond the frustrations of Somali and expatriate lives—that imposed itself upon my field of vision and shaped the year was the "fact" of July 14, 1989. On that particular Friday government troops opened fire as worshipers, whom they regarded (or were ordered to regard) as demonstrators, left the city's main mosques. Hundreds, possibly thousands, of people were killed and further violence occurred on the days that followed. This had a searing effect, not only on the local population but on the donor community as well. It placed Mogadishu on a cusp: either things would get so bad that the place and populace would burst out of this temporary blister or people would become inured and callow—as has happened in so many other metropolises in the world.

No small occurrence at all, July 14 brought violence to Mogadishu, a city that could have been described as sleepy when I first arrived. By the time I left it was sleepless for far too many. Chaos was beginning to roost—not only in people's minds but in the city's streets.

ROAD MAP

There are at least two different ways to read the results of July 14 and this book.

I have tried to build a picture of Somalia falling apart by shuttling back and forth between micro and macro frames, historical and everyday practices, expatriate and Somali experiences. In Part 1 Somalis are described as the expatriates regarded them: opportunists incapable of a functioning state. Part 2 explores how this state came about, what role westerners themselves played, and what their effects have been. In Part 3 Somali-non-Somali interactions are examined in greater detail, with July 14th presented as a pivotal point in the chronology of dissolution. Part 4 sets the context for how life was lived in Mogadishu, both before and after July 14. Part 5 then reveals some of the ways in which a number of practices and institutions (relating to marriage, kinship, and connectedness) were both changing and changed by the state into which Somalia was dissolving. Finally, in the Conclusion (Part 6) I return to the question of Somalia as a state and Somalis as a nation—and to the accuracy or inaccuracy of the expatriate stance.

But this book does not have to be read according to this particular structure. One of my main points is that there may not be quite so much sequence to dissolution as we assume. A different reading would find greater congruities between Parts 1 and 6, where I describe how Somalis have been framed, how Somalia has been thought about and treated by others, and what outside interventions (including those by expatriates in Somalia) have led to. Alternatively, the Introduction, Part 4, and the Conclusion offer thoughts about tribalism, nationalism, and the broader issues Somalia raises concerning these.

Parts 2 and 3 can stand together because they specifically describe how dissolution occurred and offer a history that, although I acknowledge may only be partial at this point, could reveal in its very partiality the fractured way in which dissolution actually occurs. One caveat concerning this section is that although understanding Somalia's history is critical to understanding Somalis, Chapter 6 is unusually dense. I include it because I consider it illustrative, suggestive, and of potential value to Somaliists, but by design it does not have to be read.

Finally, the ethnographic present during 1988–1989 is split between expatriates in Part 1 and Somalis in Part 5.

My intent is for theory to inform the whole work; however, given the complicated nature of trying to describe, explain, question, and explore dissolution there is a wide range of material to cover. Consequently, I have attempted to blend together two types of investigation: results of fieldwork in Somalia and research of the relevant literature.

The literature on Somalia is often conflictual, scattershot, and spotty. If there are not enough specific footnotes it is because I attempted to make sense of the whole out of many disparate parts. Also, just as anthropologists can never precisely reconstruct their coming to understanding I cannot always disentangle how others' understandings and misunderstandings have separately (or sequentially) informed my view.

However, I do not want to suggest I am being only interpretive. As with all stabs at science I believe someone else using the same tools could duplicate my results. Certainly, the written works are available and listed for scrutiny. Less fortunately, though, the Somalis I quote cannot be so easily traced. I promised everyone I spoke with that I would change their names, and I have. But that is hardly the stumbling block. Events are. I am afraid that the anonymity I grant only flies in the face of the far worse anonymity recent chaos has imposed.

I do not know where most of the Somalis in these pages currently are, or how many of them still live, still hope, still despair. But it is for them that misunderstandings have been most costly. And it is for everyone that they should be undone.

• 1 •

Mogadishu: The Hardship Post

Whereas the vast majority of Mogadishu's Somali residents came to Mogadishu either from the bush or another (lesser) town, or were born in the capital, virtually all expatriates arrived in Mogadishu relatively effortlessly, by air. Inevitably, no matter where expatriates had previously been posted, what their country of origin was, or how they had been forewarned, Mogadishu was immediately discernible to them as a hardship post. Too little was Western, familiar, or comfortable, either culturally or materially, although the material setting was initially most obvious.

To begin with, streets were unsigned and driving was a free-for-all. Municipal electricity was erratic and unpredictable, telephone service ineffectual, and local news unavailable.

For most expatriates little was familiar about Somalia. It was not particularly African; it was rare to be accosted on the streets solely because one was white. Children did not follow westerners asking for money or "bonbons" or "bics." Instead, they were far more likely to throw stones and to jeer what non-Somali speakers took to be insults. If children did approach without rocks in their hands, it was usually to ask for baksheesh.

But certain practices aside, Somalia seemed no more Middle Eastern than African. There were no glaring amalgams of West and East. Without an infusion of petrodollars there had been no giant construction projects; there was no blatant materialism. There were few of the juxtaposed incongruities one reads about in descriptions of the Persian Gulf. For instance, the presidential palace was behind walls well-guarded by an elite branch of the military (commonly referred to as Red Hats because of their oversized berets). But there was nothing outside the walls to suggest that the inside was ostentatious or extravagant. In fact, one of the jokes among expatriates was that as soon as the $32 million American embassy compound was complete the Americans would be asked to leave Somalia and the president would move his entourage there.[1]

As for Somali enterprises geared to expatriates, only a few hotels accommodated most Western visitors and short-term contract workers. However, these same hotels were likely to be just as crowded with visiting Arabs and Somali businessmen—not just people on their way in or out of the expatriate community. The Maka was one of the more popular and most centrally located of these.[2] As an important meeting place it boasted two long-distance telephone lines, a telex machine, and air-conditioning. However, perhaps the most telling mark of Mogadishu's place in the world was that there was no hotel gift shop and no Somali souvenirs for sale in the lobby save one small rack of postcards.

Tourist art, despite the lack of tourism or a tourist industry, could be had in Mogadishu though—some of it Somali in origin but much of it imported. A considerable proportion of this stock was sold in small shops jumbled along the Lido, where store fronts abutted various discos and clubs. However, expatriates did not have to visit the Lido, because dealers would visit them at home. This was probably the safest way to exchange money on the black market and it is also how ivory, especially, could be surreptitiously bought then shipped stateside via the diplomatic pouch.

With money purchased on the black market any item was a good buy in Mogadishu and often expatriates prided themselves on what a deal they were getting compared to what they would have had to pay in Kenya or elsewhere. However, this was small compensation in many people's eyes for having to spend time in Somalia at all; one could easily purchase the best stuff Somalia could offer within a matter of days. Nor did months increase anyone's appreciation for either the art or the culture the art came from.

Ironically, whatever people did buy was embedded in Somali culture, whether it was a tiger's eye necklace pieced together in Thailand or amber formerly worn by a Somali pastoralist. This is because, despite its catering to westerners and Somalis with Western vices (i.e., drinking), the Lido was still of a piece with the rest of older, downtown Mogadishu—crumbling stucco, pastel walls—while just past the storefronts and bars was the ocean, with simple wooden and fiberglass fishing boats riding the waves and Somali boys swimming regardless of sharks and unmindful of those sipping beer, watching them.

Overall, from virtually any spot in Mogadishu, it would have appeared that the postcolonial West had had little stylistic impact on the city. Clearly many Somalis owned VCRs and cameras and other imported, luxury goods, since video stores rivaled pharmacies and tailors for shop space. However, these electronics were within people's homes. On the streets, and as far as most expatriates would be able to tell, there were no sure signs that any significant percentage of the population was seeking a Western makeover. Perhaps this was simply a matter of finances. Nevertheless, as soon as most Somali men left their offices for the day they shed pants for *mawiss* [traditional Somali dress], and despite interest in Tracy Chapman and Michael Jackson, Somali music was inarguably louder, more common, and certainly more noticeable to westerners.

From the expatriate perspective, then, Mogadishu was not only *not* cosmopolitan, it could not even be called provincial. It was not even that open or exciting. Instead, to many people, it was a marginally exotic, definitively alien (and alienating) backwater. Because Mogadishu was never "home" to the overwhelming majority of expatriates, it was far too easy, given the construction of their lives and days, for them to forget that it was home to Somalis, and in fact, was probably the finest town most could hope to ever see.

In many ways Moagadishu can perhaps best be described as a city of walls, from police barriers on the outskirts of town, where the police and soldiers were armed, to compound walls surrounding all elite homes within the city, thus hiding the Somali elite (and those Somalis expatriates might have had most in common with) from expatriate view. The Somali language, for most expatriates, was another barrier preventing the free flow of goodwill. Few expatriates made the attempt to learn anything more than "kitchen" Somali. The fact that Somalis often addressed one another in the imperative also made it particularly convenient that the expatriates happened to learn only the gruffest of commands.

Islam, too, presented walls. Mosques were off-limits, both practically and psychologically speaking to non-Muslims. Few expatriates knew more about Islam than that it was an "Arab" religion that caused people to bang their heads on the floor five times a day; that Muslims could have more than one wife; and that women were second-class citizens and often cloistered (although this was patently not the case in Somalia). There was little curiosity about what the religion actually did dictate or about what the Koran might say. It was acknowledged that—in part due to Islam—it was not really possible to socialize with Muslims, since they were forbidden to drink alcohol, *the* social pastime of expatriates. Hence, Islam was not only blamed for the lack of Somalis' sociability toward expatriates, it was also thought to set westerners apart and circumscribe them as infidels as far as Somalis were concerned.[3]

This was particularly clear whenever expatriates discussed the meaning of the word *gaal,* which is how westerners heard themselves being tagged and described.

Gaal, in its uses, is similar to the words *mzungu* in East Africa and *hawaja* in the Sudan. Whatever it means literally—"non-Muslim, infidel; European; cruel person" (Luling 1987)—it was used as an identifier especially by children to alert one another. They used the term because they did not otherwise know how to talk about or address the white person (although at least some children seemed aware that *gaal* actually did gall

Westerners). Otherwise, *gaal* was used by adults as a shorthand descriptive. Most often it was not meant by Somalis the way expatriates understood it. Because expatriates did not hear the terms Somalis used to describe or identify one another (which were often just as impersonal and sometimes insulting), they drew conclusions about the Somalis' disdain for their religion (and thus, their very being) from the fact that this word, which they translated as "infidel," was used. They did not listen to how it was used.

In part, then, due to the dynamics set up by the impenetrable Somali language and the not-to-be-penetrated Muslim religion, it was exceedingly easy for expatriates to accept the traditional outsiders' stereotype of Somalis as arrogant xenophobes. Grounded in the history of traveler accounts as well as in the eternal romanticization of proud nomads eking out their existence in a pitiless environment, there was still enough "evidence" in present-day Mogadishu to perpetuate this view of Somali aloofness. After all, Somalis spoke in commands, were always arguing with one another, and were fueled by Islam, which gave them the power of their convictions—that others were not as worthy. Thus, they even sounded as though they believed themselves to be superior.

Again, despite their consumption of Western goods, such as VCRs, televisions, and other luxury electronic items, Somalis certainly did not appear to visibly admire the West either. Not only were Somali styles of dress the preferred fashion after hours but there were relatively few indications of just how many Somalis had traveled West: Few restaurants catered to Western tastes (there was a grand total of six in 1988–1989) although beauty parlors and boutiques did sell Western styles, but surreptitiously. Thus, without the obvious signs of, or bows to, westernizing influence it was all too easy for westerners to assume that Somalis did not aspire to their same world, or share their same developmental goals.

For many reasons, then, it became natural for expatriates to manage to ignore Somalis as individuals. Most expatriates, no matter what their nationality—U.S., British, German, Finnish—were living a "white" existence anyway, and it was this existence that attracted supplicants—a further cause for alienation.[4]

Most westerners were treated as sources of giving by many of the Somalis with whom they came into contact. Indeed, this is something that westerners were quick to recognize and to identify as one of the culture traits that they found most difficult and dislikable about Somalis. That Somalis' solicitations were rooted not only in westerners' relative wealth but also in a Somali matrix of what Somalis asked or demanded of one another is something few outsiders considered. Rather, expatriates tended to take these demands personally and to be as offended by them as they would have been had they been asked by mere acquaintances for money or goods at home.

Money, in almost every regard, was *the* major sticking point for expatriates when it came to Somalis. Corollary to the expatriate view that Somalis did not know how to handle money properly (which explained why they were always soliciting it) was the universal belief among expatriates that Somalis lacked the ability to maintain anything—roads, equipment, offices, projects, or, essentially, themselves. This lack of maintenance was epitomized by the phrase *inshallah,* which, to most expatriates, stood for and summarized Somali laziness, irresponsibility, and lack of vision. Not only did expatriates tend to interpret *inshallah* literally to mean, "if Allah wills" or "if Allah says" (which is also how Somalis translated it into English for non-Arabic speakers) but they also often understood it to mean something like mañana.

It was common to regard *inshallah* as an all-purpose excuse used consciously and willfully by all Somalis. Many expatriates disregarded the fact that there were always extenuating circumstances that were beyond the control of any given individual, which is what, in large part, *inshallah* was meant to acknowledge by many Somalis who used it as a closure in conversation. Expatriates thought that Somalis either actually believed Allah would intercede and provide—a sentiment expatriates could easily scoff at—or that they knew in advance they would not follow through on a promise and, therefore, voiced *inshallah* as a preemptive excuse.

Not only was this "out" not considered honorable by expatriates, it was openly mocked. People made fun of what they regarded to be a blatantly ill-intentioned Somali (or Muslim) penchant for using Allah as a pretext for relying on something—anything—other than themselves.

Self-reliance, then, in at least three senses was at the root of what expatriates believed Somalis were missing. First, they would not fix anything themselves because someone else was always there to help them (i.e., expatriates). Second, Somalis could not manage anything properly because they did not have the capacity to (although it was also acknowledged that willful mismanagement in the form of corruption was what made some of them so rich). This fed directly into the third sense in which Somalis lacked self-reliance: They had no civic motivation or drive to better themselves in any but corrupt terms. Remarkably, few expatriates viewed nonmaintenance and mismanagement as clever strategies. Instead, they were thought to prove the worthlessness of not only aid to Somalia but of Somalis.

In sum, what fueled Somalis—as far as expatriates could detect—was unbridled opportunism (the flip side of which was nonproductive activity or laziness) and the attendant fatalistic attitude-cum-crutch that "Allah will provide." In their manifestations, these were precisely the two things that caused Somalia to *not* work for most westerners—the very two things that made daily life possible for many Somalis.

• 2 •

First Encounters

Actually, the dialectic of expatriate-Somali interactions was triple-stranded. Three streams conditioned English-speaking expatriates. First was the colonial legacy. Second was socialization of expatriates by expatriates. And third was daily practice—working in bureaucracy. It was here, where expatriates and Somalis actually met, that expatriate views not only crystallized but hardened.

THE WRITTEN LEGACY

Throughout Africa published accounts by the first European explorers and travelers have often colored the view of those to follow. Somalia has been no exception. Virtually all soldiers, administrators, and observers who wrote in English about colonial Somalia cited passages from Richard Burton's *First Footsteps in East Africa* (1894/1987) to affirm their own points of view and then subsequently built on accounts by one another.

According to these accounts, Somalis lie, cheat, and are quick to anger. They are proud, vain, and think highly of themselves.[1] At the same time, they will act courageously, faithfully, and are capable of enduring great hardship as well as intolerable pain—"Today composed, thoughtful, diligent, and resourceful; tomorrow excitable, thoughtless, lethargic, and foolish" (Drake-Brockman 1912, 105–106).

Many authors explain away these traits as a result of Somalia's harsh environment, holding pastoralism and nomadism accountable for the Somali character: "Were the accident or influence of environment entirely ignored, and this people judged by purely European standards, it might well be classed as a race of maniacs" (Rayne 1921a, 58). "If you were to take the average Englishman, deprive him of all his worldly possessions" and only give him what a Somali had, "there is little question that, should your victim still be alive a couple of years later, he would fully understand why the Somali seems so shamelessly avaricious to the well-nourished European who, comparatively speaking, has not to take thought for the morrow" (Jardine 1926/1969, 24–25). Regardless of explanations, impressions never really altered.

Noting at the outset of his journey that the Arabs called the Berbera coast *Bilad Wa Issi*—the "Land of Give Me Something" (1894/1987, 1:79)—Burton eventually found himself concurring with the Arabs: "Of course the Somal take every advantage of Europeans" (1894/1987, II:81). Nearly one hundred years later one expatriate who had never read Burton (or anyone else) would summarize Somalis thus, "Somalis come in four types: liars, cheats, thieves, and a combination of the three."

Still, there are some differences worth observing. First, despite overt and public chauvinism allowed under colonialism, colonial accounts reflect a genuine level of interest in Somalis and their culture. Clearly British civil servants felt themselves integral to commitments made by their government and took an interest in Somalis if for no other reason. By contrast, expatriates in the late 1980s filled a much more ambiguous role, harbored much more ambivalent (if not cynical) feelings toward their jobs, and were far more sanguine and unconcerned about the future of a country they knew they were merely passing through. Second, and connected to the lack of real interest in Somalia, was the lack of desire on the part of most latter-day expatriates to read about Somalis. Unlike colonial officials who assiduously read (and in their writing seem as if they were quoting from) their predecessors' accounts, few modern-day visitors seemed to have learned much of anything about Somalis before arriving and once in-country would have found almost no works available.

Ironically, one of the only books that could be obtained in Mogadishu in 1988 was *Sisters in Affliction: Circumcision and Infibulation of Women in Africa* (Dualeh Abdalla 1982). Despite the fact that this book was allegedly banned by the government, Somali vendors had numerous copies, which they always thrust at westerners who ventured through the central market. No other nonfiction works about Somalia were available—and *Sisters in Affliction* is probably among the least flattering. Although some expatriates were familiar with I. M. Lewis's work—principally because he once wrote an introductory guide to the Somali Democratic Government for USAID (1978/1981), of which some copies could still be found—and Gerald Hanley's memoir, *Warriors and Strangers,* had recently been reissued and was widely available in Nairobi, most expatriates tended instead to rely on other expatriates for knowledge, tips, and advice about Somalis.

ORAL TRADITIONS

In fact, such brokeraged information was all but inescapable. It was what greeted new arrivals to Somalia as soon as they landed at the airport and were met by longer-term residents. Consequently there was no real need or requirement for self-education; socializing among their own kind automatically clued newcomers in about work conditions and Somalis before they ever had to fully encounter either. Plus, the collective wisdom was well-honed by this point, and if not straight out of Burton, it at least represented one hundred years of similar sentiment.

It was this legacy, and the attendant routinization of misunderstanding, that lay at the heart of most expatriates' experiences with Somalis, coloring their vision and preconceiving for them their view.

Even before the first day of work, then, opportunity for independent judgment may have been lacking for new arrivals, although this was bound to be so for other reasons as well. First, many expatriates were professional expatriates. As professionals they knew that the easiest way to save themselves time and unnecessary effort on arrival in a new post was to learn the ropes from other expatriates. The logical expatriates to turn to were those they were replacing. However, people on their way out of Somalia were hardly objective. Rather, on the brink of leaving, the only nostalgia or fondness for Somalia many old hands evidenced was for the ways in which they had gotten over on "the system" (whether they considered this to be the home office, the official currency rate, or whichever government had paid their salary). Thus, having managed to derive some unforseen benefit from having been in Somalia they were usually only too happy to pass their methods of having done so on, since in the telling they could gain a second windfall—of prestige for having been clever and resourceful.

At the same time, people about to leave were also often jaded, eager to be gone, anxious about their next job (or lack of job), and no longer at all interested in either the fate of the project or task they had headed or shepherded, or Somalia itself. They were mentally already on their way to the next place, and Somalia could now be backdrop for "in-Mogadishu-we-didn't-have" stories, which would serve as future capital for self-promotion in other foreign settings. Newcomers, by definition, made the perfect audience on which to test such stories.

In addition to being swept along by such macho one-upmanship, which did revolve around local hardship, inefficiency, corruption, and absurdity, there were structural reasons why newcomers would be predisposed to disregard the uniqueness of the Somali situation and consequently mistake many Somali intentions. This is because expatriates came already plugged in to bureaucracies of one scale or another. Most worked for one—an embassy, an aid agency, a PVO (private voluntary organization), an NGO (nongovernment organization), or a "church." The contradictory, confusing, often ineffective nature of any bureaucracy—for someone who has already spent time working in one—would not be too difficult to figure out. That Somali bureaucracies would be doubly bad was only to be expected, since they represented a conflation of two inefficiencies: that inherent in bureaucracy itself and that implicit in anything located in the Third World. That Somalis were in charge in Somalia only meant Somalis were blameable.

BUREAUCRACY: CRDP

One such Somali bureaucracy, which was actually many bureaucracies coexisting, was the Central Rangelands Development Project (CRDP). It was Somali-run, World Bank–funded, and staffed by Somalis under the nominal direction of expatriates, many of whom had been hired by a variety of outside agencies.

Implemented in 1980, the $50 million project was funded by the International Development Association (IDA), the International Fund for Agricultural Development (IFAD), the United States Agency for International Development (USAID), the Deutsche Gesellschaft fur Technische Zusammaenarbeit (GTZ), the World Food Program (WFP), and the Government of Somalia.[2]

As written, CRDP's objectives were threefold: to consolidate and improve rangeland and livestock production, to improve pastoralists' income, and to encourage the gradual concentration of pastoral communities in the central portions of Somalia (considered to comprise one fifth of the country) (Mascott 1986). The project had a time span of six years.

The Central Rangelands Development Project was housed in a three-storied, Chinese-designed building sitting just downhill from a major hospital and along a main *caasi* [bus] route. Still it stood more or less by itself on the edge of one of the villa-filled, but indistinguishable-looking expatriate/elite neighborhoods. There were no shops, no services, and (for a time) no restaurants anywhere, although when I first arrived two "bush teashops" operated just across the street.

Bush teashops were temporary shelters constructed from branches and sometimes cardboard or other materials designed to give shade and partially conceal primitive kitchens where women prepared simple meals for watchmen and civil servants. Most bush teashops were not occupied for long, although arrangements were always quickly made for people to buy their meals or tea on credit. The two bush teashops near CRDP disappeared as soon as a daytime restaurant opened in a storehouse next door.

On an irregular basis cigarette and gum vendors—usually young boys or girls—would also park their wheelbarrow stands outside the National Range Agency building. Two older women dressed in *maros* (sari-like cotton wraps) sold cigarettes and homemade sesame sweets daily on the building steps. Whether that is all these two women were doing was never clear, because they certainly had a word for and with everyone.

CRDP's cleaning lady was the only other woman to wear a *maro* wrap rather than a *dira* or tailored full-length gauzy dress, a clear sign that she engaged in menial work. She, too, was very friendly with most people, always swapping stories or voicing her opinion. But in her case it was fairly common knowledge that she was somehow related to the project's general manager. She spoke with him frequently and people knew he could potentially get wind of what was occurring in the offices through her. This was the very sort of relationship that evidenced the kind of connections people were not supposed to discuss.

CRDP's offices took up most of the first and much of the building's third floors. Managers and expatriates occupied individual offices equipped with desks, cabinets, and chairs, although it was rare to find only one person sitting in an office. Expatriates generally had a secretary, assistants, or counterparts crowded into their offices with them since most of the Somali staff did not have assigned space. There was one computer room (with two IBM computers) and a documentation center (with project papers, reports, miscellaneous related material, and a xerox machine). There was also an herbarium in an office on the first floor.

The general manager's office was noticeably different from the others. This was not only where staff meetings took place but also where meetings between donors, World Bank officials, Ministry officials, and other important people and the manager were held. It was a very large, carpeted room, curtained ceiling to floor in a style common to elite Somali homes.

When business was being conducted at the manager's desk conversation was always subdued, yet audible on the waiting area side of a carved wooden screen; there was no real privacy. Yet, the opaque glass door to the office itself was always locked, even when the general manager was in. A doorman had to let visitors in and out. And because the glass was opaque it was always necessary to knock if the doorman was not already on your side, summoning him to peek out (if you were without) and screen the urgency of your visit.

Unfortunately, there was no good way of knowing in advance whether or when the general manager (or the next echelon of managers) would be in. Only when their cars were in the parking lot could anyone be sure that they might be found somewhere in the building. Nor were the expatriates always around. Although the general manager and other Somali managers were often away attending to impression management around town, the lack and unreliability of telephones in Mogadishu meant that anyone who needed to speak with someone else generally had to physically visit or track them down. This made for unpredictable absences. As a result, many staff members spent hours, if not whole mornings and workdays waiting for their supervisors to appear before proceeding with their work.

Having to wait, feeling stuck, being part of a bureaucracy that was clearly inefficient not only aggravated expatriates but frustrated staff, all of whom felt caught in a situation they would remake if they could. Indeed, such frustration suggested that people actually did want to work, or that, for a wide range of reasons, they wanted to at least give the appearance of accomplishment. For example, although doubtless some of the Somali staff felt a need for daily purpose and others believed in the project, virtually everyone hoped that if they did a good job and proved themselves hard-working enough they might be among those fortunate enough to win a ticket out of Somalia via a scholarship or study tour. In fact, this last was *the* motivating factor behind most Somalis' employment at CRDP: A ticket out was the only sure way to move up. Given that salaries were so negligible, the hope for a scholarship—despite the slim chances of receiving one—was overwhelmingly compelling. The fact that a few lucky individuals had already been sent abroad for advanced degrees and that the top managers had come to CRDP with fellowships as part of their credentials only encouraged everyone to think a scholarship might be possible for them, too. Ironically, though, despite being *the* imperative for the Somalis hired by CRDP, scholarships were only incidental to the project's larger design. As conceived, CRDP had far greater ambitions, regardless of its staff's motivations or needs.

EXPATRIATES

When I arrived in November 1988 CRDP was midway through its sixth and final year. Phase II of the project, again under the auspices of the World Bank, was in the process of being finalized. It was expected to begin as soon as Phase I ended—in June 1989. The last of the expatriate experts, both USAID contract employees, were due to leave the country in June. Meanwhile, the decision had already been made at USAID not to participate in Phase II.

Consequently, rumors were rampant about just what and who Phase II would employ. So far only one of the expatriate experts, a Canadian botanist, was seeking to be rehired. Perhaps not coincidentally, he was the only expatriate to have had his family with him throughout his two-year stay in Somalia. When he, his wife, and two sons left Phase I for home leave they quite confidently left behind all of their personal belongings as well as freezers full of meat that they had purchased as "official Americans," knowing that they would no longer have access to the U.S. commissary once they left the USAID umbrella.

In addition to this botanist there would probably be at least two other non-Somali Phase I holdovers. One was the project's accountant, a native Indian and World Bank employee. The other was a Tanzanian national who had come to Somalia with her Somali husband, divorced him, and then remained in Mogadishu's small secretarial and accounting pool. She, in many ways, was perhaps the most interesting expatriate at CRDP, since she was unusually masterful at creating, then juggling and manipulating spheres of influence in the project. She managed to do this among Somalis and expatriates alike, in large part because she could operate in English, Somali, and Swahili (which she was able to use to advantage with the general manager's secretary, who had grown up speaking it in Brava).

The Indian accountant, in contrast, consorted almost exclusively with the Somali management. Consequently it was assumed by virtually all the CRDP staff that his hand was in the till and he and the managers were cooking the books. Whether this was true, or whether he was thusly accused because he was an Indian and Indians had this reputation in Mogadishu, was unclear.[3] People did openly talk about him in this light.

Nor was the mosaic of actual funding for CRDP ever made completely clear to me, since various expatriates were paid out of different contractor pockets with different arrangements for their attachments to USAID. In general, however, this is how it seemed to work: Louis Berger International (LBI) had won the bid tendered by the World Bank to supply most of the expatriate staff as well as to run several workshops for the Somalis; GTZ directly supervised its own components, which provided veterinary and forestry functions; USAID directly funded the Range Management program at the University of Somalia and also supported eight Somali masters' and Ph.D. candidates abroad.

LBI had been one of several companies (U.S., British, and German) to bid for the project by submitting a package of resumes of personnel suited for the particular jobs stipulated for in the project design. This design had been conceived for the World Bank by yet another company. The World Bank had no expatriate experts (other than the accountant) of its own on site and did not directly salary or support the members of the LBI team (USAID did). Nor was there an LBI management expert attached to CRDP. Instead, an animal production expert was appointed team leader and expat manager.

No expatriate was in overall charge of the Somalis. Rather, the project's general manager (who was a Somali) was in charge of all CRDP employees, whether Somali national or expatriate, and he ultimately seemed to make the critical decisions about which company should win which bid and who, therefore, should be hired or fired. It is only to be assumed that the minister of livestock and other high government officials shared in these decisions. There were many rumors about how bids, in general, were awarded in Somalia, although the general assumption among expatriates and Somalis alike was that there was a fair amount of gift-giving, including the presentation of such things as Land Cruisers, Land Rovers, Mercedes-Benz four-wheel drives (although Mercedes all too clearly hinted at German involvement), or other items (or sums) of substance.

Also in concert with Somali government wishes, the LBI team was composed of middle-aged (or older) men, all of whom had considerable professional training and expertise in the areas for which they had been hired. Here it should be noted that there were several reasons why middle-aged men were preferred over other candidates. One is that their experience level tended to be higher than that of younger recruits, thus they were seen as having more expertise to impart. A second is that it was assumed that older men would be less likely to question decisions made by Somali project heads. This was a calculation made by the contract companies—that older men had little tendency to rock the boat since they were making mortgage and other payments at home and were clearly (still) working the developing country circuit in order to earn significant salaries, the last thing they would want to jeopardize. This was one of the great, unspoken collusions. Indeed, because it was the standard presumption that Somali management preferred hiring older, perhaps less energetic, but also less idealistic employees in order to minimize or altogether avoid public criticism, contract companies were known to alter resumes (particularly concerning age and work experience) in order to better meet these unspoken criteria and win bids.

Certainly, most of the men hired by LBI for CRDP had spent at least a portion of their careers working in other developing countries. Although most of those who I knew came to the project midway through its tenure, their career records proved surprisingly representative of expatriates hired by other projects in Somalia.

For instance, the team leader, the animal production Ph.D., had worked for one organization most of his professional life, and it was this organization (the Food and Agricultural Organization of the United Nations) [FAO]) that had sent him from project to project (to, for instance, the Dominican Republic, Iraq, and Mexico). However, when his last FAO contract ended and no other project offered an opening, he had been forced to turn to LBI and the other contracting companies that make it their business to put together expatriate teams. The team's range management expert, by contrast, had restricted his work to East Africa and had joined CRDP on the demise of IPAL (Integrated Project in Arid Lands), an arid-lands project funded by UNESCO (United Nations Educational, Scientific and Cultural Organization) in northern Kenya. CRDP's rural sociologist (hired long after the team's younger anthropologist had been ordered out of the country for interfering in politics) was a university professor who, through the international development program at his university, had worked elsewhere in Africa. The U.S. director of the range management program at Somali National University was likewise a professor, and the soil and water conservation expert was retired with professional (but not professorial) expertise in his field.

In all, there were between three and twelve expatriates attached to CRDP at any one time. Each expatriate was assigned at least two Somali counterparts and had numerous other Somalis under his supervision. It is many of these counterparts' lives that are examined in later chapters. It is their interactions with expatriates that must be taken into account here.

COUNTERPARTS

Most of the Somali counterparts at CRDP were Somali National University graduates, although some had received their range management training at the Range Institute in Burao and others had studied agriculture at special institutes or secondary schools around the country. Those who held bachelor's degrees in range management were graduates of the recently formed Range Management Program (sponsored, funded, and staffed by USAID). Therefore, they were not only familiar with U.S. range management techniques but also proficient in English (in addition to Somali and Italian, the language of instruction at the university).

Nevertheless, the word *counterpart* is a misnomer. These young Somalis were not experts, unlike the expatriates. The expatriates were supposed to be training the Somalis *to be* their counterparts and to eventually have the level of expertise whereby they would be able to staff the project themselves. However, the Somalis had not yet achieved a level of education (or the experience) to put them on par with the expatriates.

Similarly, although the counterparts all spoke English—as their third or fourth language—their command of English was hardly up to a native English-speaker's. Thus, they were not counterparts to the expatriates in this sense either.

Neither the expatriates nor those who were designated as their counterparts were fooled by the appellation *counterpart*. Although expatriates and counterparts did work together on field logistics, the expatriates generally used the counterparts as gofers and sources of information and did not treat them as coequals or colleagues. The counterparts, for their part, tended to regard the expatriates as bosses and as people to please more often than they treated them as mentors or people from whom they could learn.

Another major factor in the shaping of this expatriate-counterpart relationship was the difference in age between counterparts and expatriates. Most of the counterparts were still in their 20s, although a few were older and married. Conversely, the expatriates were middle-aged men with gray hair (if they still had hair) who projected all the other signs of age, which, in a non-Western society, still commanded a modicum of respect. In addition, most expatriates were in Somalia without their wives and children, rendering the situation that much more lopsided; these men clearly had no intention of staying. And even though assistance was definitely being rendered, it was obvious that investments in relationships were not being made.

Other dynamics also made for skewed relationships. With every expatriate assigned at least two, often more, Somalis as counterparts there were not only more counterparts than expatriates on the project but far more Somalis than non-Somalis throughout the building. As a result, expatriates were highly visible as an important minority and well known and recognizable to all staff members. The expatriates, however, did not always know all of their team-members' counterparts, let alone all the Somalis on the project.

EXPATRIATES AND PHASE II

Obviously, the expatriates, as individuals, had different personalities and filled their roles differently. However, in general, and due in large part to the most basic of reasons—age, language, First World/Third World distinctions—the African colonial and post-colonial tradition of Somalis as "uneducated natives" and the expatriates as "authoritative white men" was played out in the dynamic between counterpart and expatriate.

Still, expatriate initiative did vary. The Canadian botanist, for example, identified dozens of new plant species in Somalia,[4] and, perhaps the most energetic of the experts—an Australian responsible for extension training—was critical in helping devise the shift in focus for Phase II.

Whereas Phase I had ambitiously sought to improve the quality of life and the quality of the range for pastoralists (assumed in the initial reports to be nomadic), Phase II was slanted much more toward bolstering and improving the lot of agro-pastoralists. I believe this came about for many reasons, some of which neither the expatriates nor the Somali staff (other than the general manager and his closest associates) were privy to. However, enough reasons can be guessed at to more than justify the switch. According to an Executive Report produced by Mascott, Ltd.:

> The CRDP, as originally formulated, was a complex, multi-component and multi-donor project extending over approximately one fifth of the land area of Somalia. Not only was management complicated and communication difficult, but there were also inadequate data available on which to base the first managerial interventions and a limited understanding of the pastoral socio-economic environment.
>
> As a consequence a consensus began to develop that the original objectives were unattainable within the six year period and that the direct and indirect benefits expected from the interventions could be insignificant. In addition,

security problems in the western areas of the CRDP dictated a change in priority districts from Beled Weyne, Dusa Mareb and Galkayo to Bulo Burti, El Dere and Hobyo (Mascott 1986, 2).

This lack of enough success is one reason why the focus was bound to shift. Another stems from the Australian extension chief's findings, which he summarized as follows:

> By 1983, the CRDP had begun to concentrate its activities on 3 eastern districts, Hobyo, Ceel Dheer and Bulo Burte, where cropping happens to be more common than in some other central districts.
>
> The author began a general investigation into private enclosure and cropping activities in these areas during 1982. . . . Shifting cultivation and the locally perceived increase in private enclosure of land was becoming controversial. Some pastoralists, local government and National Range Agency (NRA) officials felt urgent action was needed to address these issues. In their opinion, shifting cultivation was reducing the availability of grazing land for those without enclosures. . . . However, since the RMR resource survey had indicated that only 2 to 3% of the central rangelands was cultivated, and the project was not designed to address agronomic development, investigations continued to be very limited until 1983/84.
>
> From initial extension department herding surveys, it was becoming apparent by late 1983 that many local pastoralists, were in fact, agropastoralists. They were integrating livestock husbandry with crop production. At the same time, the Ceel Dheer District Ecologist [another expatriate] . . . was beginning to suspect that the vegetation of over 90% of the shrubland, which covers most of this district, had been changed more by shifting cultivation practices than by livestock (Holt 1985: 84–85).

In other words, what Holt was pointing to (other than his own significant discovery), was the fact that the practice of the people did not quite fit the assumptions of the project designers. I believe Holt's discovery was then allowed to preempt those assumptions for several reasons: Holt was extremely dynamic, not only as far as the World Bank officials were concerned but also according to many of his Somali extension staff. He had clearly spent more time in the field than most of the other expatriates and had a working knowledge of spoken Somali. Whether this intimidated the other expatriates, or whether they just didn't care as much as Holt did, his views held sway. Nor was it as though all the other resident experts agreed with him. Not all the range ecologists believed that agro-pastoralism was the bogeyman it was portrayed to be, nor did they think of it as the wave of the future. Indeed, some felt quite strongly that Phase II, with its heavier emphasis on the agricultural end of agro-pastoralism, was not only misguided but mistaken. However, they did not have Holt's voice within the project or Holt's charisma in the eyes of the World Bank.

In many ways Holt's view of the central rangelands accords well with Abdi Samatar's contention that during times of economic disjuncture more pressure is put on the land. It is not just pastoralism that becomes a survival strategy, people turn to anything that will take advantage of all available resources, including the soil (A. I. Samatar 1989). Another factor in the acceleration of enclosure may well have been new land tenure policies (Hoben 1988). However, Holt's lobbying for more attention to be paid to agro-pastoralism also fell into the development trap common for assessments of pastoral nomads. Despite virtually universal lip service paid to the dominance of pastoralism as both national ideology and economic mainstay in Somalia, nomads (by virtue of their mobility as well as the harsh conditions of their life) were rarely considered a viable focus group. Thus, it was easier to define and work with the more settled agro-pastoralists, and ultimately agencies lacked the will—in terms of manpower—to expend the necessary amount of time and energy on nomads. This, in some ways, was merely reinforced by urban Somali attitudes, since those Somalis who would have been responsible for pursuing work in the bush had either never spent time in the bush, and thus had no interest in it, or had themselves escaped rural life with the purpose of never returning.

Meanwhile, although the shift in project focus may not have been wrong or mistaken given realities such as these, the fact that Phase II was purposely designed to veer away from the aims of Phase I was significant, with far different implications for the Somalis on the project than for the expatriates, principally because most of the expatriates knew they were leaving whether their work was finished or not and whether Phase I could be deemed a success or not.

Still, whatever controversy Phase II may have generated, any debate about it was, for the long moment, academic. For reasons having to do with donor financing (explained by World Bank representatives and Somali managers alike as the bank's inability to release funds until the Government of Somalia settled its account with the Africa Development Bank), Phase I fizzled out without Phase II beginning. Then the hiatus between the two phases was further interrupted—by the repercussions of July 14. However, by then there were no Western expatriates at all attached to the project. Nor were there any signs of the Canadian botanist returning from home leave to reclaim his possessions. Indeed, as more and more U.S. citizens began to pack up to leave Mogadishu in the aftermath of policy decisions related to the human rights abuses of July 14, it became clearer and clearer that his clever calculations to hoard meat were causing problems in peoples' freezers; no one was sure what to do with it all—perhaps an ironic metaphor for Somalia.

PART TWO

Histories

Why *were* expatriates in Somalia? After all, Somalia had little of value to offer the world. Its three most unique resources are meerschaum, frankincense, and myrrh. Yet, even these can be found elsewhere. As for its main export—livestock—sheep and goats from Australia and New Zealand were already out-competing Somali animals in the lucrative Gulf State markets (Janzen 1986, Cassam 1987). Granted, Somalia purportedly had the world's largest camel herds, but these were in limited demand outside the region. Much of the country is semiarid, suited for little beyond livestock production. So far, nothing has proven more efficient than pastoralism for exploiting semiarid areas (Western 1982), and according to CRDP experts Somali production could likely only be improved by 10 percent at best.

Those areas of Somalia that could be farmed were already being farmed. Indeed, vast plantations supplied Italy with subsidized bananas. The area between Somalia's only two permanent rivers, the Juba and the Shabelle, had long been overexploited as had, more significantly still, its population.

Nevertheless, despite years of British and Italian experiments designed to figure out how to goad Somalis into producing more (whether they were producing enough livestock for subsistence already, or overproducing agricultural goods under exploitative conditions) and after a decade of Soviet attempts to engineer state farming and jump-start various forms of industry, a veritable avalanche of Western aid continued to pour into Somalia throughout the 1980s—as though the West could suddenly make Somalia over and Somalis much better off. . . . Well, some it did.

As we will see, the Siad Barre regime pursued a multitude of agendas for encouraging expatriate involvement: to earn foreign exchange, to keep Somalia intact, to keep itself in power. Nor was it only members of the president's own party or clan who were interested in seizing whatever moment they could. Expatriates felt that all Somalis, whom they dealt with endlessly, ceaselessly and selfishly sought assistance, money, goods, and favors. Nor did it matter to expatriates what this annoying Somali behavior was rooted in. Whether this was a matter of average Somalis mimicking more successful members of the elite, or how people had to respond when a corrupt government did not provide them with a social welfare net, or whether it emerged out of much older strategies for coping with conditions of uncertainty, none of this would have interested most expatriates who dismissed the entire greedy-seeming enterprise. As a result, the most commonly expressed prescription for Somalia at the time was that Somalis should be cut off from all aid sources for at least twenty years. Then, once Somalis had rid themselves of corruption and begun developing the country on their own, aid might do it some good (a suggestion offered by individuals garnering generous salaries in order to dispense aid).

However, despite their being full of advice for the future, most expatriates knew little about the Somali past. They, thus, would not have understood how maybe it was this past that had conditioned Somalis. At the same time, there was much that even many Somalis would not have been aware of concerning developments in the worlds of international high finance and diplomacy—occurences well beyond their purview but nonetheless affecting them. Still today, much remains only partially documented. It is for this reason that the following chapters should be read as context at the broadest level, in two senses. First, I try to suggest conditions and confluences rather than claim to fully reconstruct chains of events. Of course, at the same time, my intention is to suggest that dissolution itself does not just make for but also emerges out of just such broken information.

Second, the context I seek to describe is of flux. This history should reveal that change was a constant—politically, economically, in terms of colonial rule, superpower patronage, on virtually all fronts. In this regard the unpredictable nature of outside interests in Somalia was little different from the unpredictable natural environment that Somalis had long had to cope with. The principles Somalis were used to living by were eminently transferable—from rural to urban, local to supralocal domains. Why they needed to be transferred at all—what made flux—is what Part 2 sets forth.

• 3 •

Involvements I

Words cannot be strung together to describe the, apparently, and sterility—to the European mind—of the hundred odd miles of country I have ridden across during the last four days. . . . In such country as this, it would be plagiarism to attempt to describe what has so often been described before. The rainy season, compared with that of more favored parts of the world, appears as little short of a drought; and a drought here, similarly compared, might be classed as "hell let loose."

Rayne, 1921a, 186–187

An adequate idea of the monotony and scenery of this country may be obtained by any one who should care to walk about in a kitchen-garden of dead gooseberry and currant bushes for a week or ten days. The soil was red instead of brown, and the vegetation larger and more thorny, but in other respects the greater part of the Haud was a dried-up African kitchen-garden, instead of an English one.

James, 1888, 87

As these two quotations—one describing the area around Zeila, and the other the Haud—suggest, British Somaliland would appear to have had little to offer the British. Why then did the British bother? This is a question that might also be asked of the Italians, the Russians, those from the United States, the Germans, or any of the other Europeans who have supplied foreign aid to first the Somalilands and then Somalia in return for something else. More often than not that "something else" has been an intangible—not minerals, not oil, not souls for conversion to Christianity, not even livestock (since most of Somalia's livestock, which have historically been the country's most significant export, have traditionally been exported to the Persian Gulf). Rather, whatever has been gained in return for the foreign aid poured into Somalia has been evanescent, and ever since the nineteenth century accession of the Europeans over the Arabs in the regional trade has had less to do with what Somalia contains than where it is located.

Only a few histories have yet been written that analyze regions of Somalia in any depth. From reading these we learn, for instance, that northern Somalia (the former British Somaliland) occupies very different terrain from central or southern Somalia. Consequently, different combinations of crops (including incense trees) as well as animals can be exploited there. Northern Somalia also more directly faces the Persian Gulf, leading to different goods, which make for different trade patterns and relationships than one finds in southern Somalia, where the practice of permanent (and then large-scale) agriculture has led to contrasting patterns of settlement, social structure, and political organization.[1]

Too little accounting is often made of these differences when Somalia is analyzed. For specifics one must invariably turn elsewhere (e.g., Cassanelli 1982; A. I. Samatar 1989). Even here I cannot fully account for the patchwork of Somalia's local histories. Still I must at least allude to the purposes difference has served. This is critical to dissolution.

FLUIDITY

Although the origins of Somali clans and clan-families are hotly debated, as are the precise order of migrations that have populated the Horn of Africa, it is nonetheless clear that migration has long been a major factor in inter-clan and inter-family politics (H. Lewis 1966; Cassanelli 1982; Helander 1988). Local movements and population shifts have had at times incremental, yet far-reaching, long-rippling effects. Indeed, although floods of recent refugees may be startling, the fact of refugees should not be. Even the vast distinctions Somalis make among themselves are rooted in migration. For instance, the exact origins of the agricultural, inter-riverine populations are murky. Are these people autochthons? Are they descendants of Bantu migrants from centuries ago? Or are they descendants of more recently enslaved Tanzanians and others?[2] Most look different from other Somalis. They speak a different language. They practice a different mode of production (agriculture versus pastoralism). And they exhibit different customs.

But such obvious distinctions aside, others exist even within single Somali clan-families. For instance, the requirements of pastoral nomadism—with grazing areas and water points often left unprotected—can lead to festering disputes over who actually controls these invaluable resources. Without being able to permanently stay put, groups of Somalis have had to work out their differences over these areas through negotiation or conflict on a seasonal basis.

Other Somalis gravitated toward Somalia's coast centuries ago. Although coastal towns were historically home to Persians, Indians, Arabs, and Swahili traders (among others), Somalis coexisted with them, acting as middlemen, guides, interpreters, and protectors. Trade sponsored a whole series of lifestyles that could be engaged in by Somalis beyond farming or herding, yet which served to link the interior (and farmers and herders) to the outside world.

Just considering the differences such a continuum—from fluidity through fixity—alludes to, there should be no question but that socioeconomic differentiation existed in Somalia well before European intrusions. Nevertheless, the Europeans' combined introduction of indirect rule, their obsession with preventing conflict, and their desire to enmesh the Somalilands in economic interdependencies meant that local migrations, local boundary disputes, and differences in local modes of production were made contestable in new ways.

For instance, colonial officials sought to curtail pastoral sources of conflict through more clearly defining which grazing grounds and water sources belonged to which groups. At the same time, the very process of mapping clear lines of usership led to intense jockeying among rival groups of Somalis before control could be established and then, once it was, over whether the new rules were just.

Similarly, indirect rule by colonial administrations required the establishment of a variety of positions staffed by Somalis. This led to individual competition among Somalis over appointments, and the employment of any Somalis created further differences among groups of Somalis. Accordingly, differential access to money, education, and property recombined with other colonial favors to single out Somalis hired as soldiers, policemen, clerks, and so on. These individuals, in turn, further consolidated their status by helping their relatives share in the benefits. Splits and realignments only intensified as everyone who could compete did so to insulate kin.

Effects from all of these impacts continue to spin themselves out today, not just in terms of class relations but in economic dependency, agrarian underdevelopment, and environmental degradation. Repercussions from colonialism have been tremendous. But like local histories, they are regionally variegated and may well tell different stories separately than they would in aggregate. Regardless, such effects (significant as they are) must remain beyond the scope of this work. Here, beginning with how Europeans arrived in Somalia, I wish merely to suggest some of the ways in which Somalia was used in international and regional realpolitik by a range of facile players: British, Italians, French, Egyptians, Ethiopians, Soviets, U.S. citizens, *and* Somalis—before turning to the effects this had on Somalis politicking among themselves.

THE BRITISH AND THE ITALIANS

Historically Somali coastal towns played a critical role in the underacknowledged Indian Ocean/Red Sea trade (Puzo 1972; Freeman-Grenville 1975; Hersi 1977; Abir 1980). Since before the tenth century various ports in Ethiopia, Yemen, Somalia, and the Sudan were in fierce competition with one another as rich, sophisticated, cosmopolitan entrepôts (Abir 1975, 1980; Gavin 1975; Dresch 1989). As part of this continual positioning and repositioning portions of Somalia had been colonized long before Europeans showed any interest in the area. However, it was only once Europeans arrived that all of what would later become Somalia was laid claim to, with the British, French, and Italians establishing relatively small coastal protectorates along Somali shores by the mid-nineteenth century. Meanwhile, what brought the European powers to Somalia—namely, one another—continued to affect events in Somalia, as the ebb and flow of alliances and counterplots between the European powers *outside* the Horn of Africa dictated levels of involvement *in* the Horn of Africa.

For instance, by the 1870s, both Egypt and Ethiopia were expansionist and predatory empires. Not only did Egypt succeed in wresting increased control over the Somali coast from the Ottomans (Berbera in 1873; Harar by 1874) but Egypt and Ethiopia began to clash over control of the Nile basin. Throughout the region the disputants, including local Somali sultans, sought to draw in European support, best achieved by playing to European rivalries. This was relatively easy to do since France and Britain were quite intent on acting on their animosities well beyond Europe, with Italy and Germany also party to the maelstrom.[3] For example, French seizure of Tunis in 1881 sent Italy into an alliance with Germany, which Britain sought to undermine. At the same time Italy was losing in the scramble for colonies, Germany's intentions in East Africa were worrying the British. Therefore, Britain invited Italy to participate in its Nile ventures—ergo Italian interest in Eritrea and Somalia.

Of course, such events can also be read through a more reductionist lens: The European scramble for control over eastern trade (with the ultimate prize being India) led to protectionist and counterprotectionist seizures across the globe. If Britain acquired Aden to protect its Suez routes to the subcontinent, then France had to acquire something nearby as counterweight (hence, Djibouti).

However, there were pressures internal to these chess moves as well. For instance, the changeover from Disraeli to Gladstone governments in Britain led to different views of empire. Under Gladstone exclusive control over the Red Sea area was no longer deemed necessary and nonthreatening Italian participation could be welcomed. Similarly, France was embroiled in local conflicts in Tonkin and Madagascar; thus, French control over Obock/Djibouti would guarantee French navies a convenient coaling station. And this is just a slice of the history.

By the late 1890s it was the Ethiopians and the Italians colliding in Ethiopia. The Ethiopians, having been armed by the French (and the Russians), overwhelmingly defeated the Italians at the Battle of Adowa. This defeat with French arms of a British ally reignited British fears and Anglo-French rivalries. In turn this allowed Menelik, his sovereignty in Ethiopia recognized, to squeeze territorial concessions out of all parties by playing to their rivalries—at the expense of Somalis and Somalis in the Ogaden especially.

Somalis duly protested as Menelik projected his empire ever eastward, deeper into the Ogaden and Somali-occupied grazing areas. But despite their appeals based on the treaties of assistance the British and Italians had formerly worked out with them, Somalis received no European assistance in the face of these Ethiopian incursions. Rather, it was left to Somali members of locally based *tariqa* [Islamic brotherhoods], under the leadership of Sayyid Mohamed Abdille Hassan, to counter Menelik's increasingly aggressive, tribute-seeking encroachments.[4] For leading this fiery, quasi-religious resistance, Sayyid Mohamed Abdille Hassan has been lionized as Somalia's first real protonationalist leader (S. Samatar 1982), although not so much for his success against the Ethiopians as for his ability to galvanize large numbers of Somalis to oppose all infidels.

WAR WITH BRITAIN AND ITALY

Definitionally the British and Italians had to be considered infidels, too. Consequently, the Sayyid's movement, which began by targeting Ethiopian troops, wound up precipitating a colonial war, perhaps as much the result of mutual misunderstanding as any master plan. For instance, the British may have quite rationally but nonetheless mistakenly miscast the Sayyid as another Mahdi, the Sudanese religious leader who had recently pummeled and embarrassed them. Their aggressive reaction to the Sayyid thus could easily have convinced him, in turn, that the Europeans were indeed aggressors little different from the Ethiopians.

As a war, the British and Italian engagement of the Sayyid (who the British dubbed the Mad Mullah) and his followers (described as dervishes) is probably best summarized as a prolonged series of encounters. Stretching from 1900 through 1919, most battles were fought in northern and central Somalia. Nevertheless, despite their relatively limited nature, these clashes had a number of far-reaching and foreshadowing effects. At least five can be traced forward to today.

First, the war was fought not only between Europeans and some Somalis but among Somalis with some clans fighting on behalf of either the British or the Italians against others fighting for the Sayyid. This, as much as anything, helped drag the war on. At the same time, to keep alliances straight, both the British and the Italians began systematically documenting clan loyalties and betrayals, setting in ink what had formerly stayed fluid among Somalis and purposely recording these for administrative use. They also selectively supplied arms. For instance, before the British temporarily withdrew to the coast after their failed 1909 campaign they armed the allies they left behind, ostensibly for self-protection. This practice was one that (like so many others) never entirely disappeared. It was a technique subsequently used in the pacification of certain tribes during the colonial period and even under Siad Barre as recently as 1988.[5]

Second, the war immortalized and nationalized the Sayyid who came to be regarded (even during his lifetime) as a legendary poet of unparalleled stature. Because his poems traveled farther and wider than his cause and resonated as consummate oral literature for all Somalis, they also served to help fuse and codify a *national* Somali identity (see S. Samatar 1982). At the same time, the Sayyid's success in battle achieved him a hero's status among many (but not all) Somalis.

Third, the war's local effects—in the north—devastated the human and animal populations. This is also when the British essentially purged the north of horses, which in turn transformed systems of raiding, transportation, and prestige—with profound, but still underexplored effects for the region.

Fourth, containment of the war in the north also brought home the regional divide that the British-Italian partition represented. Notably, too, Djibouti, which had become the region's largest arms market, provided a ready source of weapons for the Sayyid's dervishes. This has also continued, with Djibouti dealers supplying both Somali rebels *and* Siad Barre through the late 1980s.

Finally, by solidifying British and Italian presences, the war served to directly and rapidly incorporate more Somalis into nonpastoral spheres (such as the army) at the same time it stimulated different types of colonization in both areas. For instance, Britain, with a larger empire, had less to gain from developing its Somaliland than Italy had. And given topography, Italian Somaliland was riper for larger-scale settlement and more intensified agriculture.

WORLD WAR II AND THE FATE OF THE ITALIAN PROTECTORATE

Once the Sayyid was defeated the European Powers had little reason to dispute in, or over, the Somalilands again until after World War I. And then the tussles were purely diplomatic; Italy felt it deserved territorial rewards for its allied participation in the Great War and was finally granted a minor one (Jubaland) in 1924.

Ten years later and Somalia was again in the headlines, although this time as the jumping-off point for Mussolini's 1934 invasion of Ethiopia. British Somaliland consequently proved the staging area for Britain's counterinvasion (or liberation) of Ethiopia in 1941, which meant that, victorious, the British suddenly found themselves in control of both Italian Somaliland and their own British Somaliland, as well as the ostensibly Ethiopian Haud and Ogaden.[6]

This was the first time in history so many ethnic Somalis had been united under one administrative writ.

However, British control—and Somalis' union—was not necessarily permanent. The fate of Italian Somalia, like the fate of Italy's other colonies, had to await post–World War II adjudication. Nevertheless, for the first time Somalis were overtly promised that they would have some say in helping determine their future. Consequently, there was much jockeying. The promise that they could be able to play a role in the decisionmaking sparked intense competition among newly emergent political groups (such as the Somali Youth League), which lobbied vociferously for either the Italians or British winning a mandate over the Somalilands (see Pankhurst 1951).

Once again, however, and despite Somalis' increasingly politicized self-awareness, Somali views tended not to matter as international relations having nothing to do with Somalis haphazardly determined their fate. Due to a variety of pressures Italy was granted a ten-year mandate over its former colony, with the British retaining control in the north.[7]

Yet, this contestation—at international and local levels—did produce two immediate results: Local lobbying during the visit by the Four Power Commission (the group charged with listening to Somalis) led to two bombings in the capital and a riot in Mogadishu that cost fifty-one Italian and fourteen Somali lives (January 11, 1948). More demonstrations followed the commission's decision (handed down in October 1949)—the first and only major outbreak of violence in Mogadishu I have found reference to until 1975.

Second, what began to grow out of the nexus of local and international politicking was rhetoric about the nation. This rhetoric in turn was made all the more realizable when two Somali-occupied regions, the Ogaden and the Haud, were handed "back" to Ethiopia as part of the commission's settlement of regional disputes and boundaries. Not only did this loss of an area traditionally occupied by Somalis crush Somali hopes for a united ethnic Somali nation but it did so at the very time Somalis were getting their first real taste of nationally oriented political power. It also buried the Ethiopian thorn that much deeper in Somalia's side.

Yet, although Italy's UN-supervised mandate was presented to Somalis as a fait accompli, the fact that it was to expire in 1960 meant that nothing was really fixed after all, except an end date. Uncertainty over everything but the mandate's expiration led, in turn, to a decade of political jousting within Italian Somalia. At the same time, it spurred Somalis in British Somaliland to agitate for their own independence, which the British finally agreed to. Thus, on July 1, 1960, the two Somalilands were able to unite a sovereign but *still* incomplete Somalia: The Ogaden in Ethiopia, the Northern Frontier District in Kenya, and French Djibouti all had preponderant Somali populations but were not under sovereign Somali control.

• 4 •

Involvements II

CLAN POLITICS

Who was a Somali anyway? For many Somalis clan or lineage was as far as their identity needed to be stretched. Certainly for everyday purposes *Somali* was a relatively meaningless term. Identity was determined by genealogy, which worked from the individual up and a progenitor down and grew more inclusive with every generation remembered.

Roots of the politicization of clans can be traced back at least to the establishment of coastal protectorates by Britain and Italy, although Puzo's history of Mogadishu (1972) describes factional rivalries as old as the city itself (dating to the tenth century). However, any history of clan interrelationships is patchy; nor has anyone yet attempted a comprehensive history for one clan, let alone explored the relationship between two clans over an extended period. Thus, it becomes impossible to reconstruct a local history at all comparable to Somalia's supra-local (essentially diplomatic) history.[1]

Until this buried genealogical history is excavated, then, only samples are available to suggest larger overall patterns. And each of these is so specifically detailed as to make it virtually impossible for anyone not already fluent in local history and geographical spread to gauge the significance of change given the norm, which is flux. For instance, here is Richard Burton's version of one local history:

> The present decadence of Berberah is caused by petty internal feuds. Girhajis the eldest son of Ishak al-Hazrami, seized the mountain ranges of Gulays and Wagar lying about forty miles behind the coast, whilst Awal, the cadet, established himself and his descendants upon the lowlands from Berberah to Zayla. Both these powerful tribes assert a claim to the customs and profits of the port on the grounds that they jointly conquered it from the Gallas. The Habr Awal, however, being in possession, would monopolize the right: a blood feud rages, and the commerce of the place suffers from the dissensions of the owners.
>
> Moreover the Habr Awal tribe is not without internal feuds. Two kindred septs, the Ayyal Yunis Nuh and the Ayyal Ahmad Nuh, established themselves originally at Berberah. The former, though the more numerous, admitted the

latter for some years to a participation of profits, but when Aden, occupied by the British, rendered the trade valuable, they drove out the weaker sept, and declared themselves sole 'Abbans' to strangers during the fair. A war ensued. The sons of Yunis obtained aid of the Mijjarthayn tribe. The sons of Ahmad called in the Habr Girhajis, especially the Musa Arrah clan, to which the Hajj Sharmarkay belongs, and, with his assistance, defeated and drove out the Ayyal Yunis. These, flying from Berberah, settled at the haven of Bulhar, and by their old connection with the Indian and other foreign traders, succeeded in drawing off a considerable amount of traffic. But the roadstead was insecure: many vessels were lost, and in 1847 the Isa Somal slaughtered the women and children of the new-comers, compelling them to sue the Ayyal Ahmad for peace. Though the feud thus ended, the fact of its having had existence ensures bad blood: amongst these savages treaties are of no avail, and the slightest provocation on either side becomes a signal for renewed hostilities (Burton 1894/1987 II, 75).

This passage, quoted at such length, suggests two things: that despite the genealogical persistence of broad groupings (i.e., clan-families), feuds and disputes were more often locale-and/or lineage-based. Secondly, it was the strength of a lineage in a given place that determined how it survived—whether it could defend its position or was eventually forced into alliance with a stronger group. Indeed, Burton's account is quite clear on the linkages between territory and lineage. For instance, time-consuming and specific arrangements for guides, *abaans* [protectors], and permission to travel had to be separately negotiated with the proper representatives of whichever territories the caravan was traversing. Hence, gaining local knowledge for Somali and non-Somali alike meant learning the local disputes and feuds in order to avoid being caught in the wrong place by the wrong group.

In contrast, by the time I. M. Lewis, David Marlowe, Saadia Touval, and the first generation of (non-Somali) Somaliists arrived in Somalia to conduct their fieldwork in the late 1950s and early 1960s, Somalia did not offer this same pattern of localisms. Rather, all areas of the country had become enmeshed in larger affairs of state. Consequently, formerly local events were receiving a new cast; politics on the broadest level were creating and then demanding group allegiances on a scale broader than local lineages could support. At the same time, the out-migration of individuals from the bush, along with the growth of towns and the scrambled nature of sedentarizing populations reinforced the growing (so it seems) primacy of clans and clan-families (not lineages) as the prime negotiating bodies between individuals and state structures.

We see bottom-up as well as top-down evidence for this—ultimately in how allegiances promoted opportunity and opportunity shattered allegiances.

SETTLEMENT AND THE RECASTING OF LINEAGE: THE CENTRAL RANGELANDS

In contrast to the fission and fusion demanded by a nomadic way of life, pragmatism alone would dictate that in settled situations neighborhood solidarity (as Helander [1988] phrases it) take precedence over segmentation. In settled communities the realities of life are that people must continually draw water and plant side by side; they can't just uproot themselves without risking their crops, their access to land, and their place in community. Essentially settlement requires a different organization than nomadism; pragmatism itself needs to be systematized. Ideologically there are any number of ways to achieve this. In Somalia one way neighborhood solidarity was attained was through religious support for upholding ties to community (*jamcaa*) over lineage. Indeed, *tariqas* [religious brotherhoods] became synonymous with settled communities throughout Somalia in the mid–nineteenth century, whereas yet other settlements were founded by non-*tariqa*-affiliated sheikhs whose appeal was predicated on their being able to negotiate between, rather than align themselves with, particular lineages (Lewis 1965).

However, much as saints in Morocco or marabouts in Senegal could not overtly align themselves politically with one lineage over another (since this would have compromised or negated their role as mediators [Gellner 1969; O'Brien 1975]), the very success of Somali religious leaders often meant that they inadvertently became the heads of their own lineages, as villages filled with their relatives and other supporters/dependents. At the very least, this prominence could lend prestige and respect to their children who, if they were clever, could turn their father's *baraka* [charisma] into their own *barwaqo* [prosperity] by either becoming sheikhs themselves or availing themselves of their father's sheikhly networks.

As Abdi Samatar, in his study of northwestern Somalia, grounds this transformation historically:

> Certain important changes in the political structure of the pastoral society took place during the first three and a half decades of colonial rule. The resistance movement led by Sayyid Mohamed Abdille Hassan had far-reaching implications for the future leadership in the pastoral society. . . . In the stateless society, each clan had an elder as its figurehead, whereas religious men were spiritual leaders and did not often indulge in the secular affairs of the clan . . . the resistance movement that he [Sayyid Mohamed Abdille Hassan] inspired and led against the infidels had upstaged clan elders and propelled the *ulema* (holy men) into a position of political leadership that was hitherto foreign to them (1989, 44–45).

However, perhaps the best diachronic study to trace the interaction between lineage elders, sheikhs, and structures of state is David Marlowe's ethnography of the Galjaal Barsana of central Somalia. Although fieldwork for this study was conducted in 1958 (around the time I. M. Lewis was first working in northern Somalia), many of Marlowe's findings and conclusions continue to shed light on the shape of lineage re-ravelings today and are particularly significant to this account since his study area is contained within the central rangelands.

Sometime during the latter part of the nineteenth century the Barsana successfully adopted *tariqa*-membership and agriculture. Although they were still able to operate as fairly successful long-range nomads whenever the rains failed them, a *jamcaa* [community] lifestyle—organized around cultivation—required them to downplay linkages through genealogy alone.

Indeed, the gist of Marlowe's sophisticated thesis is that it was the codependency of the sheikh, *tariqa* members, and lineage elders (along with everyone's dependence on agriculture) that was critical to maintaining *jamcaa*. For instance, the sheikh (who embodied the community's religious center) would risk losing his followers if he alienated the elders and the lineage elders would risk losing ritual efficacy (and, they believed, the rainfall only a sheikh could bring) if they offended the sheikh (155–156). Although analytically such interdependencies may have appeared consensual and engineered, what Marlowe's work points out is that they really worked because no one could afford risking their not working.

This was more than apparent in 1942, when the then-sheikh's younger brother denounced the sheikh to the British as a Fascist collaborator in order to be appointed headman in his stead. Unfortunately for the usurper, the year he engineered his coup the Barsana suffered a drought, proof to the Barsana that the former sheikh was more powerful than his upstart brother; the former sheikh was thereafter reinstated. However, although this reinstatement may have reestablished ritual harmony (and secured rain), it could not repair the breach in the broader social system. What the Italians had wrought by designating the sheikh their Barsana representative in the first place was to politicize the role; this politicization of a religious position could not be undone.

As subsequent administrations continued to alter the sheikh's role, and as independence rapidly approached—promising even greater political and economic opportunities—Marlowe found himself witnessing the further corruption of a decreasingly impartial leader:

> Governmental recognition and validation as the central judicial and ritual authority in the sub-clan, has served to make the lineages more dependent upon the sheikh than before. Yet, at the same time, this intensified governmental support has moved the sheikh's arena of action further and further away from Barsana life. It has changed his self image, from that of sheikh of the Barsana, dependent upon and depended upon by the lineages, of a holy man

> and a saint in Islam, to that of a politician. The sheikh's ends and desires have been oriented to the life, goods, and comforts of the town and the quest for advancement through the government. He talks constantly of the desirability of a government stipend and "house in Mogadishu."
>
> In consequence his primary use of this new political power has been the pursuit of advantage for himself and his kin (178).

Indeed, it was this irreconcilable tug between the sheikh's allegiance to his family and allegiance to maintaining extra-familial *xeer,* which directly led to the dissolution of the *jamcaa* as a religious community. *Xeer* is the pastoralists' counterbalance to segmentation. More specifically, it is a set of norms and laws (in short, a contract) formally agreed to by adult males who may or may not be closely related, designed to ensure peace and prevent bloodshed within the group they self-define. It is purposely intended to override lineage differences and is critical to preserving order among those who mutually seek it—and was especially critical to securing *jamcaa* in permanent settlements.

But *xeer* was also in the way when it came to the sheikh's family (*reer* Hassan) being able to further its own ends. Not only did the sheikh's family become increasingly rapacious for the material benefits to be gained by exploiting the *jamcaa,* but family members also sought to use their privileged position vis-à-vis the *jamcaa* as a stepping stone for access to other arenas. For instance, in 1953 the family managed to have the *jamcaa*'s agricultural lands confirmed as *reer* Hassan's personal property, and by 1959 the family was seeking to convert the *jamcaa* into little more than a tenant farming organization.

Meanwhile, although it had been colonial administrators who had privileged the sheikh (and *reer* Hassan) in the first place, colonial administrators also were the ones who replaced the sheikh in his role as supra-local arbiter. This meant the sheikh's traditional role was being diminished from above as well as from within. As Marlowe explains, "whereas formerly the Barsana system was self-limiting and closed due to the absolute status interdependence of the sheikh and the lineages, it is now open and non-limited since Barsana *xeer* can be contravened by appeal to the stronger law of the Government" (172). Thus, at the same time the sheikh's family found itself well-positioned to reap benefits from sheikhly status, members of other lineages within the Barsana alliance began to realize that their dependence on the sheikh was no longer necessary for their physical protection. Thus, "through the sequence of actions by which the power of the *xeer* to control behavior and order commitment to the sheikh was shattered, normative segmentary process was enabled to reassert itself" (254). In other words, association by lineage again came to hold sway.

Although Marlowe ultimately holds the sheikh and his weaknesses to blame for this Barsana-wide devolution, he also recognizes that with changing roles the orientation of the community's key players had to shift (238).

Indeed, recognition of structural change, along with a more comparative reading of the Barsana situation would seem to map a wider pattern: Once the sheikh's family began to consider its interests apart from the interests of the *jamcaa*—thanks to benefits accruable to the sheikh through his government role—and the sheikh reacted by favoring those interests preferentially, the inter-lineage alliance was bound to dissolve; the sheikh was supposed to be impartial, balanced, and removed from secular affairs. After all, the whole point of a sheikh's position was to bridge, not embody lineage differences. Once the sheikh began acting just as anyone else would—putting his family first—he and his family's *successful* scramble for advantages set in motion reactive competition, previously suspended for three generations among the Barsana.

Or, to put this differently, as soon as the sheikh's family set itself apart as a predatory corporation in control of Barsana resources, the Barsana elders were bound to reassert their rights and lineage members realign *them*selves, in order to reestablish security in the face of so many destabilizing and (literally) unsettling changes. In addition, the fact that the sheikh's family was behaving in this way at all indicates that it was being drawn into wider arenas of competition, and that similar breakouts must have been occurring throughout rural Somalia.

Indeed, competition for new, state-constructed opportunities were turning rural areas into resource preserves and folding economics into the political equation across the landscape, only for elites, newly emerging out of the rural areas, to then have to compete with one another at the center. According to the political histories already written (which I would refer interested readers to, see Pankhurst 1951; Kaplan 1960; Touval 1963; Lewis 1980; and Samatar 1988) such re-sorting came to define "national" politics—the eventual politics of dissolution.[2] In a decade of jockeying for representation under the guise of democracy, politics came to be about gaining access not just to the levers but to the resources of the state. The state, we must remember, putative democracy or not, itself amounted to Somalis' most concentrated source of resources. As Lewis describes it:

> In national politics, the most abiding interest of each major local voting block is to place a kinsman in a "chair" (as they expressively put it) in the national assembly. Under what political party banner this is achieved is of secondary importance, for even if it turns out that a member is returned on a minority party ticket, he can always change his party allegiance once he is home and dry (1969c, 353).

This degree of self-interest was most evident in the March 1969 presidential election. Only ten years after Marlowe witnessed the breakdown of

Barsana *jamcaa* 62 parties put up 1,002 candidates for 123 seats at the national level.

This was the last democratic election to be held in Somalia. The following October, only a few weeks after a similar coup boosted Colonel Gadhafi to power in Libya, Major-General Siad Barre became head of government in Somalia.[3]

REGIONAL POLITICS

One of the principal causes cited for Siad Barre's bloodless coup, and one of the reasons for the initial euphoria over his arrival at the head of a military government, was the level of blatant and extensive political and economic corruption being practiced prior to, and during, the 1969 national elections. In a sense, a decade of representative government had worked too well in Somalia. Too many people vied with one another to represent too few interests. Basically, too much came to pivot around kin. However, Lewis (1972) also indicates that discontent over Somalia's foreign policy—increasingly conciliatory toward Ethiopia and Kenya—may have been another factor in the military's takeover.

Again this returns us to the supra-local level, regionally first. Since Independence Somalia's various political parties had steadily committed themselves to a certain rhetoric, which increasingly looked to Nasserine Egypt and not just the colonial powers (Britain and Italy) or the superpowers (the United States and the Soviet Union) for inspiration. The resultant rhetoric represented both irredentist belief and device: Somalia needed to recoup lands inhabited by ethnic Somalis. Such a message not only reflected but helped fan pan-Somali sentiment, which proved politically significant at election time. Internationally there was a different payoff: Somalia could project a larger image. At the same time, however, such rhetoric was not always practicable. Yet it came to be expected, as were the goods it promised.

In concert with Egyptian President Abdel Nasser's message of active non-alignment and proactive self-determination (heard in Somali on radio broadcasts from Cairo and augmented by significant economic and military assistance), all Somalis notionally sought the return of the NFD (Northern Frontier District) from Kenya, along with the Haud and Ogaden from Ethiopia. After all, there was a continual reminder on the national flag that these points belonged to Somalia's star. But certain Somalis, particularly those with relatives across these borders, more actively sought the liberation of these areas than others. Thus, the rhetoric of pan-Somali irredentism aside, degrees of commitment varied between clans, with implications (as usual) for the future.

THE "SHIFTA" WAR

In a virtual repeat of the way in which the Four Powers Commission went about deciding who should be awarded the UN mandate over formerly Italian Somaliland after World War II, an internationally composed commission visited Kenya's Northern Frontier District just prior to Kenya's independence in 1963 (see Lewis 1963, 1980; Drysdale 1964; Earl of Lytton 1966). And again, although the commission's visit stirred up local expectations (indeed, made clear that the majority of the population preferred union with Somalia to incorporation in Kenya) the British government nonetheless decided to essentially ignore Somali sentiments. It did so by deferring resolution of the issue (over who the NFD should belong to) to Kenya, which it was about to free.[4]

Clearly, Somalis realized, this move was designed to cement relations between Britain and Kenya, but doing so betrayed promises made to them. Consequently Somalia broke diplomatic ties to London. At the same time, local Somalis began to take matters into their own hands. Yet despite Somali incursions within the NFD, which drew Kenyan troops into battle shortly after Kenya's independence was declared, the *shifta* (bandits) war (as it is called) never developed into full-fledged conflict. The skirmishes between 1963 and 1967 did, however, have three major impacts on Somalia.

First, the *shifta* war isolated Somalia within the Organization of African Unity (OAU). The Somali precedent of demanding territorial adjustment to achieve ethnic unity threatened the territorial sovereignty of virtually all other African states; none could afford this threat. In turn, diplomatic isolation in Africa drove Somalia to seek increasing support from Arab countries. To do so the Somali leadership assiduously played up Somalia's Muslim identity.

Second, the *shifta* war ensured mutual distrust between Kenya and Somalia, setting the stage for Kenya to be able to conveniently blame Somali *shifta* for its own internal problems in the NFD (which it continues to do) and creating a no-man's land between the two countries from which bandits *have* been able to operate. The tension this has fostered periodically flares up into diplomatic incidents requiring international intercession and allowing mediators to apply their own direct pressure on the two countries (e.g., Saudi Arabia on Somalia).

Finally, dissatisfaction over failure to attain the NFD left segments of Somalia's population frustrated not only with the Somali government but with a perceived Somali defeat. Somalia's lack of success must also have encouraged those clans pressing return of the Ogaden to consider handling the situation themselves, rather than allowing the Somali government to do (or not do) the job.

RELATIONS WITH THE SOVIETS, RELATIONS WITH THE UNITED STATES

Meanwhile, throughout this period—which was one of post-independence trial and error throughout Africa—there was intense superpower competition under way involving political and ideological tests of will worldwide. Not only were Egyptian President Abdel Nasser and other ostensibly nonaligned leaders busy striving to make their own marks by steering independent, opportunistic courses gratis the superpowers, but the U.S. and USSR were heavily engaged in the Cold War business of lining up allies, buying friendships, and trying to unseat one another around the globe. In the wake of these various tugs and opportunities, Somalia's leaders persistently tried to play and then beat the odds.[5]

For instance, both Ethiopia and Somalia used the Soviets as a trump card whenever possible with the United States, since the United States was usually the ally of first choice. Both also used arms buildups by the other to agitate for more military aid. Ethiopia had the more substantial United States commitment first—more a matter of timing than perhaps anything else (since Ethiopia regained its sovereignty well before Somalia became independent and began leasing Kagnew Naval Air Station to the United States in 1953, as soon as the British withdrew their military assistance). Thus, the United States did not really need Somalia in 1960, except to ensure that it did not fall into the Soviet camp. Ultimately, too, the United States could not sufficiently please (or arm) both the Somalis and the Ethiopians at the same time.

Meanwhile, shortly after taking power, Siad Barre introduced his own brand of pragmatism to Somalia: scientific socialism. In part this interjection of socialism must be viewed as a genuine, reactive response to the corruption that had plagued Somalia's free-market democracy, particularly as Siad Barre strove to ground his ideology (at least initially) in indigenous terms. However, it also had to have been a shrewd political move to concentrate (nondemocratic) power in the hands of a centralized few as well as a calculated ploy by which to appeal to the Soviets (and worry the United States).[6]

Once committed to Somalia (which they were by 1970) the Soviets were then able to influence domestic policies in turn: Siad Barre established a centralized party, the Soviets contributed economic aid for large state farms and industrial projects, they and the East Germans established an extensive secret service branch, and most significantly, they allowed Somalia's army to grow. As a result of this last effort, the army easily outstripped its former rival, the police force and, locked into a mutually supportive relationship with Siad Barre, became the most powerful institution in the country.

Meanwhile, as Marina Ottaway notes:

> Somalia's foreign policy in the five years following the coup was quite complex and marked both by deep contradictions and brilliant attempts to safeguard the autonomy of a very small and weak country while deliberately thrusting it into the arena of international politics. Siad preached peaceful coexistence with Somalia's neighbors but built up the army. He repeatedly asserted Somalia's dedication to Islam and brought the country into the Arab League but proclaimed scientific socialism and depended on the Soviet Union for military aid. He entered into a Treaty of Friendship and Cooperation with the Soviet Union—which appeared logical enough under the circumstances—but even while doing so announced to the Soviets he was not completely on their side by praising China in the very speech hailing the signing of the treaty (1982, 71).

This became typical, as we shall see, of tactics that Siad Barre maintained through the 1980s. Just as he allegedly practiced a version of divide and rule domestically (by carefully balancing his ministry appointments between members of different clan-families), he selectively pursued different strategies in his foreign relations such that he never *seemed* too dependent on any one patron, yet always in need of others.

THE OGADEN WAR

However, Siad Barre could not completely control all events. Although the Somali government quite dramatically and successfully mobilized the nation to combat the devastating regional drought of 1974–1975, it was this drought (referred to as the *Dabadheer* drought in Somalia) that helped bring down Haile Selassie's government in neighboring Ethiopia. The resultant turmoil in Ethiopia made liberation of the Ogaden—always an irredentist/nation-building dream—suddenly seem feasible and, thus, attractive. For domestic reasons irredentism had been on the rise in Somalia anyway.[7] Fanning the flames: Natural gas deposits had been discovered within thirty miles of the Ethiopian-Somali border in 1972, subsequently inciting Ethiopia and Somalia to build up their respective troop strengths in that area—leading to "incidents."

At the same time, although the Soviet Union did not encourage active Somali bellicosity, the Somalis must have counted on eventual Soviet support since the two countries had only recently signed their Treaty of Friendship and Cooperation, which the Soviets, more than the Somalis, had sought.

However, as incidents bled into running battles, and the more successful the Somalis were, the harder Ethiopia's new Marxist leadership pressed the

Soviet Union to intercede; the Soviets could have Ethiopia as an ally if they would stop the Somalis. For a brief time, then, the Soviet Union actually found itself supporting both countries, and though efforts were made to seek peace between them (and bring both into an alliance with South Yemen) the Somalis still sought the Ogaden. Consequently, once Somalia formally invaded in July 1977 the Soviets had little choice. Ethiopia was simply the greater prize.[8] Unfortunately for Somalia this meant that just when Somali troops were making major gains on the battlefield they found themselves without a major military patron or a steady resupply of arms.

However, not even this withdrawal of Soviet military support would have been so ominous for Somalia if the Soviets had not decided to *actively* militarily support Ethiopia. It was this support that sealed Somalia's fate.

The USSR supplied arms, pilots, military advisors, and Cuban troops to the Ethiopians. This sudden Soviet reversal, along with the lack of immediate Western support (and the United States' stipulation that Saudi Arabia not transship U.S. arms to Somalia) placed Siad Barre in an untenable position. For one, the Ogaden War exacerbated relations with Kenya, which viewed the Somali invasion of the Ogaden as proof of recidivist irredentism. But also this set off alarm bells in other OAU member-states, which still opposed any threats to the idea of territorial sovereignty in Africa. Thus, Somalia found itself increasingly isolated on the international front, which was humiliating and, on top of defeat, only added to problems already simmering internally—with the population now suffering from the effects of the war without yet having fully recovered from the depradations of the 1974–1975 *Dabadheer* drought.

Although Somali forces withdrew from Ethiopian territory and Siad Barre's government conceded defeat in 1978, by early 1980 Somali and Ethiopian troops were again involved in cross-border fighting. Somalia lost this second round of skirmishes, too, which forced a second withdrawal. And because Siad Barre perceived this second involvement as the result of his having caved in to domestic political pressures he now responded by reconsolidating his grip and one-party rule.

Agitation in the north—as much effect as cause—also contributed to this political crackdown and with a number of opposition groups being founded, their establishment only served to justify further government repression.

Criticism grew. Among initial reasons for disgruntlement was Siad Barre's handling of the war, which, it was argued, "centered on his overreliance on administrators and decision-makers from the Marrehan, from his mother's clan (the Ogaden) and from the Dulbahante (to which his son-in-law, who is head of the National Security Service, belongs)" (ACR 1978–1979: B377). Opposition really gained momentum, though, after the execution of six high-ranking officers immediately following Somalia's

1978 defeat. Accounts differ as to whether these six officers were executed for criticizing government failures or were executed because the government required scapegoats in order to shunt blame for the war from the politicians to elements within the army. Regardless, their punishment was subsequently considered to be the catalyst for a thwarted coup attempt, which either involved a preponderance of Majertein (disgruntled over the execution of the officers who were their clansmen), or was portrayed as a Majertein plot by Siad Barre in order to divide political opposition along clan lines (Sheikh-Abdi 1981).[9] The resurgence of segmentation had begun.

• 5 •

Into the 1980s

In many regards Siad Barre's reactions were typical: The more his political foes voiced their opposition the more he relied on people he knew he could trust—namely his relatives—and the more he rewarded his relatives the more distrust this sowed within the population at large. This is the pattern that also presents itself if clan-family politics are read structurally.

Here is one reading: Because Siad Barre was at the top, he was able to manipulate downward, along the lines that fed up to him. Those he manipulated had to look sideways to gauge their dispossession, invariably viewing their loss as the result of someone else's gain, which it was. Because it was individuals, and not whole blocs of individuals, involved in ministerial and other personnel shifts the public was left asking not only why X was demoted and Y promoted at this particular point in time but who (and what) X and Y really represented to Siad Barre.

Ambiguity, in this regard, contributed to Siad Barre's initial successes; he did keep everyone guessing. However, the more people were forced to guess the more they were able to (rightly or wrongly) reduce the puzzle presented to them to a series of rationales. Inevitably these were couched in terms of how X and Y were related to Siad Barre (or the other permanent power brokers) and, since genealogy was traceable for all Somalis, these relationships inevitably came to be comprehensible in terms of family at the most local level, clan-family at the broadest.

Allegiances were thus continually being tested and retested in public thinking—bringing to the fore past instances of competition and memories of having been cheated, but also setting individuals to reconsidering the recent urban past in terms of the more distant rural past and feeding into persistence of "clan" as the ultimate (because it was the most encompassing) determinant in the public eye.[1]

This is one interpretation of how clanship reemerged politically in Somalia. Doubtless there are, or will be, others. For instance, in 1982 David Laitin felt that Siad Barre was caught by forces beyond his control and that initially—coming from a clan that did not have a commanding presence in the Somali state—he sought to downplay clannism:

> Those clans—such as the Majeerteen and Hawiye—which had been key members of ruling coalitions before the 1969 coup suffered *relative* losses. Egalitarian policies necessarily appear discriminatory to groups that had been in the previous period the leading social strata. Their leaders interpreted their relative decline as persecution, and they sought to undermine Siyaad. Siyaad found himself fighting clan-based opposition by relying ever more for protection on members of his own clan. This was interpreted by the opposition as proof that Siyaad was a tribalist (1982, 61).

Nevertheless, whether Siad Barre consciously manipulated clanship, as his detractors have longed claimed, or whether this was merely the most sensible reading available to the disenfranchised (when in reality other struggles—of class or ideology—were taking place), the power inherent in clans and their potential for either being built up or broken down at the national level led to contestation, by opposition groups as well as the regime.

THE AID AVALANCHE

It is from this period that many Somalis date the beginnings of tribalism, of dissolution, and the hollowing of the state, with the regime increasingly looking out for its own membership, not for the nation. But there is a second flow that is also significant for the subsequent current of events. And this is the aid flow.

Significantly, the Soviets had emphasized large industrial and state farm projects and tended to supply equipment (both industrial and military) rather than infusions of foreign exchange. Because of this, the Western aid influx, which began during the late–1970s, amounted to a new occurrence. Even more to the point, just as the government was going about the business of subverting nationalism, the economy was being treated very much as a national entity by donors, who flooded government coffers with funds. Indeed, it was as much the suddenness and timing of this late–1970s aid flood, as it was the amounts of aid that led to crisis in the 1980s.

A large portion of the initial aid that poured into Somalia after the Ogaden War was targeted for assisting refugees from the fighting. Throughout 1978 and 1979, 1,000 refugees a day were fleeing into Somalia (ACR 1979–1980: B306) so that by 1981 it was widely recognized that "the accumulation of, perhaps, 1.5 million refugees in Somalia, making up about 40 percent of the total population is possibly unprecedented in modern times" (ACR 1980–1981: B307). As a result, unprecedented amounts of aid had to be funneled into Somalia to help the government cope; UNHCR alone shipped more than $100 million worth of food to Somalia (Tucker 1982, 22). In hindsight, it now seems that it was *this* avalanche of aid—and the influx of aid workers and Western diplomats accompanying it—that bent the system.

Although it may be impossible to fully reconstruct all of the factors that contributed to the siphoning off of refugee assistance, one major source for corruption in Somalia was the concomitant arrival of expatriates. Newly arrived Western expatriates had to be housed. Somalis see no coincidence in the arrival of relief to Mogadishu and the construction of expensive villas to be rented to expatriates (or lived in by Somali project heads with access to aid money). In 1988–1989 it was widely acknowledged that these villas were built with public moneys by top government officials (many of whom belonged to Siad Barre's immediate family) who then rented them out to diplomatic and expatriate missions. Indeed, one outlying subsection of Mogadishu was nicknamed *Bolle Qaran* [National Theft/Loot], since it was money from government coffers that provided for construction of villas there in the late–1970s.

Also not to be overlooked was the model presented by Saudi Arabia and the Gulf States throughout the 1970s. This was the height of the oil boom, with the region awash in unbelievably large sums of money. Many wealthy Somalis not only performed the hajj [pilgrimage to Mecca] but had business associations with Gulf Arabs. During the early 1970s, too, Gulf Arabs visited Somalia on hunting and falconing trips. Thus, the new "Arab" style of spending money on consumer goods and extravagances must have made an impression on just that class of Somalis who were most able to follow suit—by taking advantage of Somalia's own sudden windfall: refugee aid and foreign assistance.

Not surprisingly, then, the government, as well as thousands of Somalis employed by the relief agencies came to depend on refugees for income. The presence of refugees helped (re-)establish the aid business in Mogadishu, which had been unwelcome during the Soviet era, and which also found itself searching for new "territory" with the refugee crisis in Cambodia beginning to wind down. Maintaining the refugee camps and inflating the numbers proved to be a lucrative business for all enterprising Somalis, including refugees themselves who participated in the sale or resale of donated food (Tucker 1982, 22).[2]

Meanwhile, this, we must remember, was taking place despite (if not because of) the fact that the economy itself was insufficiently recovered from a combination of devastating events just prior to the Ogaden War. Indeed, as the aid money poured in, domestic tensions were building on a variety of fronts, which the distribution of aid money made that much more visible, and troublesome.

First, the 1974–1975 *Dabadheer* drought proved how devastating prolonged environmental degradation could be, evidenced by pastoralists suffering from climatic effects that previously would not have affected them so severely.

> Gross overstocking of sheep and goats was encouraged during the 1960s by rising market prices, especially for sheep. This led to the irresponsible multiplication of cement-tank reservoirs; these in turn, to further overstocking. There was lots of money to be made from these tanks. Their installation became "big business": largely the business of parliamentary deputies during the 1960s who sold their votes for cement-tank permits, and who built the tanks with embezzled government funds.
>
> The revolutionary government installed by President Siad and his colleagues in October 1969 soon put a stop to all that. But the damage was already great. In 1954, for example, the now very hard-hit Burao District had one such tank-reservoir. By the time the revolutionary government moved to ban the installation of such reservoirs Burao District had no fewer than 18,000 of them" (AD Apr. 2–8, 1975: 7373–7374).

As a consequence, the 1974–1975 drought permanently destroyed pastoralism for many nomads (20,000 of whom died)—with the loss of 5 million animals, half of Somalia's sheep and goats, and one-third of its cattle (Ragsdale and Ali 1988). Although the Soviets helped Somalia's government initiate a resettlement scheme that could boast initial success, large numbers of destitute pastoralists simply fled to relatives in the urban areas. This in turn only exacerbated conditions in the towns, where people were already suffering from food shortages—as much due to the drought's direct effects on agriculture as the loss of livestock-earned foreign exchange.

Urban food shortages resulting from the drought subsequently led the government to nationalize a variety of businesses and to initiate food rationing. However, "with the pegging of food prices in the capital, and with the whole of the food and retail trade controlled by the State, the inevitable black market developed" (ACR 1976–1977: B329).

Already an informal market of sorts existed legally. This was the *franco valuta* system.[3] *Franco valuta* was an arrangement whereby Somalis working or trading abroad were able to invest their earnings in consumer goods to be imported and resold in Somalia. Although serving "to alleviate the lack of foreign currency to pay for imports," *franco valuta* was faulted by economists on two counts: It cost the banking system control over imports and it allegedly encouraged inflation, since it affected the black market rate for the Somali shilling (ACR 1980–1981: B319). For these reasons and because it was considered a parallel market, *franco valuta* was terminated under an IMF (International Monetary Fund) agreement in 1981.[4]

However, abolition of *franco valuta* had far-reaching impacts. With the intercession of the IMF (itself a sure sign of an attempted Western makeover of the Somali economy) and the termination of *franco valuta*, northern merchants felt particularly targeted, since it was they and remittance earners abroad (many of whom came from the north) who had especially benefited (ACR 1983–1984: B264). Indeed, the government's abolishment of *franco valuta* is cited as having provided a boost for the Somali National Movement (or SNM, a northern, Isaq clan-family-oriented opposition group) founded in 1980. Nor can it be considered a coincidence that the SNM achieved a number of military successes in 1982 (AC Mar. 2, 1983: 6).[5]

Historically, northerners had long felt they had not received their fair share of attention or assistance from Mogadishu. The new influx of aid moneys only further convinced them that the central government was less interested in pursuing progress in the north than its own projects in the south. In early 1982 popular (allegedly self-help) demonstrations in the northern town of Hargeisa met with a brutal government response, thus beginning a pattern of regional civil disobedience leading to violent government reactions. Increasingly violent government responses, in turn, fueled SNM (and other northern opposition group) reactions, which themselves then invited increasingly violent and broad-based government crackdowns. A vicious cycle had begun.

Nor were all of these crackdowns military. For instance, in 1983 the government banned the production and sale of the stimulant *qat* (a northern crop). This was publicly explained as a move to preserve Somalis' physical and economic health, although it was also widely believed that profits from *qat* were buying arms for northern rebels. Of course, the outlawing of *qat* made its smuggling a lucrative enterprise—and one from which the army and police, especially, could profit. Thus, whereas one setback led to another for some Somalis, others were able to wrest profit from seeming misfortune.

On a broader scale, other events affected virtually all urban Somalis, since the 1970s boom in the Persian Gulf oil economy provided jobs for hundreds of thousands of migrant workers, who funneled home their wages as remittances. As we shall see in a later chapter, these remittances were critical in enabling most urban-based Somali families to stay afloat. In a sense, their doing so made a mockery of the national economy. Despite the latest Western economic fashions and efforts made to devalue currency, restrain consumer demand, liberalize, and privatize "the" economy, it was these remittances (and other earnings from parallel economic activities) that allowed civil servants to continue working for negligible salaries and permitted families to persist in being able to buy imported staples despite climbing prices.

On the one hand, then, it was family-level Somali assistance from abroad that, alongside large sums of foreign aid, helped perpetuate a system (or set of systems) that, by virtually all accounts, *should have been* dysfunctional yet managed to continue operating through 1989. On the other hand, the pastoral sector was also integral—not only because urban kin were able to make ends meet thanks to their access to rural produce but because a sizable segment of the population was able to remain comfortably outside the "national" economy without threatening (or necessarily interacting with) the state.

This is Vali Jamal's controversial thesis: Inaccurate and unsubstantiated statistics have yielded a false picture of rural and urban poverty in Somalia. In a much-debated series of articles he argued that estimations of milk production in Somalia were wrong; as a result, Somali nomads were much better off than they had been reported to be and played a much larger role in assuring a functional Somali economy. Similarly, "official figures of GDP and wages fail to convey an accurate picture of the Somali economy," which, reliant as it had been on remittances, found no reflection in any of the official reports (1988, 807). Although Jamal argued that the Somali economy was in practice very much a free-market economy, thus not needing World Bank/IMF tutelage in order to become free, his criticisms are more significant for my argument in terms of his recognition of the significance of localism (represented in this case by the pastoral sector) on the one hand, and supra-localism (represented by the remittance diaspora) on the other, which assured Somalis' survival but threatened insolvency for the country.

Thinking chronologically and not just structurally we also cannot ignore the effects of change, or the frequency of changes in economic policy (from Soviet to Western models and then whatever was favored by World Bank/IMF officials at any given time). This is without even taking into account particular Somali agendas or changes a finance minister might initiate. Given such flux the question looms: What rational choice *did* people have but to persist with alternate economies, as they continued to count on what they already knew (by practice) would work?

However, even this sketchy accounting cannot do justice to what such changeability meant to Somalis. We have touched on only some of the ways some of the pieces of the puzzle may have fitted together (e.g., the coming of Western aid and participation by Western agencies in the reorganization of the Somali economy; the Ogaden War resulting in food shortages leading to rationing and acceleration of the black market; the banning of *franco valuta* and the impact this had in the north where people already felt slighted by the Mogadishu government). But this is just one set of explanations for how regionalism cracked the national edifice. Presumably other views from within other regions (as well as consideration of other policies—on agriculture, marketing, local government, etc.) would reveal different chains of events.

Nonetheless, why focus on regions? With the Isaq predominating in the north why not focus on tribalism? Or with merchants backing opposition movements why not focus on class struggle instead?

The problem with choosing only one strand by which to interpret events is that although this might simplify what otherwise is a nightmare in forensics, only an artificially neatened history would result. As it is I am probably presenting too streamlined an accounting of Somalia. If we were to examine a single Somali life, we would find that class, region, and clan play shifting, confusing, obfuscating roles; they can't be separated out; and they clearly reflect incredible flux. But life still got lived and somehow individuals managed. Indeed, one lesson that emerges from the following case is how unimportant (on a daily basis) fissures between regions, or clan-families, or classes could prove to be, so long as flexibility meant most people *were* still managing.

THE EDUCATION OF ROBLE

When I met him, Roble (49) was an interpreter employed by the American military in Mogadishu. He was a northerner originally from the Las Caanod area, where his father's father had served as a sergeant in the British army and been killed fighting Sayyid Mohamed Abdille Hassan (or "the Mad Mullah" as Roble prefers). Instead of joining the military like Roble's grandfather, his father—who only went to Koranic school—sold a portion of his inherited livestock in order to travel to Aden, where he joined his half brother, a trader.

By 1945 Roble's father's half brother operated a fleet of ten trucks between Dire Dawa and Harar in Ethiopia and Somalia and was considered one of the richest men in the region but poor, because he was childless. When he died, Roble's father inherited his wife—according to tradition (*dumal*)—who bore him no children either.

In the course of business, Roble's father traveled to the Persian Gulf, India, and Indonesia, selling hides, skins, and live animals and buying cloth and material in return. He owned a shop in Burao, which is where, looking for a second wife, he approached a good family and received Roble's mother in 1935; she was *reer miyi* [nomadic] according to Roble. In 1954 Roble's father moved from Burao to Berbera.

Roble's mother more than made up for her husband's barren first wife, by giving birth to ten children. Three sons and five daughters survived. Of Roble's brothers and sisters only the boys were educated. Roble's older brother was trained by British veterinarians and worked for the Somali Veterinary Service between 1958–1975, when he quit to travel to Qatar, where he now works for that government's livestock service. Their younger brother is also in the Persian Gulf—in Saudi Arabia—working as an electrician, having learned his trade in intermediate school, which he attended in Mogadishu with Roble's support.

Roble, the second oldest son and fourth child, entered elementary school in Burao and did well. Subsequently he was sent to the intermediate school in Sheikh (where he boarded) and then entered the secondary school in Boroma, British Somaliland's sole secondary school at that time (with eighty students). In 1960 a new secondary school was built in Sheikh, and Roble transferred there.

Between intermediate and secondary school Roble spent five months with his brother in the Somali Veterinary Service. He continued to work with that service during his holidays in order to earn his school fees. After graduating from secondary school he was able to join the British Wildlife Service, but stayed only briefly before joining the army in early 1962. Because the Somali army was a new army he thought he would be able to do well as a career officer.

In 1963 Roble and another Somali were selected to attend cadet school in Britain. Between 1963 and 1965 he attended the Royal Military Academy at Sandhurst. On his return to Somalia as a second lieutenant, Roble filled various important positions in the army until April 1970 when he joined the National Security Service and was sent to the USSR for six months of training. Having returned home newly indoctrinated, Roble served as chief administrator of the NSS for the next six years.

Once again, in late 1976, Roble was sent to the Soviet Union. This time he was supposed to learn political science at an institute in the Ukraine. He and three other Somalis were the only foreign nationals to receive this education, and at one point, disillusioned, Roble threw a statue of Lenin from his fifth floor dormitory window. He was subsequently deported from the Ukraine and sentenced to sixteen years in prison in Somalia.

Roble remained under house arrest between January and April 1977 in Mogadishu's military police compound. But then, on April 22, Lenin's birthday, he was formally incarcerated.

Roble specifically requested the maximum security section of Mogadishu's central prison, knowing that there would be better facilities and more people like him imprisoned there. Indeed, he wound up sharing an eight-man cell with a district commissioner, an ex-attorney general, a doctor, a merchant, and an ex-minister.

Roble was imprisoned until September 1977, when the president "suddenly" pardoned him on the stipulation that he help the government prosecute the Ogaden War. With Somalia's defeat, Roble sought to resign from military service the following year, but was refused. Instead, he was transferred to the civil service where he was made a director (responsible for "planning and costing") of the State Constructional Material Agency. When that agency was abolished in July 1981 he was subsequently shunted to the State Sugar Factory at Johar as a commercial director. He remained in Johar until November 1983 when he finally successfully resigned from the civil service for "personal reasons"—these personal reasons having to do with increasing anti-northerner sentiment and suspicion that Roble was antigovernment.

Having been trained initially by the British (who were the dominant force in the north), and then retrained by the Russians (the superpower of choice during the 1970s), Roble finally gained employment with the United States (the most conspicuous new donor) in mid-1987.

Interestingly enough, in Roble's own analysis of the government positions he held he says that it made sense for him to be appointed sugar factory commercial director since he had been a finance officer with the NSS. As he put it, with his educational background he and others like him—that is to say those educated men of his generation—could fit anywhere in Somalia. As a postscript, it turns out that Roble was also (still) in the employ of the NSS while he was working for the United States.

What is interesting to consider given this life history (which may or may not have been substantively self-edited) is *how* Roble managed. In some circumstances he suffered because of his known allegiances. In other situations he profited. All that is really clear is that when he was able to manipulate the past, which he had both lived (as a single individual) and embodied (belonging to a particular clan-family, coming from a particular region, etc.), he did so to his advantage. By contrast, when it was to the advantage of others whom he threatened (either because of who he was related to, where he came from, or the opinions he held) any of these same advantages could be turned against him. He could be jailed, he could be fired, he could be made to feel threatened, he could be coopted.

As backdrop to others this history also counterpoints a number of struggles. For instance, in his ability to find employment it did not seem to matter that although Roble was initially trained by the British, he had to be retrained by the Soviets, only to wind up working for the United States (and Somalis). Of course, what worked in his favor throughout was that he was a member of Somalia's earliest postcolonial elite, a limited group. This is one reason his employment record offers such a sharp contrast to those of much younger individuals who attained even more education than Roble (as we will see). Unfortunately for them, their starts came in a different era. First of all, the number of educated Somalis was much greater in the late 1980s than in the late 1950s. Second, Roble's timing was better: He achieved his schooling just as differential access to education was itself becoming one of the foundations for nationwide but still genealogically legible networking.

Roble's life is interesting not only because it spans the abrupt lurches brought about by changing colonial and postcolonial arrangements but because it also illustrates how impossible planning could be. The changes that most seriously affected him, time and again, were way out of his control. Yet, he was deeply embroiled in them, supporting their machinery, even living out their contradictions—and succeeding.

Perhaps this is why dissolution was staved off for as long as it was in Somalia. At the most local of levels enough people like Roble were able to make do after all. It was only after people like him, who had known success, found themselves slowly losing their access to the means of success, that finger-pointing began (and genealogies got traced). Meanwhile, once finger-pointing got going there was no stopping it until everyone was reminded of who they did or did not owe their position to. By working for the United States yet reporting to the Somali secret police Roble merely exemplified this at the broadest end of the scale. At the smaller end, who his patrons really were among Somalis remains unclear. Was he an Isaq northerner in league with the government, or an SNM spy? Or, was he simply situationally flexible throughout?

COMPRESSION

As the 1980s progressed, instances of Somalia using and being used for its geopolitical significance increased, whereas specifically Somali features, such as lineage allegiance and clan-family affiliation, proved not only durable but insistent. Even history could be suggestive. For instance, early on Siad Barre was often paired with Sayyid Mohamed Abdille Hassan (the renowned poet and warrior) as a comparable national hero. It could only have furthered Siad Barre's purposes to foster such analogies.

Meanwhile, Siad Barre had to have also been influenced by his forebears and peers in the world of military dictators: Mussolini (whose impact on Somalia he had experienced firsthand), Nasser—an ally, Gadhafi—another ally, Nimeiri—again someone whom Siad Barre dealt with, and a host of other neighbors, acquaintances, and even foes. Certainly, Siad Barre had much to gain from paying attention to dictatorial successes elsewhere. It may not be mere coincidence that Yemen banned tribal clubs in 1970, with Siad Barre subsequently outlawing clannism in Somalia, or that Yemen adopted Family Law (which emancipated women) in 1974, something the Somali regime also enacted despite much conservative Islamic criticism in January 1975. Similarly, the nature of nonaligned power plays exemplified by such countries as Yugoslavia and India had to have suggested a range of possibilities for milking the superpowers and appealing to their bloc allies.

At the same time, just as first the British and the Italians, then the Soviets and the United States sought Somalia as a setpiece in larger struggles, regional players exercised their supra-local ambitions via Somalia. Clearly, members of the Arab League saw something to be gained from granting Somalia Arab League membership in 1974. Nor should oil be ruled out as a very real interest for all parties in the postcolonial era. For instance, the French oil company ELF gained significant contracts for exploratory drilling. But the French also had a keen interest in Somali politics vis-à-vis Djibouti, particularly since Somalia's relationship with this fifth point of its flag's irredentist star was always touchy (and especially so as northern Somali opposition movements began to gather momentum).

At the other end of the European spectrum, the Germans arrived in Somalia largely by accident. In 1977 a hijacked Lufthansa jet was landed in Mogadishu and the Somali government granted German special forces units permission to storm it. Out of gratitude the German government became a major donor. However, perhaps this was not entirely gratuitous. It must be remembered that it was the East Germans who trained the Somali National Security Service—who knows what propaganda (or other) benefit West Germany would have received by replacing them?

Throughout this period, too, reports about conditions in Somalia written by academics and nonacademics alike predicted Siad Barre's imminent demise. In 1982 *Africa Report* published an article entitled "How stable is Siad Barre's regime?" (Paul Henze, Mar.–Apr.) In 1985 it printed a piece that began, "President Mohamed Siad Barre has been getting a rather bad press lately. The president himself is reportedly ill—heart disease, throat cancer, liver problems, and depression are some of the suggestions. For the first time, the media has been speculating on the country's future, with headlines referring to 'a nation in tatters' and 'patriarch about to depart'" (Barre's Balancing Act," Antony Shaw, Nov.–Dec.: 26–29). In 1987 a subheadline again echoed impending demise: "parallels with the last days of Haile Selassie are emerging in Mogadishu. Interclan conflict over the uncertainty of presidential succession, an economy in severe crisis, human rights violations, and continued military clashes have left President Mohamed Siad Barre in a weakened political position" ("An Embattled Barre," Richard Greenfield, May–June: 65–69).

Back issues of *Africa Confidential* paint a similar picture. In June 1981: "President Siad Barre is looking increasingly isolated, as he pushes his oldest confidants [sic] (sideways or downwards?) into new jobs, ignores his party, and relies more and more on his own clansmen" (June 17, 1981: 3). In March 1983: "Somalia: Barre hangs on" (March 2, 1983: 5). In July 1983: "President Mohamed Siad Barre's 14-year-old regime appears again to be in its last stages of viability. Politically and in terms of security the regime is losing control: large regions of the country are now in a state of virtual anarchy. For several months fierce clan fights have raged in different areas of northern and central Somalia." (Jul. 20, 1983: 3).

However, by late 1983, *Africa Confidential* was reversing its predictions: "organized opposition to Siad Barre's regime is in danger of complete collapse. The two main opposition groups, the . . . Democratic Front for the Salvation of Somalia (DFSS) and the . . . (SNM) are now both riven with factions" (24/24).

Not until 1986 did crystal ball gazing resume, precipitated by Siad Barre's brush with death in a near fatal car accident.

Taken as a whole, two factors stand out in these reprieves for the regime: first, Siad Barre's continued ability to rally support both within and without Somalia by mixing and baiting "allies"; and second, dissension and factional fighting within the opposition movements themselves. According to *Africa Confidential* as well as virtually all other sources, it was the lack of a united opposition that prevented Siad Barre from being toppled; as unpalatable as his government was, no viable alternative presented itself.

Here it seems important simply to reconsider what was described at the start of the chapter: the differences between top-down manipulations and bottom-up views. Whereas Siad Barre successfully manipulated and realigned the clan-families on the broadest (i.e., national) scale, the opposition groups were predominantly composed of lineages from within single clan-families. Thus, there were no realignments outside the opposition group for most of these lineages to realistically consider. As a result, whenever struggles for power and control took place *within* movements, such inter-lineage fighting only weakened their overall structure and purpose. *Africa Confidential* describes one of these power struggles, in which military members wrested control from civilians within the SNM. In this instance, the SNM's military members felt that their leaders (then taking refuge in Ethiopia) were out of touch with the front in Somalia. In addition,

> there were two more important reasons for dissatisfaction with the previous leadership: it was regarded as ideologically too close to the United States and Saudi Arabia—an inclination which was unacceptable to Ethiopia and Libya [the two countries supplying the SNM with arms]; and the army officers resented the fact that the majority of the SNM's guerillas are from the Habr Yunis subclan while the leadership revolved around the Habr Awal subclan. Not that this division was illogical: apart from being the largest group within the Isaq, the Habr Awal traditionally provided most of the SNM's finance—largely from the Isaq diaspora in the Arabian Gulf, Britain and East Africa (Nov. 30, 1983:7).

Hence, potential tension inhering in both past and present power relations between the lineages was available for manipulation by both individuals (who wished to lead or enhance their own power) and those who had leverage over the movements: namely, their backers. For example, *Africa Confidential* suggested that Ethiopia sowed much of this discord purposely: Although Ethiopia's leader Mengistu Haile Mariam backed the Somali rebels in order to bring down the Barre regime, he did not want to help establish a united front powerful enough to pose the same sort of threat to him that Siad Barre posed. Meanwhile, something as "simple" as the reestablishment of diplomatic relations between Somalia and Libya (in 1985) was enough to throw the opposition movements into turmoil again. In short, the game was played from all sides and angles with very little letup.

There was also a more local context to the ups and downs of the opposition movments: Mengistu was opportunistic vis-à-vis the Somali rebels, encouraging whichever group (either the SNM or DFSS/SSDF[Somali Salvation Democratic Front])[6] he thought stronger at the time, only to then back off. Additionally, much of his commitment was determined by his own wrangles with Somali-supported Ethiopian rebels as well as with the timing of Sudanese commitments to either Somalia or the Eritreans (since Sudan also played a role in supporting Ethiopia's rebels and could apply the dictum, "the enemy of my enemy is my friend" to Siad Barre).

Of course, at higher levels the Soviet Union had to have had some say in Ethiopia's role, particularly since Siad Barre was again making overtures to the Soviets during this period. But, ultimately, on the most local of levels, Mengistu may have had far less control over the Somali rebels than his regional commanders did—whose own personal agendas could have dictated all sorts of divergent strategies. Hence, the picture is confused.

It is further complicated by such factors as climate—whether rebels and government troops were able to supplement their food supplies by living off the land or whether they instead were forced to "disturb" the local population, and if so, how this spun out. In addition, how well equipped the forces were and whether fighting appeared worthwhile determined strengths on both sides. For instance, when salaries did not reach government troops in time, weapons could be sold. If the rebels could not subsist, defection became an option. The nature of what was, essentially, a war of attrition (with skirmishes, ambushes, and running battles but no front lines) across a border permeable by the rebels, but impermeable to troops in government uniform certainly only enhanced the appearance (if not the substance) of flux.

Nevertheless, the ongoing fact of opposition and the forceful manner in which the Somali government responded did eventually touch most Somalis in Mogadishu. Given the corporate nature of Somali families almost everyone had a relative who was somehow caught up by one side or the other in the struggle between Siad Barre and the SNM or Siad Barre and the SSDF:

as northerners or members of the army, as conscripts, or simply by working or living near northerners in Mogadishu. Also the national economy (i.e., Mogadishu's merchants) felt the effects of soldiers at war and dislocations in the north, and government politics became ever more attenuated with imprisonments and reshuffles.

Thus, it is not so much a lack of information about what was taking place that renders the picture so muddled. Rather, it is that the patterns of action and reaction that emerge reveal no single all-unraveling thread. Instead what we find is a variety of courses being set that guaranteed that a point of no return *would* be reached. That it was definitively reached sometime between 1986 and 1989 now seems clear. However, what exactly constituted this point, or when it was passed is much less certain. Nor may it ever be certain. And this is important. In fact, what I try to demonstrate by accounting for a multitude of possibilities in the chapters that follow is that there may be two roots of dissolution to which hindsight and the neatening of history normally blind us. One is uncertainty. The second is the partial logics people contruct to cope with knowing-but-never-really-knowing.

PART THREE

Chronology (1988–1989)

Here we look at the process of dissolution itself: encapsulated in the coming of violence to Mogadishu on July 14, 1989. This particular day—on which the government perpetrated violence against civilians—was a watershed for Mogadishu during the time I was there.[1] Not only did it mark the culmination of expectations for change by the public as well as release of frustrations by public and government alike but it also rendered previously submerged sentiments quite visible.

Although the very fact of July 14 clarified some positions (who was opposing whom on the broad scale—the public versus the government), it confused others (who, individually, was taking part—with widespread and indiscriminate arrests). But perhaps most importantly, just as July 14 signified (at the time) the end of peace and (in hindsight) the beginning of violence, it also became representational as an Event, invested and reinvested with a variety of meanings for all residents of Mogadishu.

As a result, it is hard to know when exactly the stage began to be set for July 14, or consequently when to begin this chronology. Therefore, I briefly outline a series of events that occurred well before 1989 with the proviso that it is difficult to know from reading the limited number and variety of accounts available how to weight the relative significances of these.[2] Hence, they should not be accepted as true or authoritative at face value; this is an incomplete and conflicted record, which parallels an incomplete and conflicted time. Indeed, part of what I want to convey is that it is broken information as much as anything that *patterns* dissolution.

As a consequence, Chapter Six is essentially little more than a sequence of news bites leading up to Chapter Seven, which focuses on July 14 and its aftermath. The microevents in Chapter Six are meant to serve as slow-motion proofs of the local/supra-local level pirouette described in Chapter Five. Also, my slowing down these frames is meant to slow down the trajectory of confused conjunctions and disjunctures that cannot be molded into a smooth or accurate narrative; that would be a contradiction in terms (and of truth). Unfortunately, this does not make for easy reading. (Nor, for those who need no further convincing, does Chapter Six have to be read.)

For instance, events occur within and outside Somalia simultaneously, variably affecting different sectors of society at various rates, but the spins placed on occurrences also differ. It is for this reason that I back up three times to reconsider 1988 (for the SNM, the Ogaden, and the economy and diplomacy). Nor is there anything definitive about this particular threesome, other than that given subsequent events, these three trajectories now seem significant.

• 6 •

The Coming of July 14

OVERVIEW: 1986–1988

May 1986

A near-fatal car accident seriously injured Siad Barre and shook up his administration, his family, and his rivals (AC May 21, 1986: 3). In the accident's immediate aftermath—with Siad Barre in Saudi Arabia for medical treatment—there was a flurry of internal struggles for power within all camps (i.e., political, military, opposition) grounded in the assumption that this accident spelled the end of the regime. However, despite expectations, there was no overt struggle between any of the camps and despite the seriousness of the injuries (and his advanced age) Siad Barre was back wielding at least nominal power within six weeks (AC Sept. 3, 1986: 6).

Either coincidentally or consciously, the SNM began to step up its activities in the north once Siad Barre was seen to be recovering and it was clear that there would be no change of government (AC Sept. 3, 1986: 7).

May 1987

The SNM continued to be active in the north, making a daring raid on Hargeisa's prison (ARB Jul. 15, 1987: 854), and the SSDF (formerly the DSSF) emerged from its own period of extended quiescence to take credit for an explosion at the main post office in Mogadishu in early April and an attack on an army brigade near Beled Weyn (in central Somalia) later in the month (ARB June 15, 1987: 8513–8514).[1]

Meanwhile, Siad Barre reacted to the scramble to succeed him by engineering a more intense Marehanization of the government and the military, sidelining more and more of his Ogadeni military leaders (AC April 1, 1987: 2–3)—the Ogaden traditionally having formed the bulk of the military and filling key leadership positions.

These government actions in turn incited a split among the Marehan power brokers—as Marehan jostled for power among themselves and because not all of Siad Barre's fellow clansmen (and women) agreed with his policies. As the splits within the Marehan widened, it became increasingly apparent (at least in some circles) that two rival camps were centering themselves around two of Siad Barre's wives and their rival sons, these sons in turn rallying their mother's clans behind them (ION July 11, 1987). In light of this split and so many rumors and machinations, Siad Barre was able to arrest several leading military and police officers in June. As the July 22, 1987 *Africa Confidential* notes, "Somalia is now reaping the harvest of the policy of divide and rule which President Siad Barre has wielded so efficiently for a decade or more. But it is a policy that depends upon the skill of the individual at the top. Without Barre, or a figure of comparable talents, it is a policy which may be very hard to carry out" (July 22, 1987: 7).

In May the World Bank published a report critical of the project aid Somalia had been receiving, which the bank claimed was far in excess of the Somalis' ability to handle (ION May 2, 1987). Also the bank (like the United States Government and USAID reports) expressed a strong desire to see more privatization. By the end of May, clearly under World Bank (and structural adjustment) influence, a dual rather than triple auction system was adopted for the exchange of foreign currency (ION May 30, 1987).

August 1987

Perhaps it was the sudden change in the foreign exchange system and other "new" interventions or perhaps it was merely an acute case of corruption on the part of individuals involved in the government purchase of oil, but spontaneous demonstrations broke out in Mogadishu in mid-August—cited as the first such public protest under Siad Barre's rule. Mogadishu residents took to the streets to protest against fuel shortages and the resultant lack of public transportation and difficulties in obtaining foodstuffs. Although the government responded by putting a local military division on alert, tension eased and no violence was reported (ARB Sept. 15, 1987: 8603).

September 1987

The Somali government unilaterally withdrew from the IMF by returning to a fixed parity between the Somali shilling and the dollar.

INTERNAL DISSOLUTION— THE SNM AND WAR IN THE NORTH (FEBRUARY 1988–SEPTEMBER 1988)

February 1988

Six prominent northerners (former ministers under Siad Barre) accused of having plotted the government's demise between 1978 and 1982 were tried and sentenced (two received the death penalty). Siad Barre then magnanimously commuted the two death sentences to prison terms in an act of clemency interpreted as a move toward national reconciliation (ARB Mar. 15, 1988: 8790; ION Feb. 20, 1988). However, in the days previous to the trial hundreds more people (principally northerners) had been arrested on charges of supplying information to foreigners or planning demonstrations (ION Feb. 13, 1988).

By late February, meanwhile, shortages of all kinds were being reported in the capital in large part because the shortfall in foreign exchange had sent the black market dollar rate soaring and because people responded to government price-fixing by hoarding while many merchants simply took their goods out of circulation in order to wait for better conditions (ION Feb. 27, 1988).

March 1988

Siad Barre met with Ethiopian leader Mengistu Haile Mariam in Djibouti under cover of an international meeting of the Inter-Governmental Authority on Drought and Development (IGADD) (ION Mar. 26, 1988). Their series of talks in Djibouti subsequently led to the signing of a historic agreement reestablishing diplomatic links between the two countries, securing their mutual border, and ending support for one another's opposition groups (AC Apr. 29, 1988). Not surprisingly, while the initial talks were taking place the SNM renewed activities in the north, in part to embarrass Siad Barre (ION Mar. 26, 1988). More significantly, although Siad Barre made peace in large part to dislocate the SNM (which received financial and logistical support from Mengistu), this agreement between the two heads of state also sent a clear message to Ogadeni Somalis. The government was renunciating irredentist title to the Ogaden. Of course, the Ogaden viewed this as a *Marehan* renunciation (AC Apr. 29, 1988). However, this "secret" portion of the agreement on the Ogaden would not be publicized for another six weeks (ION May 28, 1988).

Of more immediate notice was that the government was now forcing the SNM's hand either to move back into Somalia or dissolve. However, a successfully coordinated SNM military offensive in the northern towns of

Burao and Hargeisa made it abundantly clear that the SNM was not about to simply disappear (AC May 17, 1988).

May 1988

This SNM offensive, in turn, sent hundreds of thousands of refugees fleeing southward to Mogadishu (as well as into Ethiopia and the surrounding bush). In response to this influx as well as to the turmoil in the north, the government began arresting hundreds of Isaqs in Mogadishu and other southern towns (AC Jul. 29, 1988: 1).

In Hargeisa the five days of particularly fierce fighting and bedlam resulted in all expatriate aid workers finally being evacuated by air in June. The United Nations engineered the flights, which rescued approximately 170 foreign nationals, less than a dozen of whom were U.S. citizens (ARB Jul. 15, 1988: 8919; personal communication).

September 1988

By late September it was being reported in the press and by the government that the SNM offensive had failed in the north, although SNM units were still operating in some areas. As many as 15,000 people were said to have died in the clashes (AC Sept. 23, 1988: 1; ARB Aug. 15, 1988: 8953), although this figure would later be readjusted to upwards of 30,000.

INTERNAL DISSOLUTION— THE OGADEN (MAY 1988–SEPTEMBER 1988)

Meanwhile, the peace agreement between Somalia and Ethiopia also led to turmoil in the army, with its preponderance of Ogadenis. The Somali government's official renunciation of Somalia's claims to the Ogaden and lack of discussion about the fate of the hundreds of thousands of Ogadeni refugees still in camps in Somalia were especially disturbing not only because the army was manned by so many Ogadeni but more specifically because many of them were refugees from the 1977–1978 Ogaden War who themselves had been recruited into the army from refugee camps. In the more recent past these Ogadeni soldiers had also been used as frontline troops in operations in the north against the SNM, while substantiated rumors continued to indicate that Ogadeni refugees in camps in the north were still receiving arms and inducements from the government to continue fighting against the Isaq.

May 1988

Government troops in northern Somalia raided local stock (in lieu of late wages from Mogadishu), further exacerbating resentments and tensions between the Isaq and Ogaden (ION May 7, 1988). Whether this was intentional manipulation on the part of the government (stirring up more resentment between clans) or not, such antagonism certainly played to Siad Barre's "divide and rule" strengths.

However, the government itself was also coming under fire. In May the (Ogadeni) WSLF (Western Somali Liberation Front) distributed antigovernment pamphlets in Mogadishu, although there were also rumors that members of a relatively recent breakaway organization, the Ogaden National Liberation Front, were infiltrating from Ethiopia into Somalia (ION May 28, 1988).

July 1988

Tensions were palpable in Mogadishu once more, with new pamphlets appearing (allegedly) from within the Hawiye camp calling for the expulsion of Daroods (Majertein and Ogaden) from Mogadishu, which the Hawiye considered within their geographical domain (ION Jul. 23, 1988).

September 1988

With these increasing interclan tensions, by September the Somali Salvation Democratic Front (SSDF), one of the oldest of the opposition movements, fissioned, with many of its Hawiye fighters leaving the largely Majertein leadership to join the Isaq SNM. Here it should also be noted that the long-time friend of Somali opposition groups, Ethiopia, probably played some sort of a role in some of these clan alignments and realignments since, as the *Indian Ocean Newsletter* suggests, a partition of Somalia could only have been in Addis Ababa's best interests, with the possibility of some sort of (non-Eritrean) Ethiopian access to the Red Sea implied (ION Oct. 29, 1988).

DISSOLUTION—THE ECONOMY AND DIPLOMACY (APRIL 1988–DECEMBER 1988)

April 1988

On the international economic front, in April the leader of Italy's Radical Party publicly accused Siad Barre and his family of extensive corruption involving the abuse and misuse of Italian aid for fraudulent development schemes. This public blame, stemming from charges leveled by an Italian magazine (*Europeo*), in turn brought Rome around to finally joining with the rest of Somalia's Western donors in freezing aid funds, which occurred once the IMF declared Somalia ineligible for IMF assistance in mid-May (ION Apr. 9 and May 14, 1988).

This took place just as the fighting in the north began to impact the economy. Continued fighting around Berbera halted much of the annual hajj export of livestock to Saudi Arabia (ION Jul. 23, 1988)—Berbera being the primary port for livestock exports, and livestock (officially) earning Somalia 80 percent of its foreign exchange, and the export before hajj comprising the bulk of this.

As a result, Siad Barre must have felt increasingly beleaguered. The only two countries visibly supporting his fight in the north were Iraq and Djibouti, both of which were thought to be ferrying him arms (ION June 25, Jul. 23, and Jul. 30, 1988). At the same time, Siad Barre must have hoped for some remuneration from the Soviet Union (Ethiopia's patron) for having signed the March treaty, and at least some accolades for his foreign, if not domestic policies, in the West—none of which had yet materialized. However, during this same period, Chevron (the oil company) was drilling its first well in northern Somalia, and Phillips Petroleum, AMOCO, and Agip were also active (ION May 21, 1988).

In sum, then, although a gradual fissuring of society was under way with attendant economic pressures building within Somalia, the situation was being exacerbated further by conscious *non*-alleviation from without. Still, Siad Barre continued efforts on the diplomatic front.

September 1988

Somalia and Ethiopia exchanged POWs, thus affirming the peace. Also Egypt expelled five military trainees from its military academy for allegedly having criticized the Mogadishu regime and Saudi Arabia arrested and deported fifty northern Somali workers at Mogadishu's request—the SNM was receiving too much of its financial support from Isaqs working lucrative positions in the Persian Gulf (ION Sept. 10, 1988). Clearly, such Egyptian and Saudi support is one indication of just how well Siad Barre was still able to manipulate the fears and antagonisms among those whom he wooed, particularly since Libya was once again looming larger and larger as an ally (ION Oct. 29 and Dec. 24, 1988).[2]

Nevertheless, although Siad Barre may have been able to present himself favorably to some, Amnesty International published a report in late September focusing on the "long-term human rights crisis" in Somalia (ION Sept. 24, 1988). Within a month, in October, *The Washington Post* gave play to several stories chronicling the continued fighting in the north and the regime's search for allies in Libya and the Soviet Union (ION Oct. 29, 1988). Meanwhile, this sort of publicity only hardened U.S. congressional resolve to continue blocking U.S. aid to Somalia, which it had halted back in July when the fighting in the north was brought to its attention.

October 1988

Trying to buy some sort of grace (particularly with northerners)—and because at this point it was an established October 21 tradition (this date marking the anniversary of Siad Barre's accession to power)—the government released six prominent politicians, two of whom had been sentenced to death and all of whom had been jailed since 1982 (ARB Nov. 15, 1988: 9048).

However, only two weeks after these annual October 21 celebrations, a crowd of demonstrators marched on Villa Somalia (the presidential palace). Led by those same Somali POWs recently returned from Ethiopia, whom the government had welcomed home as heroes but never adequately compensated (despite public promises), "the crowd protested against rising food prices and shortages, as well as against government actions in the north" (AC Nov. 18, 1988: 3). Inspired by the returned POWs, soldiers injured in the May and June fighting in the north then also took to the streets (ION Nov. 11, 1988).

Despite earlier assertions (ARB Sept. 15, 1987: 8603) that the three days of demonstrations during August 1987 had been the first popular political protests to erupt during 19 years of Siad's rule, an identical claim was made for these October marches by *Africa Confidential.*[3]

As *Africa Confidential* noted:

> The demonstration reflected a worsening economic situation. Food prices have risen sharply since price controls were imposed at the beginning of the year. The controls led to hoarding and shortages and by mid-year the government had to back down, privately telling merchants to ignore controls. Food returned to the markets but at a high price. In addition, inflation has been rising sharply, and the black market rate for the U.S. dollar is now 500 Somali shillings, against an official rate of SS 260. Civil service salaries were doubled at the end of August but it doesn't seem to have made much difference. There are now believed to be over 200,000 unemployed among Mogadishu's population of 1.5 million (AC Nov. 18, 1988: 3).

Despite tours of the north (and Hargeisa specifically), organized to prove to Western ambassadors and NGO and PVO representatives that the government still maintained control, *The Washington Post* articles and other adverse publicity were having effects. As a result, the military aid, which had been in the pipeline from the West for years, began to dry up just as Siad Barre needed more materiel to secure his position in the north. This vacuum, in turn, provided Gadhafi with the opportunity to become Siad Barre's main weapons supplier; and at least two transport planeloads worth of light arms were landed in Mogadishu (AC Nov. 18, 1988: 4).

November 1988

In mid-November the United Nations High Commissioner for Refugees, citing the peace treaty with Ethiopia and Somalia's "deliberate overestimation of refugee figures" announced UNHCR's phase-out of assistance programs. According to the *Indian Ocean Newsletter* this would cause Somalia to lose aid equivalent to the amount allocated to Somalia by the United States—at a time when Somalia was no longer eligible for IMF assistance. Clearly this decision, whether it was really meant to be implemented or not, signaled UN displeasure over the level of corruption involving UNHCR funds and the arming of refugees in ostensibly UNHCR-supervised camps (ION Nov. 19, 1988).

Knuckling under to some of the international pressure, Siad Barre released eleven prisoners on November 15, and ninety-two more detainees on November 20 (ION Nov. 26, 1988).

December 1988

An article in the British newspaper, *The Independent,* reported that Libya recently supplied nerve gas to the Mogadishu government, although SNM forces had been claiming this since late summer (ION Dec. 3, 1988).

Also in December, the European Economic Community (EEC) extended credits to the Somali government, purportedly so that Mogadishu could work out a revised structural adjustment program with the IMF (which would then allow the release of already-allocated funds from West Germany, the United States, Japan, the World Bank, and the African Development Bank). "Out of a total of $137.7 million worth of commitments scheduled for 1988, Somalia received only $21 million. In 1987, real aid had already been reduced to $67 million from the $109 million announced" (ION Dec. 10, 1988).

By December the price of sugar had risen 450 percent since May, while the price of corn rose 650 percent (AC Dec. 16, 1988: 6).

1989

January 1989

At the end of January the government released some 400 political prisoners (ION Mar. 4, 1989). Then, as Somalia's Prime Minister, Mohamed Ali Samatar, was meeting with Secretary of State James Baker in Washington in early February, Mogadishu released 104 more prisoners, despite (or perhaps because of) Human Rights Watch's public accusation that Mogadishu was detaining up to 1,000 political prisoners (ION Feb. 11, 1989).

February 1989

Also in early February, the minister of defense, General Gabiyu—an Ogadeni—was demoted. At the same time it was becoming increasingly clear that General Mohamed "Morgan" Said, Siad Barre's Majertein son-in-law, and General Maslah Mohamed Siad, the president's son by his first wife, Khadija, were indeed emerging as the government's strongmen—signaling a further rift between the Ogaden and Darood (ION Feb. 4, 1989).

In the same month a new, largely Hawiye opposition group formed in Rome, the Somali Unity Congress (SUC), many of whose members had previously belonged to the SSDF (ION Feb. 4, 1989; ION May 20, 1989).

On the international front, Italy's president visited the Somali capital in the second week of February—the first visit by an Italian president—signaling Italy's return to a benign stance on Somalia. Immediately after this visit, the commander of the Libyan Armed Forces flew into Mogadishu—the first visit by such a high-ranking Libyan (ION Feb. 18, 1989).

Meanwhile, tensions continued in the north where fifty chiefs (constituting a Council of Elders) met to discuss the formation of a provisional government for the north. And although infighting continued within the SNM, skirmishes between the SNM and government forces also took place (ION Mar. 4, 1989).

At the other end of the country, in mid-February the Kenyan government reported a clash between its soldiers and Somali troops. Nairobi accused Somali soldiers of having crossed the border after members of a new opposition force, the Abris. Apparently this latest group (formed under an old name) arose in response to the government's attempt to resettle Marehan—who had come under attack from Hawiye on the borders of the Hiran and Mudug regions—near Afmadu (ION Mar. 25, 1989).

March 1989

Disaffected Ogadeni troops in the south of the country, inspired by a mutiny at the Kismayo Military Academy, staged a revolt—apparently centered around General Gabiyu's dismissal—precipitating a flurry of negotiations between Siad Barre's Ogadeni government allies and these estranged officers (ARB May 15, 1989; 9256–9257; ION Apr. 1, 1989). Student demonstrations later in March ended in violence in the capital; one student was killed and eight people injured. According to *The Indian Ocean Newsletter,* the students "were not only demonstrating against their examination formalities, as the official press agency, SUNA, said, but also against the poor living conditions and shortages of all kinds which stem from hitherto unseen economic hardship in Somalia. Foreign currency is also a subject arousing antagonism as it has become increasingly hard to find since the government broke off relations with the IMF" (ION Apr. 1, 1989).

April 1989

The SNM made a surprise attack on the northern town of Erigavo, which it held briefly before retreating (AC Apr. 14, 1989). By the end of the month the SNM was resurfacing in attacks throughout the north near Djibouti. However, *Africa Confidential* asserted,

> this latest fighting is in fact less part of the SNM struggle against the government than an attempt to prevent control of the lucrative trade between northern Somali towns and Djibouti passing out of the hands of the Isaq (who provide the SNM's main support) and into those of another clan, the Gadabursi. Last year, hundreds of thousands of Isaq fled over the border into neighboring Ethiopia to avoid government attacks. This allowed the Gadabursi, who remained essentially neutral in the conflict between the government and SNM, to move in and take control of food supplies to army garrisons, of Djibouti-Somali trade in general, and of the lucrative business in the banned narcotic, *khat,* from eastern Ethiopia. (AC May 26, 1989: 7).

By June *The Indian Ocean Newsletter* was offering a somewhat different take on the activity in the north: "The SNM has apparently for the last few months been actively preparing to take over power in Mogadishu. This is a new strategy resulting from, so it appears, the realization that no other opposition force is sufficiently organized to overthrow Mohamed Siad Barre's government and that secession of North Somalia cannot be recognized internationally" (ION June 3, 1989) although the SNM had historically maintained that they were never a secessionist movement.

May 1989

The [Hawiye] United Somali Congress (formerly the Somali United Congress) held talks with the [Isaq] SNM in Saudi Arabia, whereas in a separate attempt to reorganize, the [Majertein] SSDF united several of its executives (ION May 20, 1989).

Ironically, just as fighting again intensified in northern Somalia U.S. military aid, which had been ordered in 1986, finally arrived in Mogadishu and was immediately distributed for use in the north (ION June 3, 1989).

Also in late May, a contingent of Marehan delivered an ultimatum to Siad Barre seeking a return to democracy and giving him twenty days in which to respond to their seven-point request. As *The Indian Ocean Newsletter* interpreted the move: "In putting such heavy pressure on Mohamed Siad Barre, it is clear that the Marehan accused by other Somali clans of having pocketed the power, want to ensure their safe future in case the current regime is overthrown. Their aim is also to show that the power is not in Marehan hands but only in the hands of Siad Barre's family" (June 10, 1989).

Meanwhile, in arrears with the IMF, whose funds the government desperately needed—not only because it was cash-starved but also because IMF support signified the stamp of approval necessary if bilateral Western assistance was to resume—the government anxiously promised reforms and reconciliation. Hundreds of political prisoners were released (AC May 26, 1989: 7).

June 1989

On June 14 Washington responded to this apparent move toward reform by granting Somalia a partial release of funds for assistance in its balance of payments, but freezing the remainder until further steps were taken toward national reconciliation (ION June 24, 1989).

However, although Siad Barre may have made some amends, by June 19 it was clear that he was not going to give in to the Marehan demands. He publicly signaled a stalemate in a speech that evening, which in turn apparently encouraged some politicians and senior officers to begin to speak out themselves (ION June 24, 1989). This airing of views happened to coincide with publicization of an open letter written by Professor Said Samatar (a Somali historian residing in the United States) who publicly rejected an invitation to the Somali Studies Congress (held only once every three years and scheduled to take place in Mogadishu June 25–30). Said Samatar wrote that he would not attend the congress as his way of protesting government actions in the north (ION June 24, 1989). Other well-known and well-respected Somaliists responded similarly, although at least four Somali researchers living abroad agreed to attend only after they had received written assurances that they would be able to speak freely once in Mogadishu (ION Jul. 1, 1989).

Undoubtedly this brief guarantee of free speech along with such a concentration of scholars whose interest *was* Somalia suddenly gathering in one place at such a potentially volatile time must have had some effect on the level of ferment and fervor in the capital.

OPPOSITION PROLIFERATION

June 1989

Yet, at the same time the ground was being laid for this Somali Studies Congress to convene in Mogadishu the SNM rejected a June 18 offer by the United Somali Congress (USC) and SSDF to participate in an opposition congress (ION June 24, 1989). Meanwhile, two more antigovernment groups emerged: the predominantly Dolbahante Somali United Liberation Front, and the Somali Democratic Movement representing southern Bantu peasants (ION June 24, 1989).

What is significant about this ongoing proliferation of opposition movements, is that many seem to have sprung up in reaction to the successes of those already in existence. In other words, it was essentially only once a few of these clan-dominated but not clan-exclusive groups finally managed to achieve successes (i.e., the SNM and SSDF) that other clans suddenly sought involvement. In many regards such responsiveness would seem to suggest posturing for self-preservation as much as any real push for power. For instance, all Somalis were cognizant of how the Marehan had promoted themselves, or had been promoted by Siad Barre (along with the Ogaden, the Dolbahante, and even, to an extent, some Majertein). Doubtless there was an implicit sense that the next group to seize power would do much the same thing, and would also maintain itself by making alliances with other powerful and important-seeming groups. Therefore, clans may well have assumed this new opposition group role as a more overt means to ensure themselves a place in the new Somali order than because they had any clear agenda for attaining order.

Also, there was nothing monolithic about any of these movements, or the clans that fed into them, regardless of the appearance they may have cultivated for those on the outside. In point of fact, the ruling coalition itself continued to fissure, with self-preservation for some of Siad Barre's family more urgent than reestablishing any sort of national stability. Thus, even had Siad Barre personally desired reconciliation or been ready to accept some sort of move toward multiparty democracy, it is likely that family and clan members who, for the sake of their own survival, could not afford to make any concessions would have overruled him.

July 1989

On July 3 the Somali Revolutionary Socialist Party's central committee rejected the possibility of revising the constitution or instituting any sort of political reform (ION Jul. 8, 1989). Some posited that this rejection was the result of Siad Barre using these old allies of his to do his dirty work for him, or as Africa Watch purported: Siad Barre falsely claimed that the central committee had rejected the reforms, when in fact they had accepted them after an unprecedented days-long debate. Certainly, far too little information is available to know what did transpire. Even less substantiation is available concerning the even more momentous (and momentum-filled) events that shortly followed.

On July 9 Monsignor Salvatore Colombo, an Italian national and the archbishop of Mogadishu, was shot and killed. His lone assailant escaped, despite a hefty government reward. Nor was a motive officially put forward. On July 14, perhaps catalyzed by the bishop's murder and the government's reward, but more commonly blamed on the arrest of prominent sheikhs and imams July 13 (still related to the bishop's murder according to many members of the public), government troops opened fire on worshipers (whom the government labeled demonstrators) as they were leaving Mogadishu's mosques after Friday's *juma* [noontime] prayer. Two days of street fighting followed. Civilian massacres, rapes, and lootings also took place.

• 7 •

July 14 and Its Aftermath

Let me first note that this chapter is based on a startlingly limited collection of printed news sources. Although there was worldwide coverage of the riots, demonstrations, and chaos in Mogadishu by July 15, most news stories were based on the same limited range of facts. Almost all reporting on "Black Friday" and its aftermath cited the Somali government's long-standing denial of visas to journalists. As a result of this policy there were no foreign journalists in the country at all at the time of these incidents. Thus, much of what the news organizations based their reporting on was what could be gathered in telephone conversations with local correspondents or diplomats in Mogadishu.

What this chapter is based on, then, in addition to these written accounts, is my own witnessing of events, what information I was able to gather in Mogadishu, and what interpretations of meaning I have been able to solicit both there and since leaving. To this day I know of no authoritative account explaining exactly why it was on July 14 that the government reacted the way it did to the potential of demonstrations, which themselves remain shrouded in mystery. Nevertheless, everyone in Mogadishu—Somali and expatriate alike—immediately proclaimed this the catharsis they had long been predicting, which, under the circumstances, amounted to self-fulfilling hindsight. However, there was some evidence at the time that certain elements within the United States embassy did have concrete advance warning that violence *was* being planned.

JULY 14

Shooting started not long after the muezzins broadcast the Friday noon sermons. However, because of Mogadishu's spread, it was impossible to know the extent of the shooting or who was involved until the U.S. walkie-talkie net began to crackle with broadcasts. These broadcasts involved a roll call, so that the embassy could account for the location of all "official

Americans," and also allow people to report on the level of activity in their areas.[1]

Because 'official' Americans lived in pockets scattered throughout the city it was possible to get some idea from listening to individuals reporting in on the walkie-talkie net of the extent of the fighting out of direct hearing range. For instance, only random shots were fired over our roof. However, people in other areas reported extensive and ongoing shooting, particularly in those parts of town known to have large concentrations of northerners (and/or popular mosques).

Even then, though—because most people were at home or inside compounds within largely expatriate and elite enclaves—it was never clear exactly what was happening throughout the city, although the embassy could confirm over the net that the Somali army *was* involved. Despite most people assuming this marked the beginning of a revolution or coup, such conjecture was never broadcast. If anything, the embassy was extremely circumspect in what it announced. For instance, when one woman called in to ask whether there was an anti-Christian element to the uprising the embassy simply responded that it would be better to avoid that topic at the moment.

Throughout the day U.S. citizens were advised to stay indoors and to keep their walkie-talkies with them throughout the evening and night. Roll calls were taken regularly. However very little new information was put out.

The watchmen on duty within the compound gates knew little more; Radio Mogadishu was not keeping them informed either. They, too, seemed to think this might be the beginning of the end of the regime. Nevertheless, none of this stopped them from trying to get home before dark.

By Saturday morning the shooting had essentially stopped. The government announced the imposition of a dusk to dawn curfew, although the U.S. embassy continued to tell its employees not to leave their homes. In terms of actual information, the BBC provided more than the walkie-talkies did, reporting the number of people the government said had been shot (twenty-three killed and fifty-nine injured, later revised to thirty-two killed) as well as opposition claims of thousands having been gunned down. The government, on one hand, maintained the position that it had responded to violent demonstrations. Opposition groups, on the other hand, condemned the government for having willfully ordered troops to open fire on worshipers leaving *juma* prayer.

Locally, most of the deaths were thought to have occurred in the center of the city, around the Ceel Gaab market area, although when the watchmen returned to work in the morning one said he had seen three bodies lying in the street in a more northern section of town.

Ambaro, the *boyessa* [or house girl), too, reported that there had been shooting all night long in her village (Medina) and that she and her family had huddled awake never sure when soldiers would burst through their doors. She and a friend had been caught downtown when the shooting first started just as, she said, many people had been out at the beaches. She and her friend had had to walk and run the long distance home, with soldiers yelling at them along their route to hurry up. Justifiably, she was terrified, although the fact that she had returned to work indicated the level to which people felt order had indeed already been restored.

Although there *was* still shooting once dark fell Saturday night, despite, or perhaps because of, the curfew, Sunday was just as quiet as Saturday had been so that by Monday the embassy was allowing most people to return to work in certain parts of the city, advising everyone to continue avoiding downtown and other areas where the fighting had been fiercest (and where there were still thought to be pockets of trouble).

By the time I returned to CRDP on Sunday, which was within walking distance of the house, many (but not all) of the staff were also there.

Not surprisingly, during the first few days following Black Friday people were extremely cagey about discussing what they thought had occurred and why they thought violence had finally erupted. Not even two northerners taking refuge in the house with us were willing to interpret events. All I was told when I asked about the present mood in Mogadishu's villages and downtown was that I should not go downtown and that, under no circumstances, should I ride the local buses. No one was sure that there was antiwhite sentiment, but they were unsure just what people were feeling and what might set them off.

It was only once it became increasingly clear that change was not going to occur overnight, although clearly change was "about" to occur (four or five days after Black Friday), that individuals at CRDP suddenly began to talk openly—for the first time—about tribalism, the regime, and the horrors it was perpetrating: by dragging northerners out of their homes, jailing, and even executing them. Indeed, people were quite eager to explain to me just how many wrongs the Marehan had committed since coming to power (and all Marehan were lumped together in these castigations). Unfortunately, though, this window of discussion lasted less than two weeks before it closed again, I believe for essentially one reason: There was nothing further happening. There was no further violence aimed at government forces, but only further violence perpetrated *by* government forces. This violence increasingly took the form of lootings and rapes, so that it was directed against people when they were at their most vulnerable—in their own homes and at night.

Indisputably throughout the first week there was a distinct heightening of expectations. People expected and talked about the likelihood of there being more bloodshed on the following Friday, the twenty-first. However, on that Friday government forces were conspicuous throughout town (imposing a de facto curfew—whereas the embassies imposed a de jure one), and from mid-morning until late afternoon at least one small scout plane flew menacingly low over the city's rooftops.

There was no trouble on July 21. Surprisingly, however, early in the afternoon on July 24 shooting was again audible. Ambaro (the *boyessa*), Mohamed, and Ahmed (the watchmen) all identified it as coming from the direction of the airport. Since this is where it was thought that Siad Barre had fled—to his bunkers within reach of an escape plane—all sorts of possibilities ran through their minds, but as the national radio shortly announced, the shooting merely signified the arrest of General Gabiyu, the Ogadeni former minister of defense who lived near the airport. And although his bodyguards had put up resistance, he was successfully captured.

The curfew was further relaxed on July 26. Originally imposed from dusk to dawn (6 P.M. to 6 A.M.), it was first shortened on July 20 (from 9 P.M. to 5 A.M.) and finally only enforced between 11 P.M. and 5 A.M.. This allowed workers like watchmen to return home safely in the evening and people to resume running errands during the early evening hours—when many people were used to being out.

Ironically, only after it became clear that large-scale violence was not going to continue did full-blown theories about the onset of Black Friday begin to emerge and circulate widely enough to compete with one another. Also, it was only in the aftermath of July 14th that the assassination of the bishop suddenly became significant.

Most stories I heard linked Black Friday directly to the assassination. However, I must first add that more theories circulated concerning the bishop (who was much more of a mystery to most Somalis) than about July 14. I heard at least four. One, the bishop was involved in the black market or some other illegal trade and his death was the result of a private quarrel. Two, the bishop was actually not the man the assassin had intended to shoot—there was another Catholic who was active in disseminating information about human rights abuses to Western governments and organizations—shooting the bishop had been a blunder. Three, Islamic fundamentalists shot the bishop, either (1) to make the government look bad, (2) because they disapproved of the bishop's proselytizing (although many people found this the least satisfying of the theories, since why shoot him now?), or (3) because fundamentalists are simply fanatics. Four, the government itself hired a killer to shoot the bishop in order to make it look as though Islamic fundamentalists had shot him. It is this last theory that seemed to make the most sense to most people I knew.

The logic connecting the bishop's death with the attacks on the mosques was never quite so tidy. Apparently it was common knowledge that leading imams and sheikhs had been arrested on Thursday afternoon (July 13). Less clear was whether, (1) they had actually been advocating demonstrations to follow the Friday noon prayer (thus leading to their arrests), (2) the imams who had not been arrested advocated demonstrations to protest their colleagues' arrests, or (3) Siad Barre had caught wind of rumors of demonstrations and therefore staged his soldiers outside the mosques in anticipation, or finally (4), whether it was disinformation put out by Siad Barre's government that led people to believe demonstrations were planned, thus potential demonstrators would gather and he could arrest them. Additionally, there were conflicting accounts as to what the worshipers *were* planning. It is unclear whether they were shot at as the prayers were breaking up or as they were preparing to march. It is hard to imagine the two being distinguishable, since there are only so many doors from which worshipers could exit the mosques and any resultant outpouring could have looked suspicious.

Some of the news accounts do cite worshipers wielding stones, knives, and sticks (BBC July 17, 1989; AP July 21, 1989). However, there should be nothing surprising about this since many Somali men always wear daggers and some Somali men (particularly older men, and particularly on Fridays) carry herding sticks.

News reports (as well as subsequent periodical analyses) also interpreted the timing and meaning of events somewhat differently from anything I heard in Mogadishu. In part this may have been due to their sources: The Somali government claimed the trouble was perpetrated by armed bandits masquerading under the cloak of religion, whereas Africa Watch, the most vocal critic of the government during this time, matter-of-factly relayed their interpretation of the truth thus:

> As a result of the arrest of the Imams, religious leaders had decided to call demonstrations after mid-day prayers on Friday which the government learned about through informers. It was apparently agreed that the phrase "Allahu Akbar" would be the signal for the start of the demonstrations. Consequently, all the principal mosques and the two main churches were surrounded by soldiers from early Friday morning.
>
> The confrontations occurred simultaneously in a number of districts throughout the city . . . weapons were seized from the soldiers who were vastly outnumbered. Some members of the public then began to shoot back and an armed confrontation developed. Africa Watch has also received reports that security force members dressed in civilian clothes fired into the crowd, aiming at specific targets. (*News from Africa Watch* Jul. 21, 1989: 1–2).

Although Africa Watch went on to cite political reasons for discontent—having to do with new strictures mandating the conscription of vast numbers of young men and the confiscation of four-wheel drive vehicles at the government's discretion—Africa Watch also intimated that religion-as-catalyst could not be ignored:

> The killing [of the bishop] is thought by many in Mogadishu to have been carried out by two members of the President's own clan, the Marehan, leading to resentment about the apparent attempt to implicate Moslem religious figures.

According to the reports we have received, when the authorities learned of these rumors, they publicized a six million shilling reward for information leading to the identity of the assassin, both to quash the rumors and to create the impression abroad that the government was determined to apprehend and prosecute the offenders. The government also promised that the perpetrator(s) would be killed. They also began a campaign that identified religious elements as the guilty parties on the basis that many of them are "fanatic fundamentalists" who had openly attacked the government's offer of a substantial reward for the killing of the Bishop. These accusations followed widespread criticisms in the mosques of the government's conduct. Many Imams advised people against seeking the reward and contrasted the government's indifference to the thousands of Somalis who have been killed in recent years at the hand of government agencies, with its efforts to please the outside world by resolving the Bishop's murder. This was seen as a cynical move given the suspicions the government itself was responsible for his death (*News from Africa Watch* July 21, 1989: 6).

Africa Confidential offered a somewhat different version of events:

The trouble started after Friday prayers on 14 July, when people came out of two mosques in the center of the city chanting anti-government slogans. The government had been expecting trouble. Units from the elite and loyal Presidential Guard and military police . . . were deployed within reach of several mosques. . . . When demonstrators trying to march toward the parliament buildings and the presidential villa were stopped, things rapidly escalated into full-scale rioting, with road blocks, burning tires and stone-throwing. It was then that the troops started shooting . . .

The trouble seems to have stemmed from the assassination of the Roman Catholic Bishop of Mogadishu, Salvatore Colombo, who was shot in his cathedral on 9 July. The government offered a reward of 5 million Somali Shillings, which led to criticism that it was larger than anything ever offered as a reward for the arrest of the murderer of any Muslim. Rumors were spread that the bishop, best known for his help with refugees and for recovering bodies from the NSS when families were too frightened, had been trying to convert unemployed Muslim youth (Jul. 28, 1989: 7).

Six months after "Black Friday" *Africa Events* suggested that the bishop's murder had indeed been carried out by the regime, in the person of a member of the NSS at the instigation of Issa Ugas—the head of a shoe factory in Mogadishu and a close relative of the president's. Issa Ugas had allegedly received the shoe factory, confiscated from the Vatican, when the Somali government nationalized Somalia's industries. According to *Africa Events,*

when the regime gave in to the demands of the International Monetary Fund and World Bank to dismantle the socialist economic policies it embarked on a more liberal economic style of management. The small industries were

> rumored to be on the verge of being privatized, and the Catholic Mission showed an eagerness to regain control of their factory (January 1990: 10).

Thus, the bishop was shot.

This is in sharp contradistinction to *New African's* assessment, written by Abdulkarim Ahmed Guleid (identified as a "prominent Somali relief worker and concerned citizen") a year and a half after Black Friday:

> I was in Mogadishu when the Catholic Bishop Salvatore Colombo was assassinated. . . . Barre was always suspicious of the bishop because he knew so much about human rights abuses and the inner workings of family politics.
>
> When Amnesty International visited Mogadishu in June 1989 and met the bishop, Barre became restless and nervous. He was afraid of what the bishop might have said.
>
> When the bishop was assassinated the first story was that he had been killed by English speaking Somalis. This story did not hold up so the government said he had been killed by someone dressed as a religious instructor.
>
> The government announced a reward of five million shillings for information leading to the assassin's arrest. Then four Imams, each in charge of local mosques, were arrested. It was a clear attempt to focus world condemnation onto the Imams rather than the government and to get rid of the religious leaders who had been opposing the government by labelling them as "fanatic fundamentalists."
>
> Investigations proceeded for five days only. The file was then closed and forgotten. But it later turned out that Barre had authorized a member of his Marehan clan to take over and build on a plot of land which belonged to the church, just ten days before the assassination. The bishop stopped the construction work by presenting official documents that the land belonged to the church. Afterwards the bishop was threatened, then killed.
>
> Even more interesting General Barre made the tactical mistake of going to the police hospital and inquiring about the condition of the bishop at least half an hour before anyone knew of the assassination. The Italian nuns did not know what Barre was talking about.
>
> Half an hour after Barre's inquiries the bishop was brought in unconscious to the hospital dying without recovering consciousness. Insiders claim that the purpose of the visit to the hospital by Barre was to be certain that the bishop had died as it would have been dangerous if he had survived the assassination attempt (*New African* Feb. 1991: 11–12).

The difference between these published accounts and discussion in Mogadishu about July 14 is that these print versions present themselves as definitive; their version of events is not simply one explanation but *the* explanation. In contrast, conversations among residents of Mogadishu at the time openly reflected doubt and guesswork. No one had complete information, therefore interpretations could be scrambled and rescrambled as new information emerged or was uncovered. However, the overriding sense was still the same; no one knew why July 14, yet everyone understood that who it affected—how—varied.

For instance, at street level religion did exacerbate some people's reactions on July 14. Yet, this may well have had as much to do with the mundane fact that July 14 was a Friday as anything else. According to a number of expatriate eyewitnesses and at least one Somali there was an anti-Christian element to some of the "rioting." At least one woman was chased down a residential street by a mob of men yelling "*gaal! gaal!*" [commonly translated by expatriates as infidel] before a Somali family pulled her into the safety of their compound, and several of the houses occupied by non-proselytizing Mennonites were ransacked by Somalis who clearly knew whose homes they were ransacking (whereas no other U.S. homes were entered).

At the same time, a Somali academic in a SOMAC [Somali Academy] Land Rover (with SOMAC's logo—the cross of the Swedish flag beside the Somali star—on its door) was surrounded by another mob as he unwittingly returned from the beach. The crowd, accusing him of being a Christian (having misunderstood the symbol on the door), was so menacing that he found himself exiting his vehicle to genuflect and proclaim "*Allahuakbar*" [God is Great] to prove to them his faith.

Because stories like these began circulating relatively soon after July 14 in the expatriate community there was a justified sense of concern that Somalis were turning or would turn anti-Western and anti–United States in particular. Although this only hardened the already-besieged expatriate mentality for many, here I simply want to point out that Somalis had altogether different safety concerns. After all, it was Somalis who were being killed by other Somalis—only one expatriate had been wounded, apparently for having been at the wrong place at the wrong time and, according to some, for having been caught photographing the fighting.

In the days immediately following July 14 it was commonly asserted that Siad Barre had armed all the Marehan living within Mogadishu. In response, other groups were apparently arming themselves—for defense, not offense. One Somali, for instance, assured me that people who were unable to purchase firearms were buying bows and poisoned arrows for protection. Another recounted the arguments taking place within her family about whether to flee into the bush or not. Already her mother had buried most of the family's gold.

Such a confused multiplicity of responses to July 14 is itself telling. Confusion was clearly rampant on the ground. Nor was anyone in a central position from which to view all occurrences. Likewise, there was no central organ for distributing or even consolidating information, especially since the government's official accounts were universally disbelieved. At the same time, there was also much wishful thinking and almost spontaneous revision of meanings.

Given all the various sides and interested parties involved, then, and the paucity of informed but disinterested observers, most if not all explanations for July 14 should be taken as just that: explanations. They are far too logical and too thought through to be truth. They also make much too much sense of a situation in which actors, who were often unwitting bystanders, admitted to having no sense for what was really happening at the time.

I would also suggest that because the situation was so much more complex than any of the accounts gathered immediately after can possibly convey, that none of these explanations can be considered particularly satisfying. This is especially the case because so few episodes of violence on such a scale had occurred in Mogadishu before. Hence, it was clear as soon as shots were heard throughout the city that something momentous and out of the ordinary was happening on July 14 and even, perhaps, indeed, that this would become *the* event that would usher in a series of other new events. Nonetheless, the stature of July 14 and how it would be described—what sort of turning point it would represent—could only come given the aftermath of July 14 and given one's reading of history through July 14 and beyond.

CHRONOLOGY CONTINUED

August 1989

Not surprisingly, diplomacy became more frenzied in the immediate aftermath of July 14. General Maslah (the president's son-in-law and commander of the armed forces) visited the Soviet Union once and Libya twice during August, apparently seeking oil (in addition to military aid) (ION Aug. 26, 1989; AC Sept. 8, 1989: 6). Arms, meanwhile, did arrive in Mogadishu's port from Abu Dhabi (AC Aug. 25, 1989).

During the same month, General Gabiyu's son-in-law along with other disaffected (Ogadeni) members of the military and police forces formed a new opposition group, the Somali Patriotic Movement, based in the south of the country. At the same time, it was reported that the SNM had Hargeisa almost entirely under its control and was working on capturing Boroma. In central Somalia, more troops and officers defected, although none of these defections could live up to the drama and significance of the July 17 defection of the Ogadeni commander of government forces in Hargeisa. Yet even while defections throughout the country continued apace, Ogadeni and Marehan dignitaries met in Bardheere "to denounce the regime's use of commandos to alternately massacre members of one or other [sic] clan so as to incite clashes between the two clans" (ION Aug.

26, 1989). However, *Africa Confidential* described a similar (perhaps the same) meeting between Marehan and Ogadeni leaders quite differently (although in this case two of the Ogaden and all the Marehan are reported to have been under government sponsorship): "A government delegation of Marehan elders, together with two Ogaden colonels, met the Ogaden rebels at Afmadu. . . . The meeting ended in shooting. Both the Ogadeni colonels . . . were shot in the legs. According to our information, this was done as a warning to other Ogaden officials who still support the government" (AC Sept. 8, 1989: 6).

Also in August Siad Barre fired the top three directors of the Central Bank of Somalia without offering a public explanation although the country had been suffering prolonged and severe shortages of cash (AC Sept. 8, 1989: 6). He also replaced the Isaq chief of police in Mogadishu with a Marehan son-in-law (ION Sept. 2, 1989). This, according to *Africa Confidential,* precipitated a further exodus of Isaq from the capital (Sept. 22, 1989: 7).

In late August Siad Barre flew to Tripoli to take part in the twentieth anniversary of the Libyan Revolution—with his own twentieth anniversary shortly to follow (ION Sept. 2, 1989).

September 1989

On his return from Libya, Siad Barre announced reforms, including promises of a multiparty system, free general elections in 1990, and the lifting of the 11 P.M. to 5 A.M. curfew (in effect since July 14) (ION Sept. 9, 1989).

Meanwhile, less than a month after General Maslah had traveled to Libya, Somalia's minister of defense returned from a visit to Kuwait. At the same time, it was reported in Saudi Arabia that gold and other mineral deposits had been discovered south of Mogadishu, at a site being surveyed for a major oil refinery due to be built by the Saudis (ION Sept. 9, 1989).

In mid-September the Somali prime minister returned from a trip to Italy. Later in the month the president's first wife, Khadija—one of the regime's major power brokers—flew to Geneva with a number of other women and children (including General Maslah's wife) (ION Sept. 23, 1989)—clearly signaling some concern over the future on the part of some Marehan.

In late September Somali troops crossed the Kenyan border at Liboi allegedly in pursuit of Somali rebels, accidentally killing four Kenyan policemen. Siad Barre immediately dispatched top government officials to reassure Kenya's President Moi that the shootings had been accidental. However, the border-crossing allowed Moi to express a modicum of support for the SPM rebels who were mostly Ogadeni—his own army chief, as well as many Kenyan Somalis, also being Ogadeni (ION Sept. 30, 1989).

During this same period, the chief secretary of the Foreign Office returned from an aid-seeking mission to South Africa (ION Sept. 30, 1989).

On September 25 the Somali Ogaden Liberation Front, which itself had split from the WSFL three years before, denounced the SPM and denied its right to speak for all Ogadenis (ION Sept. 30, 1989).

October 1989

In early October a variety of economic measures were introduced by the government in the hopes that these would successfully liberalize the economy and ultimately woo back donors. According to the *Indian Ocean Newsletter* these reforms were also necessary because "in the space of one month, the price of one kilo of rice has doubled, and now exceeds 800 shillings (about $1.30) while the price of sugar wavers between 700 and 1000 shillings per kilo. The average monthly wage of a civil servant is between 3000 and 4000 shillings" (ION Oct. 7, 1989).

In London a new, essentially Majertein political opposition movement announced itself—*Talawadaag*—although many Majertein remained in the militarily active SSDF and others continued serving with Siad Barre's army: Thus, the Majertein were split into at least three opposing factions. Meanwhile, the USC claimed responsibility for its first armed actions, which took place in central Somalia. The USC also denounced the government's claims that eleven thieves had died while in temporary detention in an empty container in the Mogadishu port, asserting that they were fifteen prisoners, all Hawiye dockworkers.

During the same week the SNM condemned the arrival of seven hundred Libyan soldiers and heavy artillery (including tanks) into Mogadishu's port. The SNM also reported that Colonel Gadhafi would attend Somalia's October 21 celebrations (ION Oct. 21, 1989).

October 21 and Siad Barre's Twentieth Anniversary. Despite the rumors—the most widespread of which was that Colonel Gadhafi had sent hundreds of bodyguards to prepare for his arrival (all of whom, some people said, were women)—no foreign heads of state attended the October 21 celebrations, which, as every year, included a military parade and aerial display. Nevertheless, foreign ambassadors and their staff members did attend the parade honoring Siad Barre's twenty years of rule despite days of vacillation during which most expatriates assumed that their embassies would impose de jure curfews once again. Rumors had also been rife among Somalis predicting more trouble on this day. Thus, many who had the means left town to "visit relatives" or "picnic."

Actually, I think that what many Somalis feared (or looked forward to) in the long run up to October 21 was a Sadat-style assassination (despite, or perhaps prompted by the antiaircraft guns dug into the area around the president's permanent reviewing stand). Indeed, on one hand expectations had been building since the letdown after July 14 that October 21 was the one day on which great change was finally bound to happen. The timing was just too perfect, given this twentieth anniversary, Somalia's diplomatic isolation, and worsening hardship throughout the country. On the other hand, there was also the undercurrent hope that all Siad Barre really wanted to do was sit through his twentieth anniversary celebration and then he would voluntarily step down; he only wanted to be able to say he had survived that long and then he would ensure a peaceful and reasonable succession.

However, nothing significant did occur in Mogadishu on October 21. As he had every year, Siad Barre promised to release prisoners (ION Oct. 28, 1989). However, he made no mention of stepping down. In fact, some people read his attendance at the parade and his having sat in the reviewing stand—since there had been widespread debate about whether he would risk attending at all—as defiance and, more disturbing still, a sign of renewed (or renewing) strength. Otherwise, nothing came of people's expectations. Nor, in the immediate aftermath, did anything come of people's frustration at having had expectations thwarted once again.

In part, this ebb and flow in expectation and frustration and the attendant lack of action after July 14 must have been at least somewhat rooted in Mogadishu residents' perceptions that they, and Mogadishu, were at the center of Somalia and that it could only be in the center that change for the country could ultimately occur. Doubtless this further reflected the "common knowledge" that a viable alternative had to exist before Siad Barre could be ousted or anything else could happen at the national level.

Certainly there was the sense that the peripheries were crumbling. The only journalist allowed into Somalia either preceding or anytime after July 14 reported on the BBC that Siad Barre was half-jokingly, half-mockingly being referred to as the Mayor of Mogadishu since he controlled so little of the rest of the country. However, precisely because Mogadishu was the administrative, financial, mercantile, and diplomatic center of the country, controlling Mogadishu still remained key to preventing anyone else from successfully controlling or being able to weld the rest of the country into any sort of serious counterweight or threat. Then, too, it was understood that the international community was only likely to officially recognize whoever it was who successfully occupied the capital.

Still, the situation did continue to deteriorate in all peripheries—with the SNM capitalizing on the implied significance of October 21 with a more aggressive offensive in the north. With continued fighting throughout the north it was being predicted in the final days of October that stocks of food aid for Ethiopian refugees in northern camps would run out by the end of November (ION Nov. 4, 1989).

November 1989

On November 6 the president appointed a commission to revise the constitution. However at the same time, with the SPM extremely active in Beled Weyn (in central Somalia), fighting spread among Hawiye elsewhere in the central regions; Dolbahante and Isaq clans fought one another near Togdheer (in the north); and Gadabursi and Isaq clans also clashed. It was at this time, too, that the Gadabursi finally formed their own opposition party, the Somali Democratic Alliance, in London (ION Nov. 11, 1989).

In mid-November there were violent clashes in Galcayo (in central Somalia) between government troops and Hawiye clansmen, and on December 5 the SNM announced it controlled Hargeisa, its soldiers having been able to make their final push thanks to assistance from Hawiye troops who had defected from the army in reaction to the government's anti-Hawiye actions in Galcayo (ION Dec. 2 and Dec. 9, 1989).

THE END OF MY STAY

Also in mid-November there was growing consternation in Mogadishu over fuel shortages of all kinds (including a shortage of aviation fuel). Cars were stoned, and one story told by U.S. military personnel involved the theft of an entire freighter. The ship, which had been carrying fuel (some of which had been ordered by the U.S. government for U.S. use), was apparently stolen after most of the U.S.-owned diesel fuel, but not all the rest of the (aviation and Somali-owned) fuel, had been off-loaded. On a somewhat lesser scale, tales also circulated of large-scale thefts of government money by high-ranking government or even Somali UN officials who cashed forged checks for outrageous sums (with, it was assumed, the collusion of friends in the Central Bank), before fleeing the country.

More commonplace still, Land Cruisers were being stolen throughout the region, often at gunpoint, and nighttime robberies were becoming virtually routine. However, there were no large demonstrations of any kind and one reason offered for why the capital was still relatively quiet was that pressure from the surrounding rural areas had momentarily fallen off thanks to an abnormally wet rainy (*dayr*) season. With such bountiful rains people in the rural areas had plenty of meat and milk and were only coming into town to buy sugar; they didn't need flour, pasta, or rice. In addition the *barwaqo* [prosperity] of spring was itself distracting and uplifting even for residents of Mogadishu.

Although there was certainly an air of increased dissolution and the threat of random violence, no westerners had been physically harmed up to this point, indicating the extent to which certain barriers of respect or caution remained intact. And Mogadishu was still holding together when I left the country November 22. It was not until March 1990 that the first European expatriate was reported killed, although expatriates did increasingly fall victim to thieves—signaling the beginning of the real siege for expatriates and marking a new low point of economic desperation among Somalis.

Doubtless too, this desperation increased as expatriates and nonessential embassy personnel began to leave the country. The U.S. government had decided (after a series of bureaucratic delays and debates in Washington between the State Department, the Pentagon, and USAID) to halve their presence in the country in light of July 14. This was done for at least two publicized reasons: to send a signal of disapproval to Siad Barre's government for its flagrant human rights abuses, and because it was no longer possible for anyone to venture far outside of Mogadishu, thus rendering most projects untenable and the expatriates associated with them idle. Even the indirect effects of this decision to disengage (which was also taken by other Western governments—most significantly the Germans and the British) had a major impact on the local economy and those Somalis who worked with or for expatriates.[2] However, the psychological effect of a Western withdrawal along with the uncertainty over who, if anyone, would help Somalia (or where the regime would seek backing next) had to have also increased anxiety, panic, and overall anomie. For instance, one of the fears on the part of many (but not all) people was that the Russians would return.[3] This assumption was of course based on the Cold War logic: If not the Soviets then the United States, if not the United States then the Soviets. Interestingly though, at the same time these rumors were afloat, George Bush and Mikhail Gorbachev were reportedly about to sit down and discuss the Horn of Africa at their upcoming summit meeting, where both sides (according to diplomats in Somalia) would agree to a new hands-off policy, since Somalia had become the same sort of black aid hole for the United States that Ethiopia was proving to be for the Soviets.

Nevertheless, despite all these signs of imminent collapse, it was not until December 1990 that organized armed violence finally made its way into Mogadishu and overturned Siad Barre and any semblance of civility left in the capital.

IMPACTS ON CHRONOLOGY

Although it is certain that most Somalis did not think in terms of even this limited chronology of events—spanning the country, involving a multiplicity of dealings at so many levels as well as the timing of decisions made by Somalis abroad and non-Somalis in Washington, at the UN, and elsewhere—most residents of Mogadishu clearly recognized the extent to which they were suffering the effects of these machinations at the household level. They were able to make limited comparisons between what they were experiencing in the present of 1989 and how they had lived in the recent past. However, just as the recasting of July 14 was so elastic (and ultimately inconclusive), these comparisons similarly proved incomplete and may reveal more about how people were feeling than what they actually knew.

For instance, economics were a day-to-day affair for most Somalis. Economically people certainly felt that their financial position was worsening and knew that, in terms of exchange rates and purchase prices, they were correct. However, people did not speak in terms of economic *patterns*. Rather, if anything, the decline was described as completely and inexorably linear. For example, in discussing the corruption of 1989 no one ever mentioned the corruption of 1969 (which had been responsible, in large part, for bringing Siad Barre to power). Food and fuel had certainly sparked demonstrations and even instances of violence before. Yet "now" was always cited as *the* worst time.

Similarly, although television and radio covered most state visits made by high-ranking Somalis to Libya, the United States, the USSR, and return visits to Mogadishu by foreign dignitaries, the *pattern* of foreign responses to the government's diplomatic maneuverings was invariably opaque: Somalis did not always know when high government officials were in South Africa, or that the administration was turning to the USSR because the US was not forthcoming enough with aid. The government always put a different gloss on its foreign dealings. At the same time, diplomatic initiatives often were trumpeted, since the more Siad Barre and his government could be seen hosting and being hosted by other governments, the more legitimate and powerful it made the regime (and even Somalia itself) seem.

Meanwhile, there was the conjunction of international finance and international finesse at the highest levels—evident in IMF, World Bank, and UNHCR policies, which dovetailed far too often with United States and even Soviet reactions toward Siad Barre's latest overtures on the diplomatic front. Although the agencies' names were themselves recognizable to many Somalis, the agencies, too, were skilled at publicly masking the real messages they were sending Somalia's government, since often the stated reason for a policy switch was not the real reason for change. Thus, the interconnectedness of action, response, and countermeasure at this supra-local level, which even this incomplete chronology suggests, was one trajectory of history well beyond most Somalis.

A second trajectory was equally hidden though much more local and again made itself felt in the household. It had to do with what Siad Barre and government officials *were* able to control: namely, physical aspects of local finances. For instance, in the first few weeks in July cash began to run short in Mogadishu. No doubt (and as other analyses have pointed out) this did exacerbate people's sense of frustration with, and anger at, the government. But it also symbolized more: not just the regime's corruption and corrosion but the sense that the government was no longer in control of even those minimal services it had been able to previously sustain.[4]

A second wave of cashlessness then occurred later in the summer, well after July 14—although for some (particularly government employees) no money was available for a full eight weeks. This second wave seems to have had different roots. Although a large percentage of Somalia's cash was thought to still be in the hands of nomads (in payment for livestock shipments prior to the hajj), there were also reports that Siad Barre was bribing potentially mutinous officers and their troops with outrageously large sums. Other rumors speculated that merchants were withholding money from the banks in order to do their part to help bring down the regime. Whether there was any accuracy to any of these rumors, there was also evidence that bank officials themselves were partially to blame. In a form of protest over their inadequate pay, clerks and cashiers began demanding 10 percent of any check a client wished to cash, or 10 percent of any sum he or she sought to withdraw. However, it also may well have been that the government purposely decided that keeping people moneyless would send them on personal scrambles for cash or credit, preventing people from having the time or wherewithal to join together in any meaningful opposition.

Although this is conjecture, there is some indication that this is how the government did operate on occasion. For instance, at times there was no municipal electricity because Mogadishu's generator plant malfunctioned, or because, it was said, there was no fuel (because someone had stolen it for private resale), or because the government ordered the electricity shut off so that people could not congregate and menace democracy at night. There were even rumors to the effect that the electricity usually went off Wednesday afternoons because this is when the BBC made its Somali news broadcast. Alternatively, during prolonged fuel shortages, when tensions rose and people who did have fuel and were still able to drive found themselves and their vehicles viciously stoned, fuel somehow magically materialized. It was almost as if the government was playing chicken with the populace. Either the regime was exceptionally clever at gauging the local temper and playing the limit, or it was continually testing the waters in order to see how much could be gotten away with.

What worked domestically also seemed to work internationally, which is part of what afforded Siad Barre so much control. As adept as his policies forced Somalis to be at soliciting assistance from one another (as we will see), he was exemplary at this himself on a virtually global scale. One way he stage-managed significance beyond Somalia's net worth was to purposely deal with countries opposed to each other in quick succession. Alternatively, he would simply woo the range, so that Israel and Libya were approached during the same time frame as South Africa (in early 1986), only for the combination to be reshuffled to Libya, Saudi Arabia, Kuwait, and the UAE (United Arab Emirates) at a later date. Similarly, as long as the USSR still supported Ethiopia and the Cold War was extant, Siad Barre knew he could keep the United States toeing a line of assistance far more often than the United States could successfully coerce him into more than the most token of human rights gestures. Also, Siad Barre was clearly masterful at keeping the press out of Somalia, and without any sort of tourist industry he had relatively little to fear from outsiders since virtually all expatriates directly or indirectly depended on the regime's largesse for permitting them to stay in-country, earning their considerable salaries.

Thus, Siad Barre and his associates were able to garner more development assistance per capita for Somalia than went to most other countries in sub-Saharan African (Ahmed Samatar, 1988: 52)—although much of this aid never reached most people. Of course, the even greater irony in this is that it was this very avalanche of aid money and the corruption it engendered that undermined the regime. Although how it did so was more stunning still: by ruining the lives of people who less than a generation before had been renowned for their abilities to survive in situations of prolonged scarcity.

PART FOUR

Pastoral Ideology and Urban Realities

Although the previous chapters set forth the parameters of the collapse of the Somali state, we have not yet considered the effect these expatriate and chronological impacts had on "traditional" Somali institutions, or how they shaped daily life in Mogadishu for the very Somalis on whom expatriates based their knowledge of Somalia.[1]

In the following chapters I examine a variety of institutions that have continued to persist in the urban setting, having been carried over from pastoral sources. Although these institutions have surely altered in meaning and purpose with the distances traveled (through space and time), the pastoral setting itself has also evolved so that pastoralism as it is practiced today is not the same pastoralism early explorers viewed or I. M. Lewis studied (Swift 1979; Aronson 1980; Samatar and Samatar 1987; A. I. Samatar 1988). Nevertheless, principles borrowed from pastoralism remain integral in urban Somali life.

I believe this is so for a number of reasons. On the ideological level we again see confluences: of a rhetorically national Somalia being assembled at the same time national politics demanded disassembly into interest groups (both prior to and ever since independence). Similarly, whereas the unifying nature of all Somalis sharing the same language and practicing the same Islam was used to help create a sense of coherent nationalism, both institutions themselves became pawns of dispute. How Somali was to be written and standardized—in Latin or Arabic, according to how it was spoken in either the north or the center of the country—invested one of the few allegedly defining features of Somaliness with both parochial and ideological overtones (Laitin 1977). So too, what role Islam would be awarded in shaping the laws and practices of all Somalis became politically freighted according to secular/religious, urban/rural, pro-Arab/pro-Western preferences.

By contrast, pastoralism alone provided terms of reference for all Somalis that no set of Somalis (not even agriculturalists) could ignore. Even given the changes in specific herd compositions and structure due to commercialization, the realities of livestock and of the bush remained unpoliticizable.[2] Both were resonant, not only symbolically but for very practical reasons. For instance, economically, pastoral production remained dominant for Somalia, with 80 percent of Somalia's foreign trade earnings based on livestock and livestock product sales.[3]

However, nothing else as strong or definitionally Somali emerged to challenge the idealization (and ideologization) of pastoral practices and demographics enhanced this choice-by-default. With agriculture traditionally considered the practice of an inferior minority it was extremely easy for the descendants of pastoralists to dismiss the least "Somali" of Somalis and thus attain a purer self-definition.[4] That there has been only a handful of urban centers—and essentially only two (Mogadishu and Hargeisa)—has also exacerbated the problem of a dominantly pastoral (or recently pastoral) and nomadic society striving to define itself in an urban-centered, wider world.[5]

Indeed, although the outer world might well have reason to regard the collapse of the Somali state as dissolution, some victims of this dissolution, aware of impending collapse, chose instead to view the slide into chaos as growing pains—necessary even, for the formation of a viable state out of pastoral roots:

> Somalis are not mature enough. They are in a transitional period from pastoralism to a modern economy. It is a rough period. . . . The only solution is that Somalia needs a new corporate structure and investment. . . . The future belongs to those with the most chips (i.e., technocratic knowledge). Siad gave his family the most chips. Therefore, even if Siad is removed, the country will still need his family. . . . And land is still unacquired in Somalia. It is still a frontier state. Once Somalia is occupied, then it will be mature" (Bashir, civil servant, 30).

Clearly not the words of a *traditional* pastoralist. Nevertheless, the person who expressed these views concerning the situation in 1989 is the grandson of a well-known pastoralist (and sheikh) and has himself been trained in Western range management techniques. Indeed, employed by the Central Rangelands Development Project, his work *was* pastoralism—but pastoralism that meant what? to whom?

Moving away from specific events, I focus on institutions in Part 4 and on how Somalis themselves shifted between pastoralist and urban settings and also shifted certain practices. In previous chapters I took an essentially narrative approach to outline how trust was growing increasingly circumscribed in Somalia. Here we look at how circles of trust were actually being drawn. Connections are key, tribalism (as I define it) is the result.

• 8 •

"The Bush"

If the bureaucracies in which English-speaking expatriates found themselves became settings for the production and reproduction of a homogenized view of Somalis, then here it seems appropriate to consider the context in which the Somalis expatriates knew homogenized their Somaliness. After all, pastoral practices were not identical across the landscape of Somalia. Even in those ecological zones where pastoralism was practiced most extensively, its focus was not uniform. Different herd structures required different management techniques, and different household sizes dictated different herd structures (Behnke and Kerven 1984; Hussein 1987a, 1987b; Elmi 1989). Varied local environments also called for varied mixes of animals. For instance, due to differences in temperature (and humidity) and consequently vegetation, more cattle were raised south of the Juba River, although historically, particularly in the Nugal (northeastern region), horses did well on the coastal plain, where small stock more recently predominated.

Hence, it certainly cannot be exact practices that linked the children and grandchildren of herders with Somalis who still herded, when not all herders tended the same stock. Rather, commonalities must lie elsewhere: in the principles of pastoralism, how the pastoral mode of production was structured, and how the nomadic way of life was organized. Commonalities also resided in the collective memory, kept alive by the fact that they continued to persist in real life—in the bush. In fact, the bush not only represented the place and condition from which many urban dwellers (or their parents) escaped but was also recognized as a refuge *for* escape in troubled times. Consequently, there seemed to exist deep ambivalence about the bush, what it was, what it represented, and what it might still offer.

Indeed, in some senses the emotions the bush could elicit for former pastoralists and the urbanized children of pastoralists tell us more about what the recent past has meant in Mogadishu than any event-laden history or chronology. It tantalized and taunted urban-dwellers who still felt partially rooted there. In the urbanized scheme of things the bush was supposed to be difficult and Mogadishu easy. In the romanticized view, town life was bad and life in the bush much better. However, by 1988–1989 it was becoming increasingly clear: conditions were not perhaps so different in either place. When bad, either place could be unlivable.

Certainly not all Somalis who forsook pastoralism to settle in towns did so for the same reasons. For some there was the push out of the bush—life was too hard; there were permanent water and shade in town. For others there was the pull of everything the town could offer; money indisputably bought more pleasures in town than livestock could in the bush.

Abdullahi Mohamed, for instance, moved to Mogadishu when he was seventeen. Around age four or five he had begun herding small stock with his older brothers. At age six he was already helping between five and fourteen other males herd anywhere from 120–160 camels. His family had camels, goats, sheep, horses, and donkeys. During the *jilaal* [dry season], when milk was scarce, they ate guinea hens, oryx, gerenuk, and gazelle. They planted beans, corn, sorghum, and watermelon whenever there was rain and otherwise supplemented their diet with four to six different types of wild fruit and by chewing three different types of sap.

Initially, Abdullahi Mohamed says, he came to Mogadishu on a visit and, as he puts it, "met with children the same age." He saw how good life was. He liked the food, sugar and dates particularly. He could wash his clothes, feel handsome, and swagger. In the bush all walking brought was interminable distances, lions, and hyenas. In town he saw pretty women. And there was money, which made everything more attainable and much easier, although he admits that the most difficult thing at the outset was knowing how to handle this abstract-but-real commodity.

Abdullahi Mohamed's wife, Hawa, came to Mogadishu at a later date and for different reasons. Her first visit was in 1959, when she arrived with two small children by two different former husbands. The bush was just too difficult for her without a husband. It was this push that drove her to Mogadishu (where she met Abdullahi Mohamed and married him).

However, according to Farax, Abdullahi Mohamed's oldest son, Abdullahi Mohamed did not just "happen" to wander into Mogadishu, (despite his own telling of the story this way). Rather, when he was herding stock near Garowe a hyena killed his grandfather's best she-camel—one of the animals Abdullahi Mohamed was supposed to have been watching. For this, his grandfather banished him. And this is why he had "suddenly" wound up in Mogadishu.

Nevertheless, whether it was push or pull that got him to Mogadishu and then beyond (i.e., Berbera for a time) Farax's father clearly preferred town life to subsistence in the bush. His wife, however, would sigh and speak nostalgically about the bush and its *barwaqo* [prosperity].

Indeed, many people who grew up in the bush seem to believe nothing is better than life there when conditions are right and there is ample milk and meat. However, nothing is worse than life in the bush during a drought, or even *jilaal* [the dry season]. Then, existence is not only difficult but overwhelmingly unpleasant—with the heat, lack of water, interminable walking. In fact, these are the very reasons most often cited for why town life is better, except during a successfully rainy *gu* season. Then, everyone in Mogadishu discusses the rains, saying "*waa buu*" [the countryside is replete]—pools are full of water, udders are full of milk, leaves and flowers are a welcome sight for sore eyes. Rainfall is rarely discussed without mention of milk (and meat) in the same breath since the three are so vitally connected in the pastoral economy. It is this brief window—whenever the pastoral ideal is realized—that makes people in town yearn for what suddenly appears to be the easier life, which they have forsaken.

Although people who had not improved their lot, or their children's lot, would return to the bush in an instant—as Mohamed, 54, a watchman with no children said of Mogadishu: "If I have livestock, why do I come here?"—many of those who were doing well in town and who *could* have purchased large enough herds to enable them to prosper in the bush clearly had not done so; they were doing well enough in town.[1]

As Ahmed, 67, puts it: "In the towns there is no thirst; there is water. There is food as long as there is money. In the bush there is the sun, thirst, heat, long walks. The people in the bush only know how to look after livestock and to farm, and the Koran. Both livestock and farming are difficult. In previous years there were no tractors. Manual work was hard. That is the main reason people hate the bush."

Indeed, until 1988 or so, many people seem to have felt they were subsisting just fine in Mogadishu. Not until the economy started to disintegrate and prospects for a better future began to dim did people begin to rethink the value of the bush. As one 38-year-old prison guard explained: "Because of tea, water, and not having to walk, life in the city is easier. At the same time, if there was a problem in the bush you could collect food, hunt, raid camels." In other words, life in the bush, more demanding and more basic, even at the worst of times presented more alternatives and possibilities than could worsening conditions in town.

In fact, once shortages of income and of cash became more common than rare (1988–1989), town no longer offered a steady modicum of comfort. Rather, it was straining people in ways in which the bush never did. Livestock started to look eminently more sensible and secure, since as long as an animal was alive it had value and this value always meant the same thing: at the very least, food. Indeed, as inflation made money far less reliable and the national shortages of cash introduced drought into the market economy, livestock as a source of sustenance clearly began to out-substantiate money. This, too, must be part of what lay behind increasing nostalgia for the bush.

The ability of older people to be able to compare pastoral and market economies and determine which would be able to sustain them better "at the moment"—with the difficulty of the moment ever-changeable—also helped explain the ambivalence that surfaced in people's views. For instance, Dalayo, a 40-year-old housewife, sounded three distinctly contradictory themes about the bush within the larger story of her life: "The bush was better than living in town today because life was happier and better (and she, of course was younger, although she does not mention this). It was the good life of milk and meat. With the *berkeds* [cement reservoirs] there was enough water."

1964 was the year in which she first visited a town (Hargeisa). "There was nothing to wonder at. Even though we were at different extremities, I didn't see anything wonderful. Nomads usually heard about things anyway." Not even the food was so different, except that initially she did not know how to cook pasta; that posed a challenge she still remembers.

However, despite the lack of novelty, Dalayo was happy about moving to Hargeisa. Why? Because she would not meet the hard work, long distances, and nomadism of rural life: "In the rural area there were many problems. For instance, when you give birth, you are supposed to stay in one place for forty days." Seven days after Dalayo gave birth she had to travel for one day and one night, after which she then had to erect the *aqal* [hut]—"Every night you have to erect the *aqal*; it is too shameful for the woman not to be able to put up her house."

But, despite the hardships she remembers so vividly and only infrequent visits to the bush today, she regards the bush "then" as better than the bush now: "Before, there used to be plenty of livestock and *barwaqo* [plenty]. Today there is hunger and people are destitute. The land is bad. There are too many *berkeds*. The land has eroded. Livestock are passing away. People used to have two hundred lactating camels in one family. These days you can't even see ten. Even rain used to be better." Clearly this last view suggests the fact of a changing ecology, colored by a dimmer regard for the present.

Not surprisingly, the bush/town dichotomy is often conflated with a past/present distinction. Given the differences between pastoralism as a mode for living versus the demands of settled life (finding employment, earning enough money, etc.), it is easy to see why this might be so.

Abdullahi voices the most common of the refrains among older people: "Before, money was little and life was cheap. Today money is much and life is expensive." As another 43-year-old woman remembers, food, especially, was cheap. In a day her husband used to give her ten shillings, which had been enough to support ten people. It went to purchase meat, ghee [clarified butter made from milk], and milk. People did not use oil, which did not become popular until 1972. "Today, 1,000 shillings is not enough for four people," the woman comments.

People's memories pinpointing exact dates for their introduction to different foodstuffs vary, probably because different foods became important to people differentially, depending on where they were living, what they could afford, and what was available. However, both pasta and oil seem to be two significant markers of change for many Somalis. As some people recount, pasta was introduced by the Italians and was made available to Somalis at very cheap prices, especially during drought years when it was often donated. Because it was cheaper than rice, another import eaten chiefly by northerners, it surpassed every other staple as well as locally grown sorghum as the main comestible. Once the population had switched though, and pasta had become an integral part of the diet, its price gradually increased. Many people describe this as a deliberate strategy on the part of the Italians to reap long-term profits at Somalis' expense.

Oil, too, was popularized thanks to drought. During the *Dabadheer* drought in the early 1970s ghee could not be produced in sufficient quantities. As a result oil had to be imported and oil gradually came to take the place of ghee in most households. Although critical for cooking, both oil and ghee play another role as well: The more oil one consumes the fatter one can become. This is a goal for certain Somali women, usually merchant women of middle age and significant income. Although it is no doubt an indicator of prosperity, bulk may actually serve these Somali women functionally too: It allows them to succeed at being domineering and imposing, lending them stature sufficient to cow men, and assert (asexual) independence.

Sugar is the third consumable people mentioned in describing how life had changed and serves as probably the most important signifier of the three. It was the price, and not the presence of sugar that people most often referred to; the price of sugar was usually the first (and most common) price cited in everyday conversation as an indicator of how expensive things had grown and how impossible life was becoming. And sugar was significant for several reasons. First, sugar was used throughout Somalia, by all segments of society, in the bush as well as towns. Second, it also spanned the diet—it was in anything baked (*mufo, angera,* bread) as well as in anything sweet (*halwa*) and, of course, is what made ubiquitous tea so life-sustaining.

In contrast, milk, interestingly enough, did not seem to play a dominant role. Whereas milk was critical for children to drink, most adults could go without it and often did, depending on the season and its availability. During droughts it was prohibitively expensive. Powdered milk was probably more widely used than fresh milk, particularly in tea in Mogadishu (whereas natural milk predominated in smaller towns). However, drinking fresh camel's milk was de rigueur when most urban males visited rural areas. It was as though having at least one glass of fresh camel's milk affirmed their Somaliness, if not virility—and this despite the general acknowledgment that fresh milk would cause them stomach pains and diarrhea. There were no ill side effects, however, for *reer miyi* [people of the bush; nomads] and people who drank it everyday.

In fact, this drinking of camel's milk very neatly epitomizes the greatest distinction between town and bush. As one of the housewives referred to earlier characterized it: "The biggest change is that before people used to be *reer miyi.* Now they are *reer magaal* [people of the town]." As sentiment and without specifying the realities, Dalayo is summing up *the* difference between town and country by saying this and then sighing. Her sigh is over a difference in ideals.

It is echoed in Hawa's comment. "My family is *reer miyi* and *reer magaal.* In the rainy season we become *reer miyi.*" Again, there is the sense that when things are good in the bush there is no better place to be. However, when things are climatically difficult, town is preferred. Perhaps with Mogadishu growing increasingly difficult Hawa longed to return to the *miyi,* but her children, none of whom remember actually living in the bush, did not. Nor did any of them ever return to subsist in the bush even for the rainy season. Yet all of them felt connected enough to still comment on the *barwaqo* rain brings and the joy this offered them as Somalis.

Some Somalis did occasionally return to the bush, although it may not have been the same bush they had longed for. Abdullahi (45) spells some of this out:

> The differences between previously and today is the difference between bush and town. Today there is more livestock, more money, more education, more knowledge. In those days, people weren't civilized. The difference between the bush and the town today is decreasing as they have shops in the bush and *reer miyi* are getting more things.
>
> Today you can go to the bush for health, as a sort of treatment. You can take milk, meat, etcetera from there, even livestock if you are having economic difficulties.

In this regard, the bush becomes a sanctuary from the rigors of urban life, as the countryside is for urban dwellers throughout the world: Life in the bush is more basic and more natural and thus restorative as well as helpful—and meat and milk are cheaper.

But the bush was also useful for escaping into for other reasons. It was the safest refuge there was for Somalis who needed to flee the law or the government. They could hide, subsist, and, sometimes, rally. Indeed, much of the formerly urban population of the northern towns fled into the bush at the onset of the civil war. It was widely felt that if one had the skills, stamina, and relatives it was better to return to the bush as a pastoralist than to have to subsist as a refugee. And on October 21, 1989, many Mogadishu residents, fearing widespread unrest if not (finally) war in the capital, went on extended drives, either to "picnic" for a few days or to visit relatives—in the bush.

Conversely, the government, too, recognized the bush as a refuge and used this interpretation for its own ends, often citing "bad elements" as a rationale for moving in to take action against lineages, subclans, or villages it viewed as politically troublesome. Because the bush did harbor so many different elements in addition to innocent pastoralists, it was easy for the government to proclaim that there were *shifta* [bandits] in the bush who needed to be eradicated. *Shifta* posed a perennial problem. Since independence, and resulting in part from government-sanctioned fighting between Somalia and Kenya (during the "Shifta war") and Somalia and Ethiopia (during and after the Ogaden War), the borders with these two countries persisted as proving grounds for bandits who played both sides of the border but were invariably considered to be (by both Ethiopia and Kenya) Somali. When it suited its purposes, the Somali government agreed (at least up to a point), thus enabling the army to take action against ethnic Somalis whom the government could always claim to be Kenyan or Ethiopian citizens, when in fact they were politically troublesome nationals.

For this reason the bush was often thought of as a dangerous place. Although there was little fear about lions or hyenas, there was fear not only of *shifta* (a catch-all in and of itself) but also of nomads. On the one hand, most Somalis would declare the people—meaning *reer miyi*—in the region where they (or their parents) were from as unrivaled for hospitality, claiming that their fellow clan members would slaughter a goat for *any* wayward traveler. On the other hand, if they were not going to their home area, these same individuals would not venture into the bush alone or unaccompanied by someone with local connections and local knowledge. Thus, implied in people's actions, and not in what they said, was the recognition that nomads lived by different rules and judged strangers suspiciously and would sometimes react violently, no matter how much hospitality was promised by rhetoric or the "rules" of Somali tradition.

If they were not in trouble of some sort, most urban Somalis would only venture into the bush if they were visiting relatives or if they were working for the government or an agency that afforded them legitimacy and protection. For those who grew up in Mogadishu and had not experienced the bush it was almost a curiosity. It was something many young Somalis thought they understood, in part because their parents knew it, in part because it was so integral to the national cultural heritage, in part because they learned about it in school. Yet, school taught them a vastly different appreciation for pastoralism than most pastoralists held: Pastoralism was portrayed as a mode of production that was vital to Somalia's economy and foreign exchange, but one that was not yet modern enough. This was only underscored by the need for so many expatriate range management experts, a degree program in range science at the national university, and the focus of so many donor-initiated projects on enhancing livestock production.

For instance, Amina, a 20-year-old student, spent one of her school vacations visiting relatives in the bush. During the two months in 1988 she was with them she says they moved three times, she subsisted on milk, meat, and tea, and bathed only once a week. Her conclusions: She was surprised by how her nomadic relatives lived, the prosperity they had available to them, and how they did not profit by it. "They have a lot of livestock. If they sold the livestock they would have a lot of money. In the dry season, when the drought comes, all the livestock will be finished; they should sell it."

Hers is a schooled reaction. Visiting her relatives corroborated what she had learned about nomads and the national economy at school. Her sentiments do not reflect anything she learned from her relatives. It is akin to the attitude that was pervasive among young university-educated, urban-reared government workers assigned to rural towns (and particularly those who staffed CRDP). More often than not they claimed they knew how nomads thought because all Somalis belong to the same culture, plus they had spent time touring through the rural regions. Thus, they often unconsciously (or sometimes wittingly) misrepresented the depth of their knowledge to expatriates who *did* assume that all Somalis shared the same culture or at least had intimate knowledge of it. Sometimes they also fooled themselves.

• 9 •

Pastoral Principles

Along lots of axes and in many senses, then, the bush and Mogadishu were inseparable. Not only did people move themselves back and forth through space (physically) and time (via memory) but they also continually compared conditions in both locales. Individuals who had lived in the bush felt that Mogadishu was becoming just as unreliable. Youth who had not lived in the bush believed one of Somalia's failures was in not properly exploiting its rural resources. Nevertheless, what perhaps links the bush and Mogadishu even more intimately than the way people were connected through them economically, historically, or familially was the viability of the principles of pastoralism in both locales.

In fact, it will be my contention in this chapter that principles of Somali pastoralism worked in Mogadishu precisely because conditions of unpredictability persisted there as they always do in the bush. As a result, the Somalis English-speaking expatriates knew did seem to respond in some instances *as if* expatriates and the projects they came with were milch cows (see Burton 1894/1987 Vol. 2: 95). But this, as our examination of history and chronology should have suggested, was often with good reason. Aid was the staff for many lives, and how long aid would last was never guaranteed.

Indeed, a number of alternative economies operated in Mogadishu in which it appeared as though the commodities circulating in them had been plugged in to some of the multivalent roles formerly (if not traditionally) occupied by livestock. The first of these is the economy of connections. The second is the more visible economy of money.

Like livestock, both connections and money served not only as resources but as sources of resources. All three of these economies overlapped, intermixed, and coincided. For instance, money could be begged, borrowed, or stolen in societally sanctioned, overt and covert ways—like camels or cattle—according to rules of connection. Connections no longer maintained through the transfer of livestock, meanwhile, could instead be carefully maintained with prestations of money.

One aim in this chapter is to stand the old question—is livestock capital? (see Paine 1971; Schneider 1979; Ingold 1980; Ferguson 1985; Hart and Sperling 1987)—on its head. Although still lively, the academic debate about the currency of livestock does not adequately tackle the everyday reality faced by the majority of urban Somalis: how to make ends meet. Rather, if we could instead regard capital *as* livestock, and then consider how money was being plugged in to connection-dependent systems of economy we might better understand how Mogadishu's still quiescent majority was (until recently) still managing to survive.

Further, we must consider the effects of such an environment on young, educated Somalis who were perhaps most caught between expectations for a brighter future (which they had been educated to achieve) and frustrations over the corrupt present (which they were being taught by their elders to accept).

With essentially no financial remuneration attached to their civil servant jobs and no discernible future working for a state and government visibly collapsing, young Somalis were left to ponder not only their future but the concept of *work*—particularly as they witnessed the corruption being practiced by their elders and recognized their own powerlessness to either alter the situation or keep themselves from joining in. This awareness, in turn, of their own impotence only added to their frustration. Impotence itself is a potentially rich metaphor, because many Somalis of this class were unable to earn enough money to attain women/wives and in addition they had been emasculated in the sense that education should have been (and was expected to be) empowering. To be educated had become a Somali, just as it is a Third World aspiration. However, in Somalia, any efforts to capitalize on this education were thwarted.

At the same time, though, because they had been unsuccessful at starting families, many of these young, unattached Somalis could still afford to be hopeful on other horizons: They might win a scholarship, they might yet get to go abroad, "something" might still happen.

Such a situation kept most Somalis I knew in a constant state of being poised, ready to take advantage of any opportunity, expectant. How such a state of expectation elided with opportunism, partook of tribalism, depended on wealth in connections and skill at connection maintenance and could still be attributed to Allah is a journey that, theoretically, will be delineated here, before being fleshed out in the next chapters.

PASTORAL GROUNDWORK

Somalia is most commonly described in terms of geographical differences bisected by climatic seasons, with bands of mountains crumpled across the northwest, two ocean-bound rivers (the Juba and Shabelle) flowing in the flat south, unwatered inland scrub rising imperceptibly as the Haud and Ogaden in the west, and an undulating coastal, coarse grass plain rimming the beaches in the east. Each zone, with its own particular gift, has supported graded modes of production—the gradient running from irrigated agriculture to rain-fed agriculture through agro-pastoralism to "pure" pastoralism.[1]

Often referred to as "pure" pastoralism, because its nomadic practitioners are usually not observed growing food crops, herding is practiced throughout the country and is the chief mode of production in those areas where there is no permanently flowing water and no other source of livelihood: namely inland, and along the coastal plain. Governed by undependable rains, even rain-fed crops (such as sesame, maize, sorghum, and millet) are unreliable as the sole source for food in semiarid areas. Only livestock, with their guaranteed mobility, allow renewable food (i.e., milk) to be produced wherever rain happens to have fallen and grazing can be found. It is for these two reasons, then, that nomadic pastoralism has proven so durable and remains so widespread in Somalia: Outside the inter-riverine region agriculture alone is insufficient and only pastoralism is optimally efficient over vast areas of the country.

There is a relentless logic to certain aspects of nomadic pastoralism as an adaptation to an unpredictable environment. For instance, a range of animals is generally kept by Somalis: camels or cattle, sheep and goats (cattle do not fare well in Somalia's harshest reaches). However, they are rarely herded together. Generally, small stock are retained by the family and not sent off great distances with young men, as are camels. This is so for a number of reasons. Small stock cannot travel the same distances camels can without needing to frequent water holes more often, nor can they always subsist on the same browse. If herded together with camels, small stock would detract from the efficiency of camels. Therefore, herders diversify their herds, never mind the simpler-seeming rationale that no pastoralist would want to keep his entire investment in one herd. In addition, goats and sheep are relatively easy for women and very young children to herd. Thus, for a host of reasons, one of which is simply that it is possible to do so, small stock are maintained at closer range than large stock.

Similarly, one reason for an animal-wealthy pastoralist to marry more than one wife is to gain more herders (each wife is one, and their offspring will add others). However, there is a give and take to the herds at marriage, with the bride's family receiving livestock as bridewealth (livestock and/or money presented by the groom and his family to the bride's father). Thus, in gaining a wife the wealthy pastoralist simultaneously sheds part of his herd. But in shedding the herd he also gains affines (in-laws) who offer vital connections and a safety net should his herd meet with disaster.

However, marriage transactions are more complicated than merely the husband's family rewarding the wife's family with stock in order to secure himself new "friends." As we shall see, in some central and northern parts of Somalia, the husband's family traditionally receives a return gift of stock from the wife's family (*dibad*). Although some anthropologists might argue these transfers occur to cement social ties, there is also a biological effect: These exchanges, literally, mix the herds. Such transfers might have more than just symbolic import since shifting female camels and exposing them to new bulls strengthens bloodlines.

Given the stringent demands of nomadism there is a tight fit between social organization and pastoral practices among Somali herders. And this close interplay is not unique to Somalia (see Smith 1992). Indeed, one device ensuring pastoral nomadism's continued systemic success has been its ability to expand and contract according to conditions. During drought the system sloughs off unsuccessful herders. In times of plenty relatives might afford the failed nomad a second chance by loaning or giving him animals.

However, a potentially significant attitudinal difference does exist between Somalis who view themselves as pastoralists and others (including expatriates) who have held to a different work ethic grounded in agriculture. It is a divide that expatriates, in practice, recognized (in their preferences for working with *agro*-pastoralists rather than nomads) and that Somalis have proudly acknowledged. Rooted in history, geography, and physiognomy, the dominant Somali view has been one of agriculturalists who live between the Juba and Shabelle Rivers, who were slaves (or slave-equivalents), and are Bantu-featured.

What is particularly striking about this spin on the classic pastoralist/agriculturalist dichotomy (Goldschmidt 1971, 1979) is the historical fact of slavery and the extensive documentation in the travel literature describing artisan castes composed of "lesser" Somalis (from Burton 1894/1987 through Hanley 1971/1987). Such distinctions tautologically helped guarantee the self-definition of Somalis as pastoralists. Pastoralists (Somalis) raised animals; others (non-Somalis) performed other essential functions (see Spear and Waller 1993 for a similar definition of *Maasai*).

Doubtless the presence and use of slaves (as well as members of the Migdan, Tomal, and Yibir smithing, hunting, and tanning "castes") for "dirty" work reinforced pastoral Somalis' cultural attitudes about eschewing dirty work themselves. Certainly, there was a fortunate historical congruity in capitalism (via a plantation and money economy) moving inland along *with* slaves in the nineteenth century (Cassanelli 1982; Alpers 1983; Sheriff 1985), such that (noble pastoralist) Somalis were rarely forced to work as manual laborers themselves, although they could choose to (for instance, in *tariqa* settlements). This not only preserved, but arguably even furthered the tautological—and thus perhaps viciously cyclical—nature of Somali self-identity with livestock as a means of (clean) production.

Believing themselves to be "more" Somali because their parents or grandparents were pastoralists could then enable many urban-based Somalis to carry on with these distinctions. Even more to the point, this might also explain their affinity for what, at a distance, could be regarded as the pastoralist idyll. Not getting involved in dirty work still influenced the behavior of people who had never lived as nomads themselves but could still draw on a mythologized and golden past, particularly since this past still lived in places. Perhaps then it is no coincidence that those behaviors that expatriates found most incommensurable with their own emerged out of pastoralism, evolving out of a disdain for manual labor and a preference for management over production or hands-on maintenance.

In many senses the expatriate take on Somalis' work habits really does represent the agriculturalist/pastoralist dichotomy. Ironically, though, it may reveal more about the settled and/or agriculturally grounded origins and biases of the expatriate work ethic (having to do with direct productivity) than make any sense about Somali realities. Certainly, many of the Somalis' most offensive behaviors in this regard were not unique to them. Even casual visitors to developing countries often comment on the lack of productivity and people's penchant for inactivity. Nevertheless, I believe it was specific uncertainties in the Mogadishu environment that helped generate these behaviors there. Because many of the underpinnings of the economy and responses to uncertainties were rooted in a pastoralist past, our understanding of pastoralism should contribute to our being able to explain how this seeming lack of action *was* productive activity—according to pastoralist criteria.[2]

Here I also want to make a clear distinction between fatalism, the passive response of people with no room to maneuver, and the inactivity Somalis I refer to displayed. After all, expectation is not about being passive. Nor does waiting have to be. Instead, waiting can be about *being* poised and about being ready to take action if an opportunity for action presents itself.

What follows is an example of how waiting with expectation worked: We are sitting at a tea shop. It happens to be the tea shop at "K-5." The shop itself, with its cappuccino machines and steady offerings of coffee, tea, soft drinks, mineral water, and snack food is bright white and inviting within. Nevertheless, unless customers are in a hurry, in which case they drink as they pay, most people would rather sit outside, even on the cement stoops, in intense, unrelenting, but not quite blinding, sunlight. There is no way the exterior of the shop is more comfortable than the incomparably cooler interior. Yet this is the pattern at tea shops throughout the city; customers sit outside, facing the street *and* traffic.

This tea shop is dubbed "K-5" because K-5 describes its location, square at the head of a T-section on Afgoi Road. The road that intersects Afgoi

Road to form the T is the major bus route to and from one of the larger village suburbs (Medina), and Afgoi Road itself is one of two main thoroughfares in and out of Mogadishu. Thus, there is always a steady stream of traffic driving past, which moves slowly enough so that it is possible to recognize not only vehicles but also their occupants. This passing—who passes, heading where, with whom—becomes informative. Meanwhile, next door to the tea shop is one of the supermarkets frequented by Europeans, boasting a popular fruit and vegetable stand out front.

Hence, K-5 presents a range of opportunities and a number of frames through which to scan for them. In the smallest frame there is what is happening within the tea shop and among the customers swigging their drinks. Then there are the clients sitting just outside. In the next frame are comings and goings to and from the supermarket, which blurs into who is walking past. Only slightly further removed are the drivers and passengers who specifically stop vehicles *at* K-5. These are generally civil servants and government workers either heading to or returning from downtown ministries. Finally, there is the largest frame, containing the traffic that doesn't stop, but that is slow enough to be taken in.

Simultaneous with so many multiple views are also possibilities for different events occurring: Perhaps there will be a road accident or, more likely, a breakdown—providing drama or entertainment and the manufacture of news. Perhaps someone the viewer knows will pass by or stop in for a drink, transmitting gossip or the latest rumors. Something is always bound to happen, and the likelihood of this "something" becoming useful is considerable enough that there is always an air of anticipation in the people who are otherwise quietly sitting.

Doubtless expectation is also heightened by the bustle of government employees who stop quickly (when technically they should be elsewhere) but whose stops are crucial for the circulation of information that may well be *the* ulterior reason people frequent this particular tea shop. For instance, no matter what the distraction, no matter how deep in conversation people might be, they are always cognizant of what is happening around them, who has come in, with whom, from where, and so on. Hence, the only real difference between people who are clearly on their way back or forth from somewhere and those who have been seated for a long time, with nothing seemingly pressing to do, is that the latter only *look* less active. They have time (which is not money in Somalia) to look leisurely. Yet, given enough time they know from past experience that something (or someone) interesting (i.e., useful) will come along. Their waiting thus amounts to tending a sort of a trapline, and it is this act of lying in wait that I think expatriates misinterpret as mere idleness.

Of course, there is also an additional reality at work outside tea shops: Expectation may be so attenuated because so many people have so little to do; there *is* rampant unemployment. Nevertheless, as we shall see, it is not jobs or employment per se that necessarily provide or secure money in Mogadishu. Rather, it is often the parlaying of job-related advantages into other advantages that can provide real income equivalents. One way to achieve solvency in such an economy is to indeed treat networks as traplines; they must be regularly—but not too regularly—tended to or they will not yield results.

Meanwhile, and not uncoincidentally, there are few activities available to the unemployed *beyond* networking. Thus, although inactivity epitomized by tea-drinking may be the path of least resistance and the easiest and least expensive "activity" to engage in, it is also probably the most productive and rewarding, providing the most popular, and thus most likely and most efficient means of working a network. Hence, the literal self-fulfillment in sipping tea becomes figuratively self-reinforcing.

Tea shop networking must be viewed as one strategy for coping with uncertainty in Mogadishu. However, before probing further avenues for urban networking, let us briefly return to a consideration of pastoralist conditions.

PASTORAL CONDITIONS

Ultimately it is the maintenance of connections between pastoralists that gives unity to social organization, makes for an economy, allows for exchange, and ensures survival of nomads in the bush. Pastoralists need to properly reproduce their herds as well as themselves. In order to balance stock and laborers, to find and hold water points and grazing areas, and to gain access to potential spouses, nomadic pastoralists have to maintain and retain far-flung ties (Lewis 1961; also Gulliver 1955; Spencer 1973).

Because these ties, by definition, are necessarily impermanent, the opportunities for their maintenance would, on the one hand, seem limited; nomads may not run into one another very often. On the other hand, with unpredictability such a given, flexibility is a necessity and, to cope, skeins of ties should be limitless. This is where opportunism—guaranteeing limitlessness—meets tribalism, which sets definite (and defining) limits on opportunity.

Certainly, opportunism appears to be a direct result of the ecological givens: In the short run, and on the local level, rainfall is too erratic to predict. Thus, livestock must be herded nomadically in order to take advantage of water sources and grazing as they occur. Because disease is as fickle as drought it is impossible for herders to know what will happen to their herds, or what has happened to others' herds. Since one way to recoup herd losses is through raiding, raids add another dimension to unpredictability in the pastoralist environment. Raiding has double-edged meaning: It is not only a reaction and response to sudden misfortune, it is also the means *to* instant fortune. It both alleviates and exacerbates the natural conditions, which, on the surface, seem so uncontrollable.

However, although environmental conditions might be unpredictable from moment to moment, the very fact that uncertainty is so predictable in this environment means that those who are dependent on nature's beneficence can also assume that sooner or later disaster will strike. For instance, if drought conditions exist once every three years (CRDP 1986) and major diseases opportunistically feed on drought, then raids are also likely to follow. Thus, although it may be impossible to prepare for these specific moments—since water and grazing are not preservable, nor diseases or raids preventable—pastoralism, as a system borne of this environment, has programmed into itself responses, which themselves, are systematic. As we have just seen, raiding is one of these. However, the obverse to raiding is even more helpful: the giving and loaning of livestock. Meanwhile, *who* the recipients are—who are either helped through loans or hurt through raids—is what tribalism, the social limit to natural opportunism, helps define. Who tribalism defines may also be quite different for Somalis than for other pastoralist peoples in Africa and the Middle East, where peoples' distinctions often rest on significant ecological niche differences, language, scarification, and other physical markers.[3]

Although there are some niche differences between northern and southern Somalia, most Somali pastoralists raise the same categories of stock with camels invariably being those that are most highly prized (Abokor 1987). Methods of pastoralism may differ regionally, but, if so, they differ in degree rather than kind. Similarly, for Somali pastoralists there are dialect but not language differences, differences in clothing style but not in what parts of the body are clothed, differences in degrees of religiousness but not in religion, differences in local culture but not in Culture as it defines Somalis *by* their pastoral practices.

What is significant about differences such as these (of degree rather than kind) is that they stand in place of more impermeable boundaries between people. They are fungible, and they can be easily denied or hidden. They leave no permanent marks, unlike tattoos or circumcision scars (although all Somalis are also circumcised), and they are composed of learned behaviors. Thus, they can be conveniently altered, remembered, or forgotten as circumstances require. Indeed, this last is, I believe, critical to understanding Somali tribalism; these insubstantial-seeming differences can be manipulated to serve as openings or as closures, depending upon mutual (and often only temporary) needs.

10

Ties

Although ties of blood might seem one of the few permanent possessions pastoralists have, the fact that people can be fictively grafted onto descent groups calls the immutability of these bonds into question.[1] Nor are affinal links always permanent. Thus, blood ties are certainly augmented and may even be superseded by social links that have been forged to complement the significance attached to patrilineage. This is particularly pronounced in urban (or settled) settings, where individuals are surrounded by unfamiliar clan "relatives" as well as familiar nonrelatives with whom they have many reasons for trying to get along (Luling 1971; Cassanelli 1982; Helander 1988).

For government-employed Mogadishu residents there were three significant non-kin networks in which individuals could participate: through school, neighborhood, and workplace ties. School bonds, whether Koranic or primary, were particularly long lasting since they tied people together not only as acquaintances or friends, but as age-mates. They would gain even more weight the longer people attended school together, and/or the older they got. This was certainly the case with secondary school attendance since admission to secondary schools was not universal, or universally affordable. University was more exclusive still. Mandatory national (military) service (normally performed after secondary school) also stratified people, although of the two trackings university was usually more significant. Still, it was during national service that many young men and women met their future wives and husbands and also established links with distant relatives (or fellow clan members) who lived in the areas to which they had been assigned but whom they had not necessarily previously known.

A different set of ties formed in Mogadishu's residential neighborhoods (commonly referred to as "villages"), which were purportedly not clan-based, although it was widely remarked that members of certain clans did favor certain villages. These residential ties were, in a sense, ties of convenience, since it was only pragmatic for people to try to get on well with their neighbors. For instance, thanks to Mogadishu's high temperatures, windows stayed open and domestic life (and cooking in particular) tended to be conducted in courtyards, thus neighbors were privy to much that they may not have seen but could certainly hear. Likewise, neighborhoods tied children together as playmates, youth then grew up as companions, and young men and women as potential spouses. Many neighborhoods also sported small shops or stands that doubled as meeting places.

Yet a third setting for the formation of connections was the workplace. The workplace was perhaps the most meaningful arena in which networks were negotiated since this is where the widest array of potentially helpful people was located. This is so despite the fact that most employees spent most of their time with colleagues who were at their same achievement level (with, presumably, identical prospects). What added worth to these relationships was who these peers could access through *their* schoolmate, neighborhood, and family networks. Certainly, being able to make connections across networks, and not just within them, helped keep all networks running smoothly. Indeed, from the perspective of individuals embedded within their immediate families first, networks provided an opportunity for brokerage beyond the family, which the extended family (extending into lineage and beyond) could exploit. Having said this it is also important to add the corollary: All families strove to exploit as many opportunities as possible at all times.

This is why many government workers, no matter what their official job, found themselves pressingly occupied with other work as well. This, in turn, had several consequences. For instance, because of the paucity of telephones people often tried to find one another in person, which left offices empty and meant that their absence caused others to search for them. There was a fortuitousness to this running around: by having to run around because of gaps in the formal communications system individuals could never be sure who they might run into and what possibilities might arise from these accidental encounters (which, interestingly enough, were never accidental in the framework of Islam, but were ultimately the result of Allah's hand).

The trick to succeeding at this "business" of networking, then, was to be able to *be* poised to take advantage of as many relations with as many (and even the same) people as possible. There were many different strategies for achieving this. One simple example can be found in the contrast between Ahmed and Mohamed, two watchmen working for U.S. citizens. Ahmed always asked for whatever he wanted outright—whether that was water or a wheelbarrow or English lessons. Mohamed, conversely, rarely asked for anything but had just as much success receiving things as Ahmed did. Neither may have been aware of how they should really have been playing the US. citizens, but certainly they were conscious (without jointly strategizing) that they played off one another. Ahmed's tactic was to wear expatriates down. Mohamed seemed surer he would be (and was) rewarded for not wearing them down.

Although their different attitudes doubtless reflected different temperaments (which, interestingly enough, other Somalis who knew them explained according to their respective clan affiliations), their different reactions to the same situation may also have reflected different levels of desperation. Ahmed's wife and children were refugees staying in a refugee camp half a day's bus ride away from Mogadishu. Mohamed's wife and children resided with him in town and were not of precarious citizenship.

Examined from another angle, success at maintaining and expanding networks also required one to allow oneself to *be* taken advantage of. However, in passing on one's own connective advantages to others one had to be careful not to pass on those connections themselves. For instance, Farax, who was "just another" CRDP employee, had schoolmates who had achieved responsible positions teaching and administering secondary schools. Therefore, his extended family used him and these connections to gain placement for their children in schools of their choice (when getting children into schools at all was no mean feat). Similarly, fellow CRDP employees, some of whom were senior to Farax, used Farax's father's connections at the central prison to provide *their* detained relatives with deferential treatment, if not release. Thus, Farax's position *at* work was immaterial. Neither his place in the bureaucratic pecking order nor his salary had much to do with determining his importance to his fellow employees or, for that matter, their importance to him.

The fact that salary was of little account in these networks is significant for several reasons. First, it must be emphasized that civil servant salaries were negligible to begin with; no one was working for their salary at CRDP. Rather, everyone was working for the advantages that would accrue through their connections to one another, their connections to the expatriate staff, or ideally, through the project's connections to scholarship and fellowship opportunities abroad. This is not to deny genuine concern about range management, desertification, or efforts to improve pastoral production on the part of CRDP employees. Nevertheless, the compensation for "work" in these areas was not really monetary.[2]

Rather, there was an alternate economy of connections and favors that required the symbolic, but not operative, use of money. In this economy money greased palms and kept the system functional but was not always important as an end in itself. This is perhaps most clearly demonstrated in accounts of sons giving their fathers half their salaries—salaries that were laughably insignificant in terms of their worth. In some instances these small amounts of money may indeed have been important, if their timing was crucial in adding to a lump sum necessary for some transaction. But by and large most fathers did not need these particular and paltry sums when they were presented. Instead, these transfers should probably be viewed as symbolic exchanges, in which ties were being reaffirmed and in which respect was being "paid."

Surely this economy, like many discussed in the anthropological literature on gift-giving, operated in terms of delayed and potential reciprocity (Mauss 1967; Bourdieu 1977). Money, clearly, contributed to survival, but the way in which the money was gathered was more important to the survival of the person's network of connections than to the person's momentary ability to eat or to feed others. In other words, money is not what made this system. Rather, people's abilities to realize the potential of their connections, to maintain their networks, and the uses to which they put themselves and others determined survivability, not only of individuals but of the system itself.

This is in sharp contrast to economies like those in the United States, where most services are bought (and where, interestingly enough, many fear the economy itself is becoming a service economy). In Somalia it was ties that bought services, or at least access to them. Access was the key link—the one link that is disposable in most Western economies, where anything from professional advice to a meeting with the president can be had for the right fee. Certainly in Somalia access was not free. Nevertheless, having money was not as critical as being able to gain access and knowing whom to go to in order to gain that access. Although money may have bought access on the lowest level—for example, entrance past a guard at the ministry gate—one always had to know who to approach in order to reach the person who could ultimately provide the desired service or assistance.

Those with access, by accident of birth, or school ties, or work connections, could certainly turn access into money. However, they constantly had to be aware of overusing a good thing. They had to weigh the value of bothering someone too much against the value of what it was they were bothering that person for.

From another angle it might appear that almost everything was negotiable in Somalia if such constant renewal and recementing of ties was so important. However, it may well be that it was the need for constant renewal of ties that made everything seem negotiable. After all, if ties ensured the ability to survive, not only in the pastoral setting but also in urban competition for access to resources, then how would one ensure, maintain, and cultivate ties? Presumably not by negotiating or renegotiating those ties. One would negotiate or re-negotiate other things, like money, and perhaps anything else *but* a relationship in order to gain assurances and reassurances *about* the relationship. Ties would remain as sacrosanct as possible.

Put differently, in a situation in which everything except the ideals of society were fluid, connections became one of the few sources of resources that people could actually possess *and* control. Nor was it as though there was no ideology to support this. Indeed, there was genealogy, which could create or buttress an ideology of connections in three ways: as an idealized version of the past, as an idealized (and idealizing) depiction of reality, and as the ideal template for how to construct connections and what connections should mean.

For instance, one would have different obligations to members of one's patrilineage than to affines (or in-laws), and obligations to members of one's "family" would also differ from obligations to mere friends or even useful acquaintances. All of this could easily be read backwards, too, so that how one behaved toward others one liked, connected with, or had a connection to out of personal choice was expected to be different from how one behaved toward those one actually *was* connected to (i.e., members of one's "family"), which also often happened to be a matter of public knowledge.

For example, employment in terms of university graduates represented a buyer's market in Mogadishu. In the West there must usually be some justification offered for choosing one applicant over another. However, in a situation in which qualified potential employees glut the market any decision becomes essentially arbitrary. This was implicitly recognized in Mogadishu, where recent university graduates understood that general managers and project heads could pick and choose and that they picked from the networks that they knew best, or considered to be the best to pick from. Similarly, promotions were generally awarded on the basis of ties and the use-value (rather than the work-value) of the individual to be promoted.

However, what threw a wrench into being able to predict an employer's network-of-choice was that he may have been drawing on his own school ties, village ties, work ties, *or* kin ties. This allowed the young jobseekers to hope that perhaps it would not be whom they knew among their employer's kin (if anyone) but whom *else* they may have known that singled them out. Of course, they could also never be sure whether or not it was kin ties that eventually undermined their chances. In other words, they could never be sure which ties achieved or attained them (or constrained them in) their position. This then set up a vicious cycle: it was the lack of sureness about the connection that also ensured perceptions that it *was* ties (and not merit) that swept people in and out of their positions.

And although nepotism was clearly a problem, it was a problem amplified (and no doubt exacerbated, even self-fulfilled) by the sensitivity, curiosity, and compulsion about connections writ (and read) according to the rule(s) of genealogy. Nor did people have much choice—if connections were the force beneath, and often substituting for, the economy of money. Uncertainties in that economy called for connections-as-underlying-safety-net, and the investment of connections with such potency automatically transformed them into a sort of elixir for everyday life, which in turn gave them what seemed to be a life of their own.

"QAARAAN"

For instance, there was *qaaraan*.[3] As one Somali anthropologist described it, *qaaraan* is assistance. The *qaaraan*-giving group is often the same group that also pays *dia* [blood money].[4] It is a group drawn up according to lineage connections, which offers members economic, but not political assistance and was one of a number of assistance arrangements existing in Mogadishu during 1988–1989 (Ahmed Yusuf Farah, personal communication).

In many ways *qaaraan* seems to complement *dia*, since it is money that is collected for someone within and not outside the group.[5] Nor is *qaaraan* something that could be denied; everyone claimed he or she (or a household head) paid it when asked (so long as money was available).

Who paid *qaaraan*, then, delimited the group. However, *qaaraan* was only selectively collected and distributed, often as cases arose but sometimes only annually (although one person told me his group collected a set fee once a month). In instances in which people I spoke with had received *qaaraan*, it was usually used to offset mourning costs (here it should be noted that mourning was public in the sense that mourners [lineage members and others] were provided with refreshments if not a meal, paid for through *qaaraan*). Other times it was collected to help the family when someone had been jailed, or it was requested because a family member accidentally caused the death of someone else and *dia* had to be offered. This last suggests the urban elision of *dia* and *qaaraan* and the complexities of assigning blame in such "modern" entanglements as automobile accidents.

Like the giving of livestock to individuals who had suddenly lost their herds in the pastoral setting, *qaaraan* appears to have been gathered in Mogadishu after unexpected turns in events, which family members could not have adequately prepared for.

> *In 1984 Idris's wife had a fight with another woman, which caused the other woman to abort. His father and uncle had to collect money (which Idris describes as dia) to pay the other woman's family. His father and uncle contributed 100,000 shillings. Others contributed 400,000 shillings. "This is qaaraan. It is the collection of money. Everyone's salary is written down and proportions taken. You can't refuse [paying] qaaraan because in the future maybe you need qaaraan."*

This sentiment is echoed by young and old alike:

"If I have some money I pay. If I don't have money, I take a loan from some other person. It is a must." (Yusuf, 30)

Roble (49) corroborates this, "It is a must. Even you will seek a loan to pay *qaaraan.*" He goes on to explain that the *qaaraan*-paying group is not necessarily restricted to the *dia*-paying group, but may involve the clan or friends as well. "Usually someone calls together a meeting of people from different sections of Mogadishu and they will come up with a list of names of people in their sections, and who can afford what. You always know how much wealth people have by how they live. Nothing is secret. You can estimate someone's wealth.

"For *dia* these days, in an accident, the charge is 600,000 shillings. You find groups to pay 50,000 or 30,000. No one pays as little as 1,000. On the other hand, if someone wants to travel to the North, people may pay as little as 1,000 or 2,000 so that 30,000 can be collected."

As Ismail, 26, explains, *qaaraan* "is our insurance. If my leg is lost, the government won't pay me. But the family or tribe will. Always I pay *qaaraan.*" He remembers his mother once paying one camel (which belonged to him) as *qaaraan* when one boy killed another. When his uncle's son was killed in a car accident in Mogadishu in 1975 the family received 150,000 shillings as *qaaraan.*

Clearly, *qaaraan* was neither a form of socialism (the redistribution of resources) nor welfare (compensation for chronic inability to perform), but instead was a public acknowledgment, via assistance, that events beyond an individual's control do take place but do not have to unduly crush the individual as long as he/she is a member of a lineage/group.

Generally *qaaraan* was organized by very old men who represented (or were) the urban heads of their lineages. These men reportedly knew how to find most members of their lineage even if those individuals had only recently arrived in Mogadishu. In part this is because most people stayed with relatives (if they had them) or at least went to relatives for assistance upon first arriving in town. Also, it was difficult for people to remain anonymous in Mogadishu; some sort of connection to someone had to be expressed, even if false and even if nothing more than a connection to neighbors; housing was too crowded and entrances and exits too difficult and public for someone to be able to remain "strange" or anonymous.

The amount of *qaaraan* solicited was calculated according to a household head's ability to pay. Evidently it was not possible to hide wealth; people who had money lived a certain way, in certain kinds of houses, and drove certain types of vehicles. Traditionally *dia* was solicited proportionately, on the basis of herd size and wealth in livestock—something else difficult to hide, but not difficult to negotiate over since not all animals in a herd belonged to the herd owner.[6] Similarly, although *qaaraan* had to be paid, its amount was potentially negotiable.

Indeed, the idea of not paying *qaaraan* was so alien to most Somalis I spoke with that their expressions of dismay at being asked such a question could have served as an indication of the extent to which *qaaraan* was deeply embedded as a cultural norm, at the same time this overarching (yet ultimately divisive) cultural norm revealed, again, how life in Somalia, if not group-oriented, was definitely group-orient*able*. But, having said this, I still have not adequately explained why it was lineage that tended to be the principle organizing factor in most *qaaraan*-paying groups.

The most obvious reason for the use of lineage as organizing principle was not only that *qaaraan*-as-assistance was rooted in the vagaries of pastoralism and the pastoralist need for organizing some sort of stability-in-fluidity but *qaaraan*-as-organizer had been transplanted, almost intact, from rural Somalia into urban Somalia with a ready-made membership. As individuals moved from the bush into Mogadishu they moved along familiar family webs. By claiming kinship ties, new arrivals automatically proved themselves to their relatives; kinship ties were the quickest and cleanest ties to recognize since lineage gave individuals a history and legitimacy that other forms of connection could not (yet) lay claim to. Because kin traditionally helped in the pastoral setting, and there was a history of assistance—ergo the lineage genealogy—it was easier to assume that kin would continue to help in the urban setting, (i.e., kin were assumed helpful until proven unhelpful).

As with many forms of informal assistance in Africa, *qaaraan* ultimately was little more than a substitute for the government's inability to respond to need or provide people with a safety net. However, *qaaraan* was also extremely specific; it provided for need only in specific instances. It was not blanket aid designed to help a certain segment of society or category of person. Rather, it was event-merited at the same time it was merit-proof. This allowed it to be selective in ways that assured its success; it was not continually demanded, there were limits on whom it was drawn from or whom it assisted, and it did not reward failure although it did compensate for acts of fate.

ISLAM

Aid for chronic failure and for temporary shortfalls, on both the larger and the smaller scale, had to come from elsewhere. *Qaaraan* was a sort of safety net, but not a complete one. This, I believe, is also a reflection of pastoralist ethics: Pastoralists were competitive; success was never assured; disaster could strike anyone—"it is Allah's will"—therefore, it was only right to help out in disaster, but it was not smart to help a competitor learn how to compete. Such assistance devolved upon the family.[7] Alternatively, if the case was chronic enough and the family could not afford assistance, it was possible for an individual to turn to religious means in order to appeal for assistance, either by teaching (if a male), by learning (and receiving support for study, if male), or by "begging" for alms.[8] Indeed, rural Koranic teachers were often described as having been failed pastoralists who turned to teaching in order to collect wages in livestock in the hopes of recouping status in two ways: by building up their herds at the same time they gained respect (and further gifts) because of having become men of religion.

Islam was also the rubric under which pocket money, or temporary help, could be solicited from kin, coworkers, and acquaintances. "Allah will provide" was the subterfuge used by people of all walks of life in Mogadishu to explain where money beyond salaries (and remittances) came from, even though it could really only have originated with either relatives or friends, and usually only after having been solicited. Because it was so often claimed that everything was already written down and preordained by Allah, it was just a quick sidestep to then rationalize that it was only "natural" that so-and-so help—this was Allah's will, not the individual's. Ultimately, then, it *was* Allah who provided. Thus, too, it was under Allah's direction that people saw themselves, and were seen, fulfilling their Muslim duty *by* providing.

Interestingly, people rarely asked others for money directly. There was a politesse involved in activating a transaction. Usually the person needing money described his or her misfortune in such a way that it became clear that money could help alter the situation. Or, someone would present a problem that clearly stemmed from lack of money and then would invite help in arriving at a solution to the problem without openly articulating a need for money itself. People rarely admitted to not assisting, if they were able to, when cases were presented thus. The view was expressed that if someone had money and was approached in these ways he or she had to offer a portion of what was available. Only rarely did someone admit to me that they sometimes said they had no money, in order to avoid having to part with any.

What is striking about these methods is that people were very careful about the image they projected when they were soliciting; it was not that they were moneyless but that in this one instance they lacked funds, suggesting that normally they would have been able to handle this crisis or problem but that they were facing abnormal circumstances and were temporarily unable to cope. Thus, they carefully presented themselves as *not* failures, nor did they see themselves chronically foundering. This was important to get across because everyone caught up in webs of connections understood the underlying conditions: One would not necessarily want to maintain (or reinforce) ties with someone who was in chronic need of help and who would consequently not be *of* any help. It also amounted to a form of mystification in the face of common knowledge about the general situation, in which no government employee but a project manager or businessman had a salary sufficient to get by on.[9]

As in most places, people would often ask as many of their friends as possible for assistance rather than turn to a single individual. The solicitation of small sums from several people cemented several ties rather than undermining only one, and at the same time, small sums were less threatening. In addition, if it was a network of assistance being cemented then not asking for a large sum avoided the precedent of setting oneself up to have to reciprocate in a big way sometime in the future.

However, there was something else at work here, too: obfuscation. Most people knew the position of those around them. For instance, everyone in Mogadishu was aware of civil servants' inadequately small salaries. However, all civil servants somehow seemed to get by using this same strategy of soliciting small sums for particular reasons when, in fact, they needed endless numbers of small sums for the very general reason that, otherwise, they would never have enough money. Even more intriguing is the fact that this resulted in an almost ceaseless circulation of small sums. For example, it was quite normal for people to borrow money from one individual in the morning in order to pay back another person in the afternoon. Certainly business would have been tidier if this had not been the case. Nevertheless, I heard no complaints about the methods that had to be used to manage survival (although, of course, I did hear complaints about low salaries). This is because, I would suggest, Islam offered a tidiness that, in turn, invested the business of small sums with other—namely, God-given—meaning.

This was particularly possible in the Somali case because of the close fit between Islamic and pastoralist moralities. There are striking correlations (and, perhaps, corroborations) between Muslim and pastoralist ideals, ranging from ideals of egalitarian communitas and *umma* to belief in the superior value of camels over other stock, to recognition of the importance of genealogy (converging, not surprisingly, in traced descent from the Prophet Mohamed). Considering the historical locus of the Somali "center"—dispersed as it was in the bush—and the relative newness of settlement, it is not surprising that some elements of the pastoralist morality were intromitted into the urban setting. That solicitations (like those I have described) were often reinterpreted, by virtue of Islam, as the righteous acts of good Muslims, though, is significant. This way, what could be interpreted as a return, revival, or fallback to pastoralist/lineage morality (involving the borrowing and begging of livestock [now money]) during moments of shortage, could instead be locally interpreted as the proper Islamic response to a modern economy's demands. In other words, by privileging the Islamic rubric people could openly deny other allegiances at the same time they were locating themselves in the modern Muslim world in which backward nomads no longer had a place. And, concomitantly, they could pretend that, if they acted correctly, they had done all that they could individually be expected to do. The larger situation was not just out of their hands but not of their making; *they* were good (and righteous) citizens.

• 11 •

Moralities

This fit (and hidden convergence of moralities) is perhaps best exemplified in the answer, "it is part of our culture" whenever people were asked why they "lent" others money. There was no deeper reason that people who participated in this continual exchange of sums could offer, nor was there an overarching explanation for how so many people were managing to survive (in comfort, despite the rhetoric) on such paltry salaries. The general explanation was a mystifying and not uncontradictory "I can't say I get money from another place, but sometimes I get the opportunity." In many instances these opportunities could not be described to me in very great detail (since they often involved some measure of illegality), however how "the means" (which is how people often referred to income) were "suddenly" available was often just as mysterious to those who had to count on them.

How money could be generated in Somalia collapses Western categories for how money is supposed to be earned and what behaviors are supposed to be practiced in earning it. In addition, money in Somalia was invested with a variety of meanings drawn from various sources within the local culture (pace Parry and Bloch 1989). Thus, a saying like: "money is spring's leaves" (*lacagtu waa caleen gu'u*) resonated at many different levels, intimating that money does not last, that money is refreshing, that money is not dependable, that money is a relief, and that money, like springtime itself, depends on conditions that, at best, are evanescent, and at worst are erratic, unpredictable, or nonexistent. Indeed, once the banking system began to fail the general public in the summer of 1989, some young Somalis euphemistically began referring to money as "rain" (*roob*) and lack of money as "drought" (*abaar*). The environment of money, then, clearly presented people with at least superficial parallels to the traditional environment of bush and livestock.

It could be argued that in both environments—whether these are conceived of as rural and urban, barter and monetary, or even precapitalist and capitalist—unpredictability has been the only steady constant. Thus, people either amassed money much as they amassed livestock, for fear of disease, drought, or raid (which can all be interpreted as lack of job tenure in an economic lexicon), or they diversified it into other resources (wives, water points, farms, real estate), or they dispersed it via the economy of affection (Hyden 1983; Berry 1984). Different people displayed different strategies, although it must also be kept in mind that money meant different things at different moments in any one individual's life, so that a civil servant from a well-off family might afford to be generous in courting young women whereas heads of household would have had far weightier and often more overwhelming responsibilities draining their pocketbooks. Similarly, money may have meant different things to the same individual over the course of a single day, moment by moment, and depending on how the size of the sum in his or her pocket increased or diminished.

At the same time, the shifting nature of local, national, and international economies throughout the post-Independence period, coupled with the studied arbitrariness of one-man rule, unquestionably spelled inconstancy in the amounts and timing of money coming into households, as a result of which unpredictability permeated the entire system. With so many shifts in policy—with the promotion of import substitution and industrialization in the 1970s, along with the continued allowance of *franco valuta,* followed by liberalization in the early 1980s and structural readjustment by the late 1980s—various pathways for profit were bound to be opened up, disallowed, hidden, occasionally re-excavated, but once established always embedded in common knowledge.

For instance, foreign aid projects like CRDP were all temporary. Likewise, who remained in charge of them was continually shifted by those in control of the government who, themselves, were often demoted or replaced. Therefore, for many people it only made sense to get all they could while they could, whether through means others would label corruption, graft, or nepotism. As a result, with money and other opportunities having been siphoned off by the men at the top, resources would often dry up for those below, as well as for those the project, agency, or ministry was intended to assist. Thus, one lesson learned by government employees attempting to work their way up the snakes-and-ladders board was to seize opportunity, and money, whenever possible.

According to folk wisdom one telltale sign that someone had acquired his or her money through cheating the government was how extravagantly money was spent. If the person in question spent money as if it would not last then the money was clearly attained illegally. In contrast, it was thought that those who earned money in the Persian Gulf used it constructively by investing in real estate and building homes; this is because they knew how they got the money (i.e., through their own labor). However, it should be noted that many ministers, generals, and other high officials (including project managers) likewise built houses and invested in businesses. This may be one reason why it was also said that every nomad could tell you the origin of his money, but no urban man would tell you the truth.

The profile of a rich man was of someone who owned five or six cars (although, for instance, the general manager of CRDP had only three). The rich chewed *qat* (a narcotic leaf), and could spend as much as 500,000 to 1,000,000 shillings a day on food and entertainment. After chewing *qat* the wealthy man would often go to the market looking for women. Meanwhile, to entertain his wives and children he would have two to three television sets and VCRs scattered throughout his home.

Although cheating the government in some way was necessary for achieving such a (mythical) lifestyle or amassing any significant amount of wealth in the urban setting, not all illicitly earned money was government money. Essentially, there were four different but not necessarily distinct sources of income people who worked for the government relied on in Mogadishu, with most people ideally striving for a mix among several of these.

CIVIL SERVICE

Salaries were paid to all government and agency employees. In 1987, according to one source "a secondary school graduate, if he can obtain work, may expect to earn some 800 shillings a month; even the salary of a minister is only 4,000 shillings—at least from official sources. Yet a soft drink now costs 200 shillings, a kilo of meat 180, a three or four kilo fish 500, or for that matter a single issue of *Time* or *Newsweek* 250 shillings" (Greenfield, AR 1987: 26–29).

In mid-1989, university graduates (most of whom were in their late 20s) working for CRDP were earning 4,700 shillings a month (and between 6,000 and 10,000 with per diem if they went into the field). The USAID librarian, who was the same age as many of these civil servants, earned more than 50,000 shillings a month. Watchmen working for the security company subcontracted by the U.S. embassy earned 15,000 shillings. *Boyessas* employed by the U.S. government earned between 11,000 and 20,000 shillings (and possibly more) according to seniority.

Depending on whether the employee was a head of household or not, a CRDP salary was commonly asserted to last between four and ten days. An ideal salary was put at either 40,000–60,000 shillings or 100,000 shillings. It was felt that this would be enough to live on.

For those who were bachelors, life may have been no cheaper than if they had been fathers and husbands. A meager (meatless) breakfast at a bush teahouse typically cost 200 shillings for two teas and seven pieces of *angera* [sorghum "crepe"]. A bush teahouse lunch of rice or pasta, milk, and tea cost 300 shillings. At some restaurants the same meal might cost 600 shillings, although it would probably also include meat. Those who smoked could also spend as much as 300 shillings a day on cigarettes. Then, there was rent for those who could not stay with relatives—sometimes as little as 3,500 shillings a month sharing a room.

As one mid-level project manager, earning 7,000 shillings a month, described the situation: He spent 5,000 shillings a day—"where can I get that?"—had not received his salary in two months, but had nonetheless "managed" to come to work in the morning with 1,000 shillings in his pocket, of which (after being asked for money by others) he had only 100 left by noon.

This sort of salary paradox was particularly striking in cases where the employee did not have access to a vehicle or any other visible project perquisite. For instance, one 39-year-old married to two wives, with seven children to support, relied on one of his wives to support him. She was the one who peddled foodstuffs between the central rangelands town in which they lived and outlying villages. With this wife needing 2,000 shillings a day, and his Mogadishu wife (with only one child) using 1,400 shillings, his salary of 4,700 shillings would last less than two days. Even augmented by per diems it would last little over three days.

Virtually all civil servants needed "outside" sources of income, whether these came from other family members or other jobs, and although many could cite friends as sources of assistance, friends were never of *direct* primary support.

Mohamud (27) has friends who have a boat. He pays them a fee to use it and can then make up to 13,000–14,000 shillings a day by fishing.

Abshir (also 27), who spends most of his time at a single field location, augments his salary by farming. He has one hectare that he plants with sesame. Harvesting the crop (two sacks-worth) earns him 70,000 shillings, from which he subtracts the cost of hiring a tractor and paying wage laborers. Otherwise, he must rely on relatives.

Faisal (31), a veterinarian, earns only 7000 shillings a month from his salary but is a member of a contraband incense cooperative through which he can sometimes earn as much as 70,000 shillings a month.

Abdulla (32), another government employee, receives money from his older brother (who works in Kuwait as a cashier), which it is his responsibility to invest for the family. He cannot tell me what he buys or sells with this money, since he admits what he does is not exactly legal, but "it's absolutely irregular. Sometimes you make a profit of 100,000.

Sometimes it is a risk of 100,000. You may sell at a low price. You can't do very good planning. We never count on the money." In describing change over time he adds: "In 1978–1982 money was going up. People could make a good profit by selling quickly. These days, every person tries to keep money in material or dollars." Thus, he himself always buys whatever it is he buys whenever there is a supply. That way, the supply is bound to diminish and he can charge more for the goods he retains. Everyone hoards, using this strategy, and then releases their goods slowly.

Mahdi (31) receives support from his wife's parents. He also works as a middleman between people seeking to buy foodstuffs and wholesalers in Xamar Weyn. He is able to earn 5,000 shillings a day doing this. His entire monthly salary is only 4,700 shillings.

Ahmed (27), who was fortunate enough to get to Nairobi on a job-related seminar sponsored by USAID, managed to save $700 from his trip, which he exchanged for shillings on his return. Some of this money he sent to his father. A paternal cousin now helps support Mahdi with money.

Given the pitifulness of salaries, it was the scholarship abroad that virtually all CRDP employees said they were waiting and hoping for. Scholarships represented exit from Somalia, entry into the West, and the opportunity for bettering one's education and, ultimately, one's position in life. Although only a handful of people had actually managed to receive scholarships so far, the knowledge that some people had succeeded and the visible proof of their continued success—with prominent promotions or, alternatively, the very fact that they had not returned to Somalia—along with being told that a handful more would receive future fellowships, kept everyone's expectations whetted. For many the promise of a fellowship was the sole reason they stayed on at projects and agencies where they earned such abysmal salaries. Indeed, one young man I knew left CRDP for a job at FAO because he was explicitly promised a scholarship if he worked there for a year. In this particular case the young man was a skilled computer operator who had learned word processing in India where he attended a vocational school on a "scholarship" supplied by his family.

Nevertheless, although people voiced the sentiment that they were only at CRDP awaiting a scholarship, there were also non-salary-related but remunerative benefits to be gained from working for the government (just as it may well have been the extra-educational value of study abroad that held the greatest allure). These advantages were not stressed, not so much because people were unaware of what else they had to gain from frequenting the workplace but because taking advantage of opportunities often involved behavior that people knew to be improper at the same time it was universally recognized that salary constraints left individuals little choice. For instance, the well-educated driver of a water tanker for the U.S. embassy readily acknowledged that his salary was much higher working for the U.S. government than it would have been if he worked for his own government in some office-related capacity. Nevertheless, driving the truck for the Americans also meant he had to work from 7 A.M. to 3 P.M., which, he admitted, left him no time to do business. In other words, although a government salary might have been more limited, the structure of government work was less limiting. Nor did there appear to be any systematic policing of what westerners would regard as systemic abuses of the workplace in most Somali offices.

BUSINESS

This open recognition that government employees earned income either directly or indirectly through their positions blurred any clear-cut distinctions between business and "work." Business per se was a second source of income many residents of Mogadishu relied on for earning or turning over money.[1] Owing to government restrictions on letters of credit necessary for import/export businesses and concomitant access to foreign exchange, and because so much of what Somalis required (for agriculture, industry, or daily living) had to be imported, manipulation around these restrictions presented a range of business possibilities that many people took advantage of. Again, it was felt that the example for how best to succeed had been set at the top, with former ministers and high government officials and their relatives being the people most commonly awarded with letters of credit (which were also valuable because they could be used to withdraw foreign currency from the banks, which could then be exchanged for Somali shillings at black market rates). Thus, anyone else who could take advantage of either a connection, or knowledge about someone else's connections, was assumed to feel "free" to do so.

Nor was it as though business, as conceived of by many Somalis, involved production. Rather, business was often a matter of buying, selling, transporting, trading, and positioning oneself as a middleman. Although there is a long history of this sort of "business" in the evolution of a middle class and the transition of Somalis from participants in productive nomadism to facilitators of livestock-driven market capitalism (Geshekter 1981; A. I. Samatar 1989), the ideal in the late 1980s appeared a variation on the same transactional (and markedly non-menial) theme.

For people with vehicles or the ability to rent them, Somalia's lack of infrastructure was itself a boon. Because of the remote nature of outlying villages, the same item—imported into the capital by a wholesaler—could be sold and resold countless times with numerous middlemen making a profit on it before it finally reached its ultimate destination: the village-bound consumer. Indeed, as a Clark University team surveying the Kismayo region discovered, "even when goods are imported from outside the region, 20–30 percent of the consumer price is retained in the region by wholesalers and retailers" (Clark University 1988, 162). This study went on to conclude that "there is an active process of spending and 'respending'—that is, of income multiplication—within the region, in which smaller towns, and to a lesser extent larger towns, play important roles" (Clark University 1988, 170).

The towns played these important roles because, as the Clark team points out, 80 percent of the households in Kismayo, Jilib, and Jamaame maintained some form of business, with half deriving at least some of their income and one-third relying primarily on business (Clark University 1988, 166). However, this should not be too surprising considering that Somali towns *were* essentially business and administrative centers. Also, as we have seen, one of the attractions of sedentarization and town life was the luxury of no longer having to work the bush, or the fields.

Although it could be argued that wealth earned relatively effortlessly represents a worldwide ideal, criteria for distinguishing earned from unearned and clean from dirty money would seem to differ for Somalis and westerners. In the West dirty money is money earned illicitly and clean money is money earned for honest work.[2] However, according to folk concepts in Somalia, dirty work has traditionally involved manual labor *in* dirt or dirtiness—agriculture, metallurgy, slaughtering—and clean work has kept people above having to perform such tasks. Business has fit these essentially idealized pastoral criteria perfectly. Without stretching the comparison too far, shady dealings in Somalia may have become so routinized that shade was sought not only because individuals had to ensure the well-being of their families, but also for the comfort (and lack of physical hardship) that shade promised. Thus, even on an idealized level, cultivating areas of shade or alternatively, seeking someone else's patches whenever possible, stood to reason.

For instance, one young businessman I first met in the Nairobi airport regularly shuttled back and forth between the UAE and Somalia. When he was in Mogadishu he visited the markets to see what was needed, and when he was in the UAE he telephoned his contacts in Mogadishu at least once a week. From Somalia he might have found himself exporting bananas, metal (from automobiles), copper scrap, shark fins, or livestock.

In his most recent 1989 trip from the UAE he brought henna and automobile tires back to Somalia. From the vantage point of a Mogadishu tea shop, where he could greet passersby whom he knew, he explained why he preferred doing business to holding a job: in business he could lose or make a lot of money, he had more independence, and he had more people under him and hence more people to support. Having more people to support was a good thing as far as he was concerned, since it made him more important. Business also gave him more friends and a wider network with which to support his parents and siblings.

Of course, just because government restrictions would seem to be so easily circumvented (evidenced by so many people in small-scale trading businesses like his), success did not mean that circumvention itself was easy.[3] Indeed, this is where businessmen and women had to actually work. Most, like Abdullahi, had to have good solid connections, either through friends or relatives of government officials who would turn a blind eye at the port or airport, foreign ministry, and elsewhere. This, again, is where one category or occupation as source for income blurred into another. On the one hand, businessmen had to know government officials who would collude with them. On the other hand, it was knowledge and information for businessmen and government employees alike that allowed them to connect and either earn money together, or earn money at one another's (and ultimately the state's) expense.

INFORMATION

Coercion (which in some instances is nothing more than failed collusion) was the third source of identifiable income in Mogadishu, although as with government and business, its boundaries, almost by definition, were ill-defined, often lying in the gray (or shady) areas between the two. Racketeering proved a major source of money for some individuals, whether, for instance, this involved the "loss" of freight on ships at sea (in order to collect the insurance money *and* profit from selling the goods [Miller 1982]) or the manipulation of information about what had already reached port. The port was particularly significant since Somalia had no rail connection with any other country and the number of weekly international flights could be counted on one hand. One quick way of making money was to know what goods had come into port and who had not paid customs. With this information one could threaten the offending merchant with "the station" (meaning he would be turned in to the police), a position from which he then had to bargain his way out.

What such a purportedly widespread practice also suggests is that having information and getting information was vital and could prove quite lucrative as a pursuit in and of itself on the one hand, whereas on the other, businessmen (aware of racketeering) had to have worked into their calculations the likelihood that there would be someone they had not counted on whom they would have to pay off. This then meant that what was not paid as customs might well have had to be paid to other demanders of duty—pumping money directly into the unstructured rather than structured economy.

Indisputably the line is very thin between this sort of outright blackmail and more subtle manipulation of others' positions, whereby well-placed individuals were able to do "ordinary" Somalis out of rightful access to such things as university placements or title to, and registration of, land. Because bureaucratic procedures required knowledge of reading and writing and exact fulfillment of the requirements, understanding these systems was key, although knowing the right people would be the only assurance that you fully understood "all" the requirements and had someone looking out for your interests (i.e., paperwork) all the way through the system.

Again, this is where networks of all sorts proved themselves invaluable and could compensate in instances of negligible salaries. For instance, Idris was working as a watchman until the position he wanted (as storeman) opened up. However, he also had significant connections through his family and one day was given 30,000 shillings by an acquaintance to arrange a meeting with someone he knew at USAID. Idris, in turn, gave the 30,000 shilling gift he received to Mohamed, another watchman. Mohamed explained to me that Idris had given him this money because Idris was good (although he used the word *khatar* [danger] in conveying this) and, because Idris' father was rich Idris did not need the money himself. Ahmed (who worked with Mohamed and knew Idris) confirmed this, adding that he would ask Mohamed for some of the money later. Meanwhile, a third witness to the transaction later explained to me that Mohamed and Idris were members of the same clan.

Essentially then, because Idris "happened" to know someone important a friend of his did not know, he gained a windfall, which he magnanimously passed on to someone else he "happened" to know from work who "happened" to be a fellow clan member (and needed the money more than he did at that particular moment). Such convergences were not uncommon, although whether it was the fact that Mohamed worked nearby and Idris liked him, or it was their shared clanship, or perhaps a history of past transactions, the exact rationale behind Idris turning his money over to Mohamed was never made explicit to those outside the relationship. Therefore, any one of several interpretations would have been available to the transaction's witnesses, each of whom knew Mohamed and Idris differently. Because the exchange itself was relatively public, knowledge of it was a common good, which, potentially, could be of use to any of these other individuals in the future.

REMITTANCES

Drawing the net of networks tighter, the fourth source of income for residents in Mogadishu was, in many cases, probably the most substantial: remittances. Virtually all middle class educated Somalis had at least one cousin—but sometimes a brother, sister, uncle, or even father—working in the Persian Gulf (in Saudi Arabia, Abu Dhabi, Dubai, or Kuwait especially).[4] Support from remittances was critical to most families; some received money monthly or quarterly, whereas others received large sums intermittently or whenever they specifically requested assistance. Up until 1981 these remittances were legally funneled back into Somalia via the *franco valuta* system, whereby anyone earning foreign currency abroad was allowed to purchase luxury (and other) items and import these into Somalia, where they could then be resold. Under IMF and World Bank supervision, *franco valuta* was abolished, although forms of *franco valuta* were also reinstated and then again banned on several subsequent occasions; even as late as the summer of 1989 *franco valuta* was reintroduced for rice and sugar when cash was not available in the banks.

As a system for generating Somali shillings from foreign exchange via the sale and resale of goods, *franco valuta* also crystallized various pathways and methods for monetary transactions, many of which continued to operate surreptitiously in the unstructured economy. Again, although the remittance economy was technically illegal far too many people relied on it for it to have remained very hidden. However, the fact that most remittances came in surreptitiously can only have fostered further surreptitiousness.

Although I describe the impact of remittances in somewhat more detail in the next chapters, let me say here that the mechanics were relatively simple. Most often earnings abroad were banked abroad. Arrangements were then made with Somalis who ran import/export or other businesses involving foreign exchange to pay off relatives in Somalia in Somali currency (at black market rates) in exchange for foreign currency deposited with their foreign-based businesses. As we have seen, many of the businessmen and businesswomen involved with foreign exchange were enmeshed in a system that was designed to cut corners (and cut out as much of the Somali government customs and banking system as possible). Indeed, the lines seem far too thin and delicate across the board—between importing, "losing goods," sloppy bookkeeping, foreign exchange, and smuggling—for there not to have been deliberate slippage.

Without impugning all business enterprises in Somalia it still seems safe to assume that those ties that were grounded in covertness were, by virtue of the danger that inhered in their discovery, more often than not that much more closely guarded, pulling people closer together and tempting them to risk more knowing that their solidarity was already beyond risk. Thus, it might not be wrong to suggest that there was a spiral of activities that, once engaged in, spun people further and further out of government control. At the same time, however, there were two very real dangers swirling beyond this spiral. The first was that, with so many people having to engage in such activities, most people knew full well it was impossible to make ends meet by legal means alone. Thus, most people who lived in a modicum of comfort were probably suspect and knew they *could* be held liable. Second (and corollary to this), there were laws on the books. Therefore, at any time the authorities would be sanctioned to arrest wrong-doers, never mind that everyone was potentially doing wrong. Thus, one constantly had to be on guard against people who would use information (which had to be case-specific but was, in the broadest senses, essentially common knowledge) for their own ends. Indeed, one way some people made money, as we have seen, was by threatening to tip off the authorities; in order to keep these people silent the "guilty" parties had to pay off these "do-gooders."

Again, it would appear that how money circulated and who it circulated among most often demarcated "the group"—in this case lending groups definition from within rather than calling attention to them from without. Once again, and for these very reasons of propriety and discretion, it makes sense that these groups should have concentrated along family lines, taking advantage of well-placed affines as well as agnates.

• 12 •

Tribalism

Given Somalia's conditions of uncertainty trust had to be circumscribed; tribalism resulted. In this chapter I sketch a theoretical argument.

Traditionally ethnographers have described tribalism in East Africa and the Middle East as structure rather than process and have done so by examining the systemization of tribes from the ground up—in terms of how they are constructed out of kin—at the same time they peer at tribes from the top down—ultimately explaining them in terms of how individuals are organized in telescoping oppositions depending on their kinship links. Both types of explanation, top-down and bottom-up, are etic, and hence pivot around a sort of societal exoskeleton without paying attention to sentiment as a glue for allegiance or belonging.

From Evans-Pritchard (1940/1978) to the present (e.g., Dresch 1989), ethnographers who have studied societies organized along segmentary lineage principles have tended to focus on the rules of organization rather than the messiness of reality. As a result it has long been a matter of debate whether the rules indeed generate the pattern, or instead simply idealize it to the local population as well as the ethnographer (see Holy 1979; Kuper 1982; Abu-Lughod 1989).[1]

There are other difficulties. The role of territoriality and the fit between locality and lineage seem to pose special problems for anthropologists who emphasize organization-by-lineage (see Marx 1967, 90, 180, for a glaring example of such a problem). Thus, it is often hard to know whether it is genealogical or geographic location that marks the individual as belonging to a particular group (for one solution see Verdon 1982). This is especially the case in Somalia, where clan affiliation has been assumed to be definitional yet it is linguistic dialect—indicating locational (not *necessarily* genealogical) origin—that has most recently served to finger individuals as belonging to such-and-such a tribe.[2]

On the one hand, this congruence would seem to give credence to the idea that there may be less ambivalence about allegiances on the ground than ethnographers have indicated; people have a variety of ways to tell one another apart. On the other hand, it might also suggest a sliding but still fixed scale in terms of what marks people as belonging. Or, alternatively it might suggest a more noteworthy error—that ethnographers have overemphasized the structure, without sufficiently considering the content of belonging.

Ethnographies addressing issues of cultural pluralism have described how groups maintain identity over time (Cohen 1969, 1981). Most often maintenance involves keeping sentiments focused inward in order to preserve the group's distinctiveness and position vis-à-vis other groups (whether for ritual, defensive, trade, or other reasons). The instruments for cohesion may be shared religion, language, culture traits, genealogy, history, and so forth (Geertz 1963). However, because individuals are invariably located within webs of different types of ties there are several different routes mobilization can take, several different levels to how identity can be realized, and several different ways in which any one individual might be recruited (Young 1976; Horowitz 1985). Similarly, there are numerous ways in which individuals can respond to mobilization, depending on which links they deem most important to them at the time.

Reflecting a years-old debate in the literature it is argued that this potential for tribes coalescing is either timeless or that tribes are recent inventions resulting from colonial policies (see Helm 1968; *Journal of African and Asian Studies,* Vol. 5, Nos. 1 and 2 1970; Vail 1989). However, in Somalia there is no local ambiguity about the long-term existence of lineages, clans, and clan-families, based on histories of genealogies and collective memories stretching back twenty generations and more, or of what identity adheres to. Instead, the question in Somalia is how widely, in any given situation, the tribal umbrella should be spread.

Virtually all descriptions of the building blocks for pastoralist Somali social organization describe segmentary lineages across which exist contractual associations [*xeer*] that Somalis freely join (pace Lewis 1961). These mutual assistance associations are entered into, ultimately, for the pursuit and collection of bloodwealth [*dia*] and are predicated upon moral bonds that disallow violence within the group. Yet, despite the significance of *xeer* [commitment through contract, not blood], Somalis continue to fit academic models of segmentary lineage opposition (e.g., Lewis 1988/1976).[3] In this regard, they are like the Nuer, *the* classic example, the significance of whose kinship has never been downplayed, although the relationship of their genealogy to everything it can be related to has been analyzed and reanalyzed (see Kelly 1985; Hutchinson 1985). Given what such scrutiny of the Nuer has revealed, though, it may well be that Somali structure actually also works more as conditioned process than rigid structure. In other words, what looks like responses predicated on principles of segmentary lineage opposition may instead be how nomadic pastoralists have had to meet the conditions of fluidity imposed by the environment on the one hand, or how they have reacted to encroaching empires and external forces on the other, rather than emerging out of any conscious "Somali" attempt *at* structure.[4]

Similarly, the ways in which the segmentary lineage model telescopes scale—up from the individual through his lineage, clan, and clan-family—does not necessarily translate into the same choices simply magnified or multiplied. The content of what is at stake for individuals as well as groups inevitably changes with size, something the model does not account for very well. Also it ignores time. As Ahmed Samatar (1988) suggests, the invigoration of tribalism may yet have relatively recent *historical* roots. For instance, Samatar argues that if traditional society specially weighted kin relationships, and the colonial and postcolonial trend has been to favor clan-family affiliation, the latter should not be regarded as simply the former writ larger and stronger. Rather, kinship has been transformed into clanship due to changes in production relations and world system interventions (Lecture at Somali Studies Congress, June 1989). Or, put differently, kinship without *xeer* [contract] has turned into clannism (Lecture, African Studies Center, Harvard University, Apr. 1991), and again we are not simply talking about a change in scale alone.

Rereading the history we can even begin to catch glimpses of this alteration of Somali identity as Samatar suggests and Marlowe (1963) much more concretely describes. Among the Barsana, we should remember, it was only after new junctures opened up and rural position could "suddenly" be translated into urban aspiration that old interdependencies were manipulated into exploitative dependencies. At the same time, once extended families (such as *reer* Hassan) proved relatively ineffectual as interest groups in the Mogadishu arena—where much larger forces had to be marshaled—new alliances involving recruitments to larger-level interest groups were called for, for which clan-families proved ready-made. Already more or less there, webs of loose clan-family ties formerly associated over space and through time (even if largely mythic) were concentrated and even, to an extent, made more manageable, realizable, and formularizable in urban settings. Then, once recruitment at such a level did prove successful, once politicking over state resources at the national level began to resemble *and* reassemble clanship, recruitment to the clan (or clan-family) level proved inescapable; everyone had these ties.

Family trees, anthropologized into kinship charts, make the nested nature of these ties clear, although by doing so they may also explain less than they reveal. What they outline—families mounting into lineages, clans, and so forth; structure; mirror-image telescoping—certainly agrees with insiders' evocative verbal descriptions of patrilineal ties forming branches, and lineages branching off, and so on (see Lewis 1961; also

Gellner 1981, 40). Nonetheless, such abstractions say nothing about how people go from living in family trees to encircling themselves in laagers, or how they drop from branches to plan raids around campfires. Or, to rephrase this, as applicable as the segmentary lineage opposition model may be to the situational nature of escalating competition and conflict, it cannot adequately account for the nonlinear nature of belonging (or *communitas*) people subscribe to once competition or conflict threatens. Sentiment is missing.

Somehow expectations based on degrees of relatedness have to be turned into compulsion. But how is that compulsion inculcated? Is it just learned behavior? Perhaps. However, the persistence of self-sacrifice in all societies seems to suggest something else may be at work. The fact that people die for causes and over issues of honor, shame, ego, and recognition, hints at a welter of emotions that can bind people in ways that have as much to do with feelings about the definitions of (the bounds of) community, identity, and reputation—and perceptions of threats—as with any calculable structural dictates. Certainly this seems to be the case if we consider how the threat of conflict may intimidate like an insult, eliciting responses that can be far more emotional than rational. Attempting to make sense of conflict after the fact, which itself is an exercise in rationality and rationalizing, then unduly favors rational choice as if it had been calculatedly engaged in at the time.

Can emotions be learned? This is a huge question. A far more reasonable proposition is that emotions are what people everywhere hide, present, play up, and play down to establish, disestablish, or reestablish trust with one another. I would suggest that as a result people do employ rules that quickly, conveniently, and unequivocably tell them how they can expect others to act and what they should expect others to be (i.e., friend or foe, reliable or unreliable).

Genealogy works perfectly as one such set of rules, mapping trustworthiness—by charting who has trusted whom in the past and where this has led in terms of thicker or thinner, and sustained or broken relationships. Or, turning this around and rethinking linear models: Breaks between lineages indicate breaks, or at the least gaps, in trust.

Meanwhile, there may be yet other reasons why organization rather than sentiment has been so assiduously modeled (by anthropologists particularly). Anthropologists believe in rules—our society's, our discipline's, our fieldwork's. This segues us right into wanting to learn and analyze others' rules. Plus, if knowing our own rules provides a shortcut to our judging others, then learning others' rules seems just as useful a shortcut to gaining understanding of them. However, without having been born into tribal societies, few anthroplogists seem to also realize the irreducible significance of belonging.[5] By focusing on rules and by not being able to ever fully participate ourselves (when it comes to being able, or even wanting to feel what tribalism evokes), we have given ourselves no choice but to offer explanations from the outside of the outside, and of structure rather than content.[6]

HOW IT FEELS

In the Somali case it becomes a matter of semantics whether the groups Somalis divide their society into are called clans or tribes.[7] Some people even refer to them as "families," the more government-sanctioned euphemism (and the term I use in the chapters to follow). Nevertheless, no matter how they are called, or on what scale beyond the individual they are being discussed, these *reer, jamaa, qabila, tol* are recognized, recognizable, and genealogically organiz*ing* (but not necessarily formally organiz*ed*) groups. In this regard the ethnographic literature is in agreement, and so am I—kin models. However, although these groups might define membership and organize members along lineage principles, it is not the bonds of blood (or marriage) per se that *cause* people to adhere. Rather, adherence and allegiance must come from something else and draw on something more deeply embedded than how people are related to one another and how their forebears interrelated as a template for how present generations subsequently *should* interrelate.

In order to define the feel of tribalism in the Somali context, let me first attempt to define tribalism as I use the concept. I believe there are three different ways in which the definition can be approached. First, tribalism is a matter of affiliation and affinity. It is a state into which members are involuntarily borne, initially according to parentage. The attachment by tribe is an automatic labeling device that is held in common and cannot be individually negotiated. In a tribal society one is for life whatever one was born. Even if at various moments exact origins can be ellided they are not permanently forgotten, but rather can always *be* remembered, which is exactly what tends to occur in moments of conflict.

Second, the outer limits differentiating those who count as tribal members from those who do not is the unspoken agreement that tribal members are innocent until proven guilty; everyone else is suspect at the outset of any encounter. Trust is what is continually tested and what inheres in, and emerges from, shared moral codes.[8]

Third, tribal members share a background that they know is shared. There is automatic acceptance and warmth among them because they hold "something" in common that others don't share but that, by definition, cannot readily be defined or else anyone could assume it. In other words, there is not much point in questioning people about why they feel what they do for one another (or the group).[9] This is a matter of feeling, emotional and emotive, and grows out of the socialization of morality, which fine tunes people's abilities to plumb for trustworthiness. This is not something that can necessarily be made sense of to outsiders (particularly people who do not come from societies so organized), yet it makes implicit sense to anyone who lives within its rubrics.

All pastoral Somali clans share breaching moral codes based on a shared pastoral mode of production (or rather, its ideology), as well as Islam. This is not the case for most "tribes" in East Africa.[10] Therefore, the criteria may be much more slippery in Somalia for determining what distinguishes one moral code from another, which may be why the social definitions (genealogy, dress, dialect) are so subtle. For instance, with the near-universality of spoken Somali among pastoralists it is a matter of accent and select vocabulary and not language that serves as available marker.[11]

Those who come closest to sharing the same moral codes are those who have been inculcated with the same values and in the same ways. In nonsettled societies these people are, necessarily, close relatives. And it is close relatives who compose families, extended ideologically into lineages and clans.[12]

Clearly, and as ethnographies describing lineage organizations suggest, if lines cannot be drawn on the ground and organization is not, strictly or accountably, territorial, then other principles must be used to identify potential competitors from noncompetitors. However, Somalis have not been able to afford to invest too heavily in unfungible structure; conditions are too fluid. Hence, situational fluidity dictates the need for flexible, expandable/contractable markers—not scarification or different grammars or missing teeth, and so on—to distinguish potential competitors (who could be kin) from potential noncompetitors. Thus, the role of subtle difference, of degree rather than kind, across nomadic Somali clan-families.[13]

Meanwhile, the genius of subtle difference is that the recognition of subtle difference is that much more a marker of belonging. The ability to sense being of the same "blood" and mind, then, is one emically acquired technique for determining moral compatability, which, in turn, proves mutual belonging. Otherwise, belonging has to be carefully constructed. Indeed, as the next chapters should demonstrate, subtle local/lineage differences in such things as customary marriage payments would have marked off groups that otherwise practiced widely similar pastoralisms and would have bespoken just enough difference so that negotiated affinal ties could have showcased the reconciling *of* difference whenever an intermarriage (at whatever level) occurred. Conveniently, and at other times, these same subtle distinctions could obversely and opportunistically be used to revive historical grievances, and people could feud (c.f. Black-Michaud 1975).

In short, there may be two modus operandi for testing and acknowledging solidarity. On the one hand, there are the organized principles of kin-relatedness that link people dyadically and hence, on the larger scale, indirectly to one another: the structure. But there is also the principle of solidarity: *communitas*. Both make use of deeds, words, and looks to signal a shared morality—what one should and should not do, with whom, when, where, how, and so forth. Ultimately, each sets different, but overlapping limits for determining trust, and for reacting to the breach of trust. For instance, when the state can no longer be trusted, and when its offices increasingly seem to be held by people who share a morality among themselves but not with others, there are various reactions. These reflect a wide range of views grounded in different socioeconomic, religious, regional, intellectual, and individual, backgrounds. Nevertheless, as conditions worsen, individuals increasingly cohere in order to depend on one another because they *know* they can, not because they *think* they should.

PART FIVE

Family to "Family"

At first glance the existence of tribalism would seem to challenge the Somali-held belief that all (pastoralist) Somalis share the same culture. Alternatively, it could provoke us to question the definition of "culture" itself.

Put logically, the development of anything approaching a "national" Somali culture could only have come about given national and state boundaries that permanently contained Somalis together. Otherwise, when would Somalis have had to identify themselves *as* Somalis? Rather, they would have been of this or that lineage/clan/clan-family in relation to one another, but never just Somali. To push this further, Somaliness only would have developed any real meaning in the face of non-Somalis invading. Certainly this is precisely what the segmentary lineage opposition model suggests. It also complements my earlier argument that the presence of Bantu Africans and Others was instrumental in purifying what *Somali* could come to mean and who it would apply to: nomadic pastoralists and those descended from them.

At the same time though, we know that thanks to the British and Italians colonialism was beginning to erode the centrality of subsistence pastoralism just as urban and national settings were demanding new interest groups. Consequently, although the subtle differences distinguishing "families" according to traditional, pastorally grounded practices should have been becoming increasingly irrelevant in the urban setting, new markers were being called for, for which these very practices could be used. Or to rephrase this, what had stood simply *as* differences before could stand *for* those differences in the more mixed-up and competitive urban setting.

Reinforcing the usefulness of such pastoralist practices in the urban environment was the fact that subtlety remained critical. Fortune and misfortune were no more certain in Mogadishu than in the bush. This was particularly true once public discussion of "family" was outlawed. Thus, there was little sense in making anything hard and fast, except for how one measured trust.

Trust was already (and in many senses, historically) implicit when it was "family" members providing funds to other "family" members. But in an urban center like Mogadishu, where "families" were all mixed up, accommodation had to be made for slippage. For instance, marriage represented one prominent arena for slippage, as youth increasingly met and mingled across "families." At the same time, marriage stood to bridge all sorts of gaps. It is where family and "family" met and where Somalia's political economy was both literally and figuratively grounded.

Indeed, working in the late 1970s, Allan Hoben analytically described Somali extended families as corporate bodies:

> Diversification of specific skills within family units seems to have gone apace with animal husbandry and pasture management being supplemented by commercial, trading, and mechanical (particularly driving and vehicle repair) abilities. Many families are pursuing diversified income-generating and risk-pooling strategies spanning livestock and crop production, trade, and wage employment, both in urban areas and abroad. To some extent these families can be viewed as multi-plant multi-national enterprises in microcosm, and the same principles of decentralized management with centralized resource pooling used by the modern corporation are employed to advantage (Hoben 1983:30).

This view of families as diversified corporate units has been adopted by innumerable analysts and consultants since Hoben first described them as such.[1]

And marriage has been particularly integral in this regard, especially as it has grown increasingly difficult for individuals to engage in without familial assistance.

By the late 1980s, at the same time youth seemed to feel ideologically free enough to choose their own spouses, marriage was costing more than any one individual could secure. Hence, much as pastoralist youth had had to turn to family members for assistance, young civil servants and others earning negligible salaries could only afford to marry when family members helped them. Economic realities thus lent marriage an old-new spin. Of course, one reason marriage was costing so much was that "traditional" marriage payments were still proving useful. They provided one way to allow families to plumb for trust, and smooth over but not obliterate "family" differences. At the same time, traditional marriage payments also kept offspring beholden to family, and kept the blurring that otherwise may have occurred across "families" more or less in check *and* under corporate control. In lots of ways, and in ways quite different than we find elsewhere, marriage proved sticky.

Of course, to unmarried youth the whole issue of marriage was a pressing one for completely different reasons. There were issues of sex, reproduction, even illusory autonomy all tied up in finding a spouse. Indeed, marriage was so central to young Somalis' concerns that for me to have ignored it would have been to ignore how people still did yearn for normalcy and still did seek to live their lives in the face of severe uncertainties. At the same time, I would have been ignoring everything else that was being described to me as people described why marriage was so difficult; marriage didn't just happen to be one overtly apolitical area I could probe. It was corrosively political. Indeed, marriage was fraught in ways that I'm not sure were fully realized even by those most frustrated by not being able to marry. On the one hand, by not being able to afford to get married these educated, nationalist-minded youth who believed they represented Somalia's future were unable to start families of their own. On the other hand, by not marrying they also weren't being of much assistance to the larger corporate units to which they belonged. Having said this, though, how young Somalis who could marry did marry gave an added twist to what the frustration really related to: marriage as one more cause of dissolution.

Elsewhere dubbed an economy of affection (Hyden 1983; Berry 1984, 1989) or the moral economy (Scott 1976), such a kin-based economy of connections as existed in Somalia did represent nothing but failure to numerous young Somalis: of the state, their society, themselves. These youth were well aware that the more kin had to rely on other kin, and family on "family" as a social welfare net, the more this undermined the workings of the state. They also knew that they had to participate in such networks themselves if they ever hoped to attain what they most wanted. What else could they do? There was certainly no escape route through merit, or service to the nation. In fact, there was no real escape route out of this frustration at all, so why not at least marry?

Those who could did, although the dynamic was pitiless: Who money defined as kin helped to define how money flowed, and money flows helped determine who could marry.[2]

In this part I continue to draw the circles tighter, as I believe they tightened around the Somalis I knew. Somalia was not just undone by supralocal and local-level politicking. Economic and political realities invaded and pervaded everyday life. To cope with this Somalis responded in ways that further cinched the networks around them. Of course, this does not mean that family tentacles were retracted. Rather, just the opposite tended to occur. Somali families quite effectively and ingeniously diversified their children, their interests, their locales. Individuals did the same with their talents. One way to read this section is as a further reduction from the macro to the micro level, and from the general to the particular. The point is to broaden the picture: Somalia came undone thanks to a conjunction of events, institutions, *and* individuals.

• 13 •

Marriage I

For reasons too numerous to mention marriage has long been of interest to anthropologists.[1] Not only does it lie as a central node in the construction of kinship relations—one of anthropology's favorite domains—but it also represents what Marcel Mauss (1967) would call a total social phenomenon. There are religious, economic, political, productive, and reproductive matters all tied up in how and why two individuals marry. Nor does any marriage only involve two individuals. Even in its most abbreviated form the ceremony of marriage itself must be performed by a third party. At the same time, whether others are present or approving or not, marriage changes the variety, context, and patterns of relationship that the couple, formerly two individuals, engage in. This is at the level of theory. At the level of everyday practice marriage is perhaps more significant still.

Marriage acts to both liberate and constrain husband and wife. It frees them to start their own family, yet burdens them with new responsibilities. It offers opportunities for limitless sex at the same time sex must be reproductive. The list of such trade-offs is potentially endless and can be either tempting for those who are not yet married or tormenting for those who already are. However, it is perhaps at the broadest levels that marriage poses choice: not *to* whom one should really get married, but *for* whom. For parents? future offspring? oneself? . . . which in turn gives shape to how people define and categorize others, as well as split yet reproduce their world.

PASTORAL PRACTICES

In the recent (livestock-dominated) past, there were clear and significant regional and "family" differences in Somalia for how marriages and bridewealths were negotiated, in what the ceremonies consisted of, and in who received how much remuneration as a result of their connection to the bride (Lewis, 1962).[2] This is evident in people's life histories, when they recount what their father's and father's father's generations exchanged for wives, what the wives were given by their families before departing for the husband's home, and who benefited from the negotiations; in some cases it was only the bride's father, whereas in others it was the immediate family, or even other relatives.

Ideally, and generally speaking among camel-keepers (and not people whose primary stock was cattle) *yarad* [bridewealth] was meant to consist of 100 camels, a rifle, and a horse. However, in only a handful of instances did individuals cite this as real bridewealth that a grandfather had paid. More often, a number of camels and small stock, sometimes a horse, and sometimes a rifle were offered instead. In a few cases the bridewealth was paid over a period of time. In the vast majority of cases it was presented to the bride's parents before the bride left home. But all of this tended to be dictated by local parameters—what was expected, what was possible, what the "family" could afford *as* the ideal.

Other "family" differences marked two related payments: *sorio* and *dibad. Sorio* was most often described as food or money supplied to the party negotiating on behalf of the bride. But it could also be food or money given to members of both parties who were present for blessings by the sheikh. In other cases *sorio* became (or contributed to) the wedding feast. Here I should explain that many people regarded marriage as a two-part affair and, indeed, often described it to expatriates as "two weddings," or a betrothal and wedding. By describing it thus people were distinguishing between the sheikh's blessing, which officially married the bride and groom, and the public party, held at a later time. Sometimes this party was held the same day, sometimes it was postponed or delayed for years.

The first ceremony was usually a small affair at which it was compulsory for the husband to pay *meher,* the money that would belong to his wife if they divorced. In the pastoral economy this *meher* often consisted of a small number of small stock so that the divorcee would always have some means of support. By decree in 1975 minimum *meher* was set at 1,000 shillings (which by 1989 amounted to only a token and, essentially, symbolic sum).

Once officially married the husband and wife did not customarily begin living together until the "family" or public ceremony had been held and they had acquired a place of their own. The husband's family would often pay for this public gathering and feast with *sorio.*[3]

In pastoral society *dibad,* on the other hand, was clearly the responsibility of the bride's family. Lewis describes this as dowry and writes that among northern Somalis *dibad* was proportionate to the value of the *yarad,* but rarely exceeded two-thirds of it (1962, 16). As *dibad* was described to me by people who knew that their mothers or grandmothers had received *dibad* and could remember what it consisted of, it was an *aqal* [hut] and its furnishings along with livestock in some instances, but more often it appears to have been lesser items—*subaq* [ghee], *oodka* [dried meat], kitchen and milking utensils, and mats—in other words, those items of equipment the young bride and her mother and other female relatives would have been able to manufacture prior to her departure. In some cases *dibad* was strictly food stuffs, whether stored (such as *subaq* and *oodka*) or on the hoof (small stock). Also, *dibad* was often described as a series of delayed prestations; the married daughter would receive *dibad* on her first visit home and sometimes thereafter, whereas women from livestock-rich families were given *dibad* whenever they returned home.

Although all of these kinds of *dibad* would seem to represent a return on the bridewealth (itself an exchange by the husband's family to the wife's father), *dibad* might also be viewed as an exchange between women, mother to daughter. From this perspective *dibad* signifies a passage: of "knowledge," given concrete form in the handicrafts the daughter received; into fertility, embodied in livestock and the woman herself; and of labor, from one hearth to another. However, *dibad* was not universally practiced and is not a term all Somalis recognized.

While the most complete descriptions of marriage and bridewealth appear in I. M. Lewis's *Marriage and the Family in Northern Somaliland* (1962), it must be noted (even as Lewis does) that the numbers of livestock that were transferred from one family to another, even within the same "family," varied widely. Perhaps this is one reason why the only conclusion he draws from the numbers is that *dibad* appears proportionate to *yarad*. Indeed, recently in Mogadishu people described even *yarad* in terms of a proportion of what one had, or what one's family was capable of raising. As Lewis acknowledges, much depended on "the standing of the parties, and according to the desirability of the match, both in relation to the personal qualities of the bride and to the aims of the groups concerned in establishing a link between their lineages" (Lewis 1962, 14).

VARIETIES OF "YARAD," "DIBAD," AND "SORIO"

Farxan is from the Galcayo region. He is 67. His parents married in 1911. They met and arranged their marriage through a sheikh. Yarad *was five female camels, one male camel, and twenty goats. There was no* sorio *in the bush, save for the slaughter of goats.* Dibad *was* subaq, oodka, *and lactating goats.*

Farxan's father subsequently married two other women, both gorob *[women who have been previously widowed or divorced], and both of whom he divorced before there were children.*

Farxan himself married his first wife in 1946. He was a soldier, saw her, and "took her." There was no yarad *because, he explained, a soldier never paid* yarad. Sorio *was 100 shillings. They divorced after only three months.*

He married a second wife in the same year. His sister and she were living in the same house, and they were close relatives. Again there was no yarad, *and* sorio *was 100 shillings. Of their two sons and five daughters, only three are still alive.*

One daughter teaches in Saudi Arabia and is not yet married. Their son graduated from the Somali National University in veterinary medicine and is not yet married, and their second daughter married but also divorced. Her yarad *was 50,000 shillings (in 1986).* Sorio *was one container of* halwa, *2 goats, 50 kilos of rice, and a party for young people at a hotel (which Farxan estimates cost a total of 200,000 shillings). The groom had graduated from university and was a businessman. Farxan explained that in towns there is no negotiating* yarad. *His daughter came to him and told him she was going to marry. He asked her to introduce him to his prospective son-in-law. When the groom-to-be came to the house Farxan asked him, "Do you need this girl?" The boy answered in the affirmative, brought his own father as well as a sheikh back to Farxan's house for the blessing, and then took Farxan's daughter away that night.*

Ahmed (31) is from the Ogaden. His father and mother are members of the same "family." Yarad *was eighty camels, 200 goats, and fifty sheep a little over thirty years ago.*

Ahmed met his wife in 1979 at a dance in the refugee camp where they were both living (he had been a "freedom fighter" during the Ogaden War). They married secretly, since he had no money at the time. However, other people informed her parents that she was married. Subsequently his father-in-law demanded cattle from Ahmed, knowing that Ahmed's father had ample livestock. Ahmed knew that if he asked his father for the livestock he would have to work for his father in return. Instead he had older relatives convince his father to reject the request. Ahmed then went to his father-in-law and was allowed to postpone the payment. Eight months after securing a job in Mogadishu he was able to give his father-in-law 3,000 shillings. Four months later he gave him another 5,000 shillings. Still, whenever he meets his father-in-law he continues to be asked for money. Ahmed tends to view this as a continuing payment, although others tell him it is simply help.

Mohamed's grandfather was a "tribal chief" in Ceel Dheer who was very rich and married to numerous wives.

Mohamed's father had three wives. His first wife was a cousin, so there was no yarad. *They divorced six years ago. His second wife, Mohamed's mother, died twenty-four years ago, after having given birth to four girls and two boys.* Yarad *was two she-camels, one he-camel, and thirty-five goats. Three goats were slaughtered at the ceremony.*

Mohamed's father married his third wife after his second wife died. Because so many livestock were used in this third marriage, the children got nothing and were initially angry. Now, however, Mohamed's father lives with Mohamed in Mogadishu and Mohamed willingly assists his father's children by this third wife.

Mohamed married in late 1977. His wife-to-be asked him to ask her parents for her hand. Mohamed paid the price of sweets, milk, and tea consumed during the negotiations, along with a 5000 shilling "gift." Negotiations lasted four hours, and Mohamed says there were no problems since his intended had wife convinced her father she should be allowed to marry Mohamed; she was the fourth of four children.

In 1982 Mohamed's father and father's brother came to Mohamed to ask him to marry a second wife, his uncle's daughter. He was told, "If you want our blessing, take this girl." However, Mohamed refused, explaining that he loved his first wife and did not want a second wife. Nevertheless, he was brought before a family meeting at which he says he was made to think that if he did not accept the offer of this second wife he would not succeed in life.

His first wife was extremely jealous of this second wife, for whom he gave 12,000 shillings out of xeshimood *[respect], not because he was asked, and to whom he gave 10,000 shillings for clothing in 1982. He managed with both wives for nine months before he divorced the first one, who has since remarried. He deeply regrets this divorce. He loved his first wife and does not like the second, whom he describes as stubborn and like a rock.*

As these cases imply, it was not only fluctuating economic conditions and change on the large scale that altered marriage patterns. Marriage arrangements differed even for members within the same immediate family. Also, individual circumstances could change through time. Just as Roble's life history, presented in Chapter 5, demonstrated how a single individual could successfully maneuver through a number of societal changes as situations around him shifted, in this next excerpt who Abdullahi marries and why similarly varies with time and circumstances. Even how he marries differs wife to wife. Yet, despite his changing needs and desires, his expectations for the content of marriage do not change. In that sense there is continuity.

ABDULLAHI AND HIS FIVE MARRIAGES

Abdullahi, 45, grew up in Garbahaare. His grandfather (*FaFa,* or, literally, father's father) was a nomad from the Mudug region who had one wife, but no fertile children other than Abdullahi's father, who had two wives and lived in the Galcayo region.

Abdullahi's father's first wife gave birth to five children, of whom only two lived. Like the first wife, Abdullahi's father's second wife (Abdullahi's mother) was a relative.

Abdullahi's parents met in the Hiran region. They conducted *shukansi* [courtship/flirting] and then *masafo* [eloped]. She was a *gorob* [divorcee or widow]. Nevertheless, Abdullahi's father paid *yarad*—twelve camels, five cows, a *tiro* [100 goats], and a rifle—around 1939. *Dibad* was some livestock. One he-camel was slaughtered for *oodka,* and a goat was slaughtered for *sorio.*

Abdullahi's mother bore four boys and three girls total (a twin boy and girl, from her previous marriage, died). Abdullahi is the second oldest child and first-born son of this second marriage. Abdullahi himself has married five wives, of whom only two have produced children.

Abdullahi married his first wife, Sofia, "in the rural area" around 1962. They initially eloped, although later there was a wedding. As *sorio* he killed a camel and goats and provided sorghum and *bun* [coffee]. *Yarad* was five she-camels, five cows, one he-camel, and twenty goats for his mother-in-law. Over the course of ten years Sofia gave birth to two daughters (who died young), and three sons.

Abdullahi married his second wife, Ubax, a *gorob* in 1972. He kept this second marriage secret from Sofia. However, when Ubax was six months pregnant Sofia "discovered" her. At the time Abdullahi was working as a watchman at night, or so he claimed. Usually, however, he would return home for supper at 8 P.M. When he suddenly stopped coming home at his usual time Sofia became suspicious. So, one night she decided to visit him at his office. But he wasn't there. The following night she tried the office again. And again, at 8 P.M. the office was closed. However, at 6 P.M. on the third night she happened to be in the market where she did see him. Surreptitiously she followed him and after watching him enter someone else's house she knocked on the door.

Sitting on a chair inside, Abdullahi recognized Sofia's voice and invited her in. But afraid that the woman whose house he was in would hit her, Sofia told him to come out instead. She added, "I know you have a wife. There is no problem. Let us go to our home."

Abdullahi told her he would have his supper at Ubax's house, then return to work. However, Sofia insisted he come home immediately with her, saying "If you are married, you have to divorce me."

Abdullahi refused to grant Sofia a divorce. He also warned her not to create additional problems, blaming her for his second marriage in the first place. He explained that he had taken a second wife to soothe him from the problems Sofia caused him by always talking back to him. He promised that in order to make things right he would visit each of them in turn, every other night. To which Sofia agreed.

Three months passed and when it was time for Ubax to give birth to her first child she returned to her family to do so. They were *reer miyi* [nomads]. Abdullahi told her that after the birth she should come find him in Balambale (Mudug region) because he was leaving his government job. The salary was too low and he had wealthy cousins in Balambale; he had complained to them that he had no livestock. They subsequently provided him with 100 goats, a male camel, and four lactating camels. And so he and Sofia moved to Balambale to become nomads.

After giving birth to a daughter, Ubax arrived to join them in Balambale. She brought *oodka* as *dibad*. But because Abdullahi already had Sofia staying in the bush with him he found Ubax a place in the village. There she became a "commercant," selling meat.

One day Abdullahi told Sofia that he was taking two fat goats to Ubax in Balambale. Sofia balked and fought with Abdullahi so loudly that the cousins they were camped with interrupted to ask what was wrong. Sofia complained that Abdullahi was in the wrong, that he either had to have both of his wives in the village or both in the bush; he couldn't treat them differently. Consequently, Abdullahi asked his cousins to take the goats to Ubax. But somehow, Sofia managed to go along with them.

Sofia stayed with Ubax in the village. When Ubax asked Sofia why she didn't return to her children in the bush, Sofia said she was sick and needed a rest.

Abdullahi himself traveled to Balambale. Before his arrival in the village Sofia went to stay with an "uncle" of hers also living there. On arriving, Abdullahi asked Ubax what Sofia had told her. Ubax said Sofia explained that she was to deliver the goats and then stay in the village until she felt better. Abdullahi then went to Sofia's uncle to see what she had told him. Sofia's uncle claimed that she had similarly told him that she was sick and was staying in the village to cure herself. When Abdullahi responded that this was untrue, Sofia's uncle confronted her, seeking the truth. She then told him that she was not going back to her children.

A meeting of relatives was convened. The uncle worked hard to try to implore Sofia to return to her husband and children. But no matter how hard he tried to persuade her, she refused. Apparently she was jealous of Ubax for getting to stay in the village, so that all this uncle could relate to Abdullahi was "I have no wife for you"; Sofia wanted a divorce.

When Abdullahi finally confronted Sofia and asked her whether she preferred divorce to her children and her livestock and she said she did he granted her a divorce, and she cried.

Abdullahi then had to tell Ubax that since he had divorced Sofia, Ubax would have to move to the bush with him to take Sofia's place. She remonstrated; the bush was difficult. But he reminded her of his sons. He explained to Ubax that his three sons would look after the livestock and that she would not have to look after the goats at all. Her only task would be to cook for the children. He would milk the camels. He told her that when times were good and there was *barwaqo* [prosperity], all they would need from the village was tea and rice. Thus he convinced her.

However, the year was 1974, and the *Dabadheer* drought was under way. Too many people were moving to the Lower and Middle Juba regions. The Russians were busy evacuating people from the Northeast. Also, Abdullahi's own goats were practically all dead, and his four female camels and burden camel were also dying.

With Ubax pregnant again Abdullahi left her in Balambale while he went to become a soldier trainee in Mogadishu.

However, Ubax did not deliver when she expected to and in fact became overdue. And because, as Abdullahi explains, Somalis say that when a woman can't give birth she must see her husband, Ubax came after him. Sure enough, after seeing Abdullahi, labor began, and as he was off asking the Italians for a car in order to take her to the hospital Ubax gave birth to a son. Ten days later he was transferred to Garowe. She traveled with Abdullahi, but after a month in Garowe they thought it better for her to return to Balambale.

Abdullahi was in Garowe six months before he requested a transfer to the custodial corps at the central prison in Mogadishu. He arranged this through a well-placed cousin married to an Italian. The year was 1976.

However, Ubax refused to make this transfer. She said Mogadishu was no good for their children. She was also pregnant again and upon giving birth to another daughter still refused to leave Balambale. Abdullahi visited her there during his leave, taking food and money to her. But she didn't need anything, and still wouldn't move to Mogadishu.

After more time alone in Mogadishu Abdullahi wrote Ubax and essentially ordered her to come to the city. He prepared everything—two beds, a table, cabinet, and other furniture in a house—and Ubax visited. However, once she was in Mogadishu she told Abdullahi that he could take another wife if he wanted to, but that she would not stay. She subsequently returned to Balambale. Seven days later Abdullahi married a third woman.

Two months after this third marriage, Ubax returned to Mogadishu. She stayed with a relative and summoned Abdullahi. She told him that she was making an accusation against him and then went to the military court to file her suit. But he preempted her by going to the Family Law Court, where he received a letter that he presented to the military court.

In military court he told the authorities that if Ubax desired, he would send the third wife away, however Ubax only wanted to stay in Balambale. At a subsequent hearing Ubax sued for divorce. Abdullahi agreed to the divorce, allowing her custody only over their youngest child.

Abdullahi had met his third wife in the custodial corps. She was a *gorob* from a different "family," with parents living in Hardere. Of two children from her previous marriage one had died and the other lived with his father in Kismayo. Abdullahi paid some amount of money as *yarad*.

Abdullahi stayed married to this third wife for seven years, from 1976–1983. Yet they had no children. Also, she became a singer so, as he says, "we couldn't stay together, she goes around." Indeed, he became increasingly suspicious of her activities and since she wasn't "useful"—having not produced any children—he divorced her while preparing to marry his fourth wife.

Abdullahi's fourth and current wife was a prisoner. She was an Eritrean mistakenly arrested during the Ogaden War. Jailed in Mogadishu for six years, it was not until the ELF negotiated a general release with Siad Barre that she was freed in 1983.

Abdullahi and Asha had been conducting *shukansi* in the prison. Seven days after her release he asked her if she still held to her promise to marry him. She told him "a false promise I do not know" and the following afternoon they made arrangements to marry. Although she was a *gorob* with two children in Eritrea, she and Abdullahi have not yet had a child.

Abdullahi married his fifth wife in 1986. Originally from Wardigle (in Mogadishu), she is the daughter of a sheikh who had been arrested and imprisoned for four months. Shortly after his release from prison the sheikh summoned Abdullahi to his house. There Abdullahi found the sheikh sitting with many other sheikhs. Abdullahi was told to sit and then the sheikh began to tell his listeners how well Abdullahi had treated him in prison. Hence, he announced, as a reward he was going to give Abdullahi his daughter, Fatuma. Indeed, he was so happy that he said, "if I give you my daughter, I will pay all the facilities in order for you to have her"—in other words, he would provide the house and pay for its furnishings. Since this announcement took place in the presence of so many sheikhs, the two could be engaged on the spot.

Abdullahi found a house in his village; the sheikh supplied the rent. Abdullahi bought two beds, a table, and four chairs. The sheikh and his wife supplied a cabinet with mirror, another table, a refrigerator, and utensils. When the sheikh asked why Abdullahi had bought anything at all when he had been told not to, Abdullahi replied, "Never mind, I am a *rage* [man]." Two goats were slaughtered for the marriage two weeks after the engagement.

Asha (his fourth wife) was suspicious of Abdullahi, but Abdullahi used his old ruse and told her he had a night job. It took Asha two months before she found out that the night job was really a new wife. The prison was too close to their home for her not to discover that he did not have night work. However, because she was a foreigner she felt it impossible to follow him, as his first wife had done. It was the village women who told her that her husband had married again, and when she confronted him he admitted that he had.

Asha grew jealous, always wanting to know where Abdullahi had been as soon as he came in the door. But not long after she found out about Fatuma, Abdullahi became ill and had to be hospitalized. This cooled Asha down and she took turns with Fatuma visiting Abdullahi in the hospital. For twenty days they rotated the duty of bringing him food.

On his last day in the hospital Abudllahi gathered up Asha's utensils and returned to her house. However, it was Fatuma's day at the hospital, and when she arrived there and found him already gone she grew angry.

The next morning Abdullahi went to visit Fatuma. However, she wasn't home. She still wasn't home by evening. So finally Abdullahi went to her mother's house, but she wasn't there either. It wasn't until the next morning that she returned home. And by then Abdullahi was angry. He began to interrogate her and then insult her, "What happened? Go back to where you came from."

This, in turn, angered Fatuma who threw a lamp at Abdullahi, hitting him. He promptly hit her. They yelled and fought so loudly that eventually the neighbors entered the house in order to restrain Abdullahi. Meanwhile, Fatuma ran outside the house and heaved a stone at the front door. The owner of the house said, "don't break the house." And someone ran to call her mother in the hopes that she could calm Fatuma.

With her mother there, Fatuma tried to apologize. However, Abdullahi refused to hear of it. Instead, he went inside and Fatuma went home to her mother's. The next day, Fatuma returned while Abdullahi was out and removed everything her parents had given, so that when Abdullahi arrived home she was sleeping on one of the few remaining pieces of furniture—one of his beds. He asked her, "Where are the things?" He had already decided to divorce her. She answered, "It's none of your business," at which point Abdullahi proceeded to Fatuma's father's house to try to settle the matter.

After listening to Abdullahi the sheikh grew angry and asked him to return the following afternoon. In the meantime he called Fatuma and asked her "Have you done these things?" Fatuma admitted that she had.

Then the sheikh called in his wife, to ask her whether she agreed with her daughter's actions. His wife denied that she did. But the sheikh scolded both women anyway, blaming his wife in part for his daughter's behavior. [Here Abdullahi interjects a proverb to the effect that "if an old woman builds a house, then the house collapses."]

The following afternoon Abdullahi returned to the sheikh, who told him "Since they tried to destroy your house I will fix it." Abdullahi thanked the sheikh but responded, "We are like father and son. I don't want Fatuma to make problems between us. Yesterday you engaged us and now you have to make the divorce, because she hit me and she will hit me again harder."

The sheikh then said, "Let me divorce you and give you another wife." Abdullahi politely demurred, saying "We will talk about that later." In the morning Fatuma and he went to court and were divorced.

At the moment Abdullahi is married only to Asha. Despite Fatuma having been a *gorob* he still firmly believes that *gorobs* make better wives than previously unmarried women. He explains that a *gorob* is easy in terms of "passing the gate" (sex), but still gives birth. He then compares *gorobs* to castrated camels. The uncastrated camel runs to other camels and cuts the rope (hobble); the castrated camel stays forever.

He also volunteers that having two wives is a problem, but that having three and four wives at once is not troublesome.

Finally, it should be noted that the one person who may be least innocent regarding the conflict between Abdullahi and Fatuma is the sheikh himself, who cleverly got rid of his troublesome daughter by "generously" giving her to Abdullahi, along with a lot of things, doubtless offered in order to sweeten the deal, but perhaps also to make the sheikh look that much more selfless in the eyes of his peers.

Abdullahi's case is more than just interesting for its parallels to Roble's. Like Roble's story this one bespeaks flexibility and shrewdness and misfortunes made good. And it, too, demonstrates how one individual can (literally) play the field. But it also begins to suggest the complex interplay between what seems haphazard and how this is institutionally addressed, by individuals. Now, what of those institutions?

• 14 •

Marriage II

"SHUKANSI"

Shukansi is flirting and courtship. Although *shukansi* was certainly not a recent development, it probably played a larger role in young peoples' lives recently than it did in the pastoral past, although even recently there was much secretiveness concerning who one was courting and why—whether for sex, love, marriage, or a combination of the three. For instance, most brothers did not know who their sisters were seeing. Most sisters were not privy to their brothers' relationships. Even brothers did not always tell brothers, nor sisters sisters, and most parents claimed to have no idea what their children were up to—nor did they wish to.

In the pastoral setting young men and women could meet as they ran across the paths of one another's family, whether at watering holes, in villages, during rainy season dances, or through travel. In the more recent past, with some men having become even more mobile through soldiering, police work, or teaching, meetings were more a matter of where the man happened to be and whom he met who caught his fancy. Alternatively, with Mogadishu's increase in size, as more and more people came to visit relatives in the capital city they met one another in relatives' homes. Perhaps as a result, perhaps only as a holdover, the urban parents of today's marriageable generation seem to have married within the same "family" more often than today's urban-based youth were managing to. Likewise, marriage itself sounded as though it had been easier to achieve previously, whether because the economy was better balanced, or the system of *yarad, dibad,* and *sorio* was better attuned to economic realities, or because there was a substantive economy, or (again) because the past is always golden.

At any rate, one clear strategy in *shukansi* in the late 1980s was to flirt without commitment. This is something that some men would unabashedly admit they practiced, and is something that women openly said they were wary of. Surely the impossible economic situation was used by at least some males as a false pretense for putting off the issue of marriage. And the widespread recognition that "proper" marriage had become financially all but unattainable for many men gave all men more leeway in pursuing women for other aims.

Ambaro (22) is a boyessa *who grew up in Hargeisa. She says she wants to be an only wife—"There is a lot of jealousy in my mind." Her husband must be calm and handsome. His "family" does not matter. She was recently jilted in an affair with a neighbor—she saw him coming out of a cinema with another woman on his arm. On another occasion she saw this same woman in a car with him. When Ambaro went to confront him she says it was obvious that he had just arisen from bed with this other woman. At any rate, he has since married either this woman or someone else. Ambaro says she now flirts and tells boys she loves them, but she will not allow herself to really love them.*

Sofia, 31, is one of the few women working in her agency who is not a secretary. At the time of our first discussion she was not involved with anyone. Several months later she was openly conducting shukansi *with another member of the staff. In a previous job at another agency she had had a boyfriend who wanted to marry her, but he would not wait for her to finish her education. Her family advised her to finish her education. Sofia has no regrets about not having married him. Nor has she been at all pressured by her family to marry, despite her age.*
Sofia's two closest friends, also university graduates, have faced similar difficulties, although one of them is currently engaged to a secondary school graduate because, Sofia says, "She wants to marry only."
In Sofia's view men only say they love you to "get you." They also go from woman to woman as soon as they tire of the same one. This is easier to do these days than previously. Also, women tend to want more (material) things from men than they did in the past.

Bashir, 29, a civil servant, conducts shukansi *with many girls, but only one is a serious girlfriend. He met her in his village. She is of a different "family," and they have been engaged in* shukansi *for three years.*
"When I get my scholarship, then I can pay yarad *and everything." If prices were to hold he would pay 300,000 shillings for* yarad, sorio, *and the celebration. He regards* masafo *[elopement] as shameful. He says that for his "family" 50,000 shillings is the normal cost of* yarad, *although some people pay as much as 100,000. He would like to be able to give 70,000 shillings, which would come from his father and out of his own pocket. He wants to pay* yarad *in order "to satisfy the girl's parents."*
As for the unserious shukansi *he engages in, he says that "All girls expect marriage. Some I tell I will marry, but I'm not going to." He goes*

to the cinema and the theater with all of them, "But the girl you are going to marry you can't touch, you can't sleep with her. Other girls you can talk to and you can touch and you can sleep with." *However, as becomes clear,* sleep with *(for him) is literal, and not a euphemism for sex.*

ABDI KARIM AND WOMEN

Abdi Karim's parents met in the Audegle region when his father was a soldier. According to tradition, Abdi Karim claims, it is shameful to ask how or where or when they met. Abdi Karim's mother died after bearing six sons, who were then raised by their father's second wife who, herself, was a *gorob*.

Abdi Karim's oldest brother is in the United States, where he went to study economics. In order to get a passport he married a U.S. citizen, although they have since divorced.

Abdi Karim's second oldest brother is in Saudi Arabia, working as a computer operator. Once he finished his computer training in India and was established in Saudi Arabia, he returned home in order to find a wife. He was in Mogadishu for about two months and was introduced to many different girls before he chose one, who returned to Saudi Arabia with him.

Abdi Karim's next oldest brother works with Abdi Karim's father in the north. He finished secondary school and is now awaiting an opportunity to marry.

Abdi Karim is the fourth son. The fifth son is in the university, studying economics. Abdi Karim "thinks" he is conducting *shukansi*. Abdi Karim's youngest brother has finished secondary school, failed his university exams, finished his national service, and is also now working for their father.

Abdi Karim himself graduated from secondary school in 1979, and from university in 1985. He has visited Nairobi and Italy on seminars, was extremely well thought of by CRDP expatriates, and has a position of some authority as a district range officer in one of the more remote districts.

Abdi Karim conducts *shukansi* with several girls in Mogadishu, several where he is stationed, and several at district headquarters. In Mogadishu there are two he is most serious about, but he has not yet discussed marriage with either of them. His excuse: "This time is very hard for all the preparations." He hasn't made either one of them a promise, although on further reflection he admits that they both must hope for marriage.

He met the first girl in 1982, at a friend's house. The first time they met he stayed with her several hours and they made an appointment for the following night. A secondary school graduate, she works in an office and is not of his "family." She has visited him once where he is stationed.

He met the second girl in 1985. He was giving two girls a lift home from a party. The one he knew he dropped off first, the second, whom he didn't know, he took home last. They, too, made an appointment for the following night. She is an intermediate school graduate, also from a different "family."

Neither girl is a virgin. He can have sex with them, which he says is a common thing to do. The biggest constraint they face, according to him, is not pregnancy, but finding a place to meet since he lives in his father's house when he is in Mogadishu. Sometimes they have a friend who loans them his/her house for a few hours. Hotels ask for marriage cards, which makes it too difficult to spend time there. Abdi Karim claims that people lie, and many men sleep with "girls."

Beyond these two, the other girls he "courts" he flirts with for fun. He will pay their taxi fare or take them home afterward unless, he says, they live in the district and they can walk. He does not give them anything or pay them anything. He says they engage in *shukansi* for their satisfaction.

Abdi Karim is unusually explicit on the subject of women and their satisfaction. He makes it clear that some women have more "feelings" than others. In his district women behave differently than they do in Mogadishu. In the district they groan so loudly that he sometimes has to put a pillow over their mouths. He assumes this results from how they have been circumcised, since "it is up to the old woman how she circumcises the young girls" and whether she leaves anything with which they can have "feelings." As for the women with no feelings, he says they only want to marry a man in order to have children. Abdi Karim believes some women must enjoy sex more than men because they make noise and cry so loudly before they climax.

Although it is hard to discover the exact content of *shukansi,* which for some was the giving of presents, visiting under the parental eye, going out to the cinema or theater, or sneaking time in someone else's house, it is clear that extra-Somali romantic notions of love infused, if not confused, male-female relationships. This is not to suggest that love was not known or desired in the pastoral setting, although many ethnographers describe how the realities of marriage among pastoralists—designed to link two families—often precluded individuals being able to marry for love (Marx 1967; Spencer 1973). Rather, it is to acknowledge the influence of romance-laden Urdu, Hindi, Egyptian, and Western films at the cinema; the wide dissemination of recently composed Somali love songs (Johnson 1974); and the experiences of young Somalis who had traveled outside Somalia and knew how "things," as well as women, were beyond the confines of home.

However, it was not just ideas from outside that rendered the ideal of love tantalizingly more available. There was also the juxtaposition of girls and boys at school and men and women in the workplace. Similarly, neighborhoods unrestricted by "family" also aided the inter-"familial" mobility, which had to have presented new possibilities, not only for the sexes meeting, but for individuals from different "families" mixing, leading to young people increasingly choosing mates for themselves.

Certainly women with more independence offered men more opportunities to flirt, although those women who experienced what independence offered—that is to say, being entertained—must have realized what flirting back could achieve them: Not only love as promised on stage and screen but visits to stage and screen (on dates) and the wealth that affording such dates suggested.

Already, this is a familiar conjunction, of money, courtship, romantic love, which should suggest another: parental worry and familial tension. And the solution? Elopement.

"MASAFO"

Elopement, or *masafo,* was not new in Somalia. However, it did seem to be used more frequently and for much the same reason from couple to couple. Despite common claims about eloping in order to spare the groom from paying *yarad, masafo* clearly also helped a couple avoid parental approbation (or a first wife's disapproval of a husband's intent to take a second).[1]

Technically *masafo* was a secret, minimalist ceremony conducted at least 90 kilometers from the girl's home. One or more sheikhs were paid for the marriage service, which included a reading of the Koran, blessing of the couple, arrangement of the payment of *meher,* and provision of a marriage certificate that, most often, had to be collected later. Most but not all secret marriages were witnessed by friends of the bride and groom. From accounts by couples who either witnessed or wed in *masafo* marriages, secrecy was usually maintained long after the wedding had taken place and was given away either by the bride's pregnancy or the groom's admission and less often by friends, acquaintances, or relatives.

Abshir (28) is conducting shukansi *with a neighbor who belongs not only to his same "family" but the same "root." He has been courting her for two years and they want to get married. She would prefer a secret marriage, or* masafo, *although he desists since "you might meet something bad if you do; the parents won't agree."*

*He describes a secret marriage: The boy and girl go before four sheikhs. There are no other witnesses. The sheikhs ask both the girl and the boy whether they want to get married. Then they ask the groom the amount of money he intends to pay his bride [*meher*]. Sometimes the girl will say she* *doesn't need money, only "one book of the Koran." The sheikhs then read passages from the Koran pertaining to marriage, and the couple is given a marriage certificate.*

According to Abshir it is middle class and poor people who "will do this system" because, otherwise, if the boy approaches the girl's parents for permission, they ask for payment, a house, or a car.

Dahir, 27, has five siblings. He and one of his sisters married via masafo. *His sister's husband came from the same "family." Yet it wasn't until she was pregnant that she informed her family she was married. They subsequently forced the couple to have a small ceremony.*

Dahir met his first wife at a small shop in his Mogadishu village as she was buying a Coke. They, too, were from the same "family." Shukansi *lasted one night. They made an "appointment" for the second night and the third night they visited a sheikh, who approved the marriage. One week later they returned to the sheikh to obtain their marriage certificate. Two and a half years later they held a marriage ceremony and not long after that she gave birth to a son. Leaving the son with Dahir she asked to return to the northeast (where both of their families lived) for a two- to three-month visit. However, she stayed in the northeast for one and a half years. It was during this time that Dahir decided to marry again, without informing her.*

He met his second wife by helping her get through the crush at a crowded concert at the National Theater. It turned out that she lived in his same neighborhood but was from a different "family." Dahir made an appointment for her to meet him at his house the following night, and it was on this second night that they decided to marry. The following day they traveled to Wanle Weyn (the requisite number of kilometers from Mogadishu) to marry before a sheikh. The sheikh read from the Koran and told them to return in ten to fifteen days for their marriage certificate.

On returning to Mogadishu, Dahir dropped his new wife far from her house so that no one would see them together. The next week he bought her some dresses and gave her some money—this was in February. Shortly thereafter she became pregnant and in April had to tell her mother that she was married.

Her parents were upset since before Dahir had come along there had been a rich man interested in their daughter, someone who had agreed to pay them a considerable amount of money. Dahir subsequently called elders from his "family" in order to help him satisfy her parents. A yarad *of 150,000 shillings (in 1989) was negotiated. After being given this money he says her family forgot about their concerns.*

At the moment Dahir is in the process of buying new furniture for her. He estimates he will spend about 350,000 shillings.

As for his first wife, when she heard Dahir had taken a second wife she returned to Mogadishu immediately, told him she refused to have a co-wife, and they divorced. Dahir now says he will not have more than one wife at a time in the future. "I had an experience. Two wives is very, very difficult."

Ahmed, 19, is now in the national service after having dropped out of school in Form 4. His father is a well-placed military officer stationed in a town outside of Mogadishu.

Ahmed did masafo *in 1987, with a girl (same "family") he met in his Mogadishu village. They did not have to travel the full ninety kilometers from town since her father was already hundreds of kilometers away in Hargeisa. Ahmed and his "wife" each had one friend accompany them to the sheikh, whom they paid 5,000 shillings to marry them. Once married they returned to town as if nothing was different; she continued to live in her parents' home. After one week Ahmed told her parents they were married.*

Yarad *was four cows and 100,000 shillings. Ahmed says his father was very happy to pay this. His father also bought the newlyweds a house and gave Ahmed's mother the money to buy furniture in Mogadishu—two beds, four cupboards, one couch, two chairs, and a dining room set.*

After two months Ahmed's wife became pregnant and subsequently gave birth to a son. In 1988 she moved to Mogadishu with her son. Ahmed divorced her not long after that, apparently because they could not manage their affairs; Ahmed admits he was too young. Ahmed's mother now owns his former house.

Actually, it may not have been the expense of proper negotiations so much as avoiding the issue of negotiation at all that sent many young people running to distant sheikhs (just as it gave married men the option of running secretly to second wives, sneaking out of private negotiations with the first wife, and public negotiations with the parents of the second). In the case of young people, though, choosing *masafo* may reveal something more: that educated youth *did* know how and where lines between "families" were drawn no matter how vigorously they denied knowledge of clans by laying claim to higher education and progressive thinking.

That *masafo* as an option was also discussed in theory by young men who feared they would not be able to marry because they would not be able to afford *yarad,* yet was adamantly opposed as an option by most of those who were already involved in serious *shukansi,* likewise suggests that something else was at work beyond just fears over gaining familial and inter-"familial" approval. In actuality this well could have been the cost of married life per se, *the* biggest financial stumbling block young Somalis faced. Indeed, men who were already married very often claimed that *yarad* was no longer being paid in the towns. It was the young men who had not yet married who pointed to *yarad* and economic strain in general as the reason they could not marry. Meanwhile, neither unmarried women nor their parents ever cited *yarad* as a "must." *Yarad,* then, served as an all-encompassing excuse. But why *yarad* particularly?—unless *yarad* had still other significance.

MORE ON "YARAD," "SORIO," AND "DIBAD"

This is where we again have to reconsider the linkages between kinship and obligation, rural and urban environments, and how trust is established.

We have already considered how trust is born out of kinship, setting apart those you can trust because ties to them have been tested through time from those you cannot be sure about (because there have never been enough ties). One thing *yarad* can do is cement loose ties or make new ones. But it cannot do so without also proving who those ties connect to and how much they are worth; *yarad* is not abstract, but a literal given. It is money or goods, although in fact it may be worth rather than wealth that *yarad* really measures: the worth of the bride (to her family, to the groom, to his family), worthiness of the groom (in the past, the present, and the future), and the worth of each family (as a gateway to wider networks). Granting this, however, raises another question: Given changes in wealth is *yarad* still worth what it once was?

For instance, the circulation and recirculation of camels as bridewealth had very real identifiable consequences for pastoralists since camel genealogies were often as well known as human genealogies. Consequently, what a particular camel brought to a herd was potentially far more than the sum of its (milk and meat) parts. If every camel's breeding bespoke reproductive potential for the future, then which *specific* camels were given would have signified much—and even more when they were considered in the context of the herd from which they came. Similarly, the redistribution of *yarad* among the bride's relatives would have been an equally meaningful event. Also, the fact that *yarad* was never only camels meant that the *mix* of livestock was another text that could be read and reread by interested parties. The circulation of cash, by contrast, could not duplicate livestock in these ways.

Cash-as-*yarad* did follow livestock in at least one sense however; it continued to lay the groundwork for relationships among new kin, which in the urban setting often meant between "families." At first glance, then, although cash-*yarad* might amount to wealth (easily measured) we already know how significant potential could be in Mogadishu—hence my sense that worth was also being plumbed for. In fact, by paying *yarad* to members of a different "family" a prospective groom would not only be showing his worth as a Somali by doing this traditional Somali thing—establishing commonality at the most basic level (since all nomadic clans engaged in *yarad*)—he was also establishing his good faith. He was displaying good faith on the one hand, in the wife he was receiving (and hence in the honor of her family), and on the other, in the future of her family's ability to have good faith in him.

How was he accomplishing all of this? Through the literal papering over of the differences between them—via money (although by coming up with money in such an environment of scarcity as Mogadishu, a potential groom was also displaying the very real worth of his networks, and underlying them *his* kin).

Still, perhaps the comments of many young men regarding *yarad*—when they claimed they were paying (or would pay) *yarad* out of respect, and why they rejected *masafo* as an option—can also be taken at face value. As one Somali who participated in *yarad* negotiations explained it, "the honorable way" was for the family to accept whatever *yarad* was offered without bargaining: "You need peace with the man who is marrying your daughter. We pay so that the father should not curse you because she is a good servant in the house. When you take her forever let them feel happy. You will see them often."

Sorio, too, should be revisited for what its recent uses might reveal about the present. This is because in some cases *sorio* and not *yarad* was paid, suggesting *sorio* as another measure of wealth and worth, and marriage. Indeed, in some instances *yarad* clearly would have secured nothing between two families, either because it would have been redundant (individuals were already closely enough related) or relationships were otherwise impracticable (parents were dead). When there was ample *sorio* but negligible *yarad* the message may also have been: Marriage is meant to secure the happiness between two individuals first and only then (and only maybe) an arrangement between their families/"families."

Certainly *sorio* represented money that could be eaten and entertained away; it was flash, the purchase price of a public ceremony-cum-party, the modern marker of "the wedding." Indeed, if *sorio* in its traditional contexts served to render public appreciation to the elders and relatives responsible for the marriage negotiations, the new shift away from public acknowledgment of the means by which marriages were arranged to celebrations of the wedding itself only underscores the degree to which individual choice and celebration of that choice were helping to undermine parental control over who should be marrying whom.

Of course, the literal and figurative constitution of urban existence in general, ranging from house construction with cement to male domination in the civil service, made for change in other senses, too. This was made more than evident in the atrophying of *dibad*.

In the rural setting women were the ones customarily responsible for the *aqal* [hut] and its contents. Not only did they manufacture mats, containers, and other necessary utensils themselves but they were also the only ones who erected the home. The division of labor, although perhaps fuzzy around the edges, clearly existed as a division; there were certain responsibilities for which each gender could be held accountable that were critical to successfully raising both children and livestock.

In the urban context, where the wife's mother could not make the house or furnishings herself—not even with the help of other women—but where it was cash money that attained such goods, it was men's earning power that would seem to dictate men now providing this equipment. The simple fact that houses and town furniture were more substantial than *aqals*, mats, and containers had meaning as well. For example, although men in the pastoral setting had to have livestock, or a share in livestock, to be able to support a family, it was the *aqal* that was incidental. In Mogadishu it was a job and an income that secured the future of a family, and having a place to live is how the future was, literally, made secure. There was nothing incidental about a house.

Young men who regarded the responsibility of marriage seriously (since we have seen instances where some did not) often assured one another as well as other interested parties, particularly young women, that they could not marry until they were able to provide a house and its furnishings for their bride. And the furnishings, usually, were a set "set" comprising bed(s), a dining table and chairs, cupboards, and chairs for a living room area as well as curtains to be decoratively hung ceiling to floor around walls (and not just windows). The cost of these items was also fairly standard (or, at any rate, ideas about the cost were fairly standardized); most people would quote a fairly universal price of 300,000 shillings (minimum) for the package they felt they had to have before they could marry.

In the next chapter I return to how this money was acquired by those who could acquire it. But in order to do so I must first examine in somewhat greater detail the breadth and range of the family as an incorporating entity. Many of the cases already presented have bespoken this spread, particularly if we consider the range of occupational niches filled, and not only rural-urban links. Nor was it only marriage that spread families. Divorce, too, played a significant and perhaps too-little recognized role.

• 15 •

Divorce and Family Spread

In Somalia neither marriage nor divorce had to be particularly difficult to accomplish. The following case study illustrates the seeming ease with which either condition could be achieved.

Mohamed, 54, came to Mogadishu from the rural areas around Johar in 1977. He has had five wives, but no children. At the moment he is unmarried. He met his first wife at his tea shop/drink stand. Shukansi *lasted one month before he married her in 1982. There was no* yarad, *she came from a different "family," and they subsequently divorced because "they could not live together." He married his second wife the same year. She was a* gorob, *from a different "family." He went to town one Friday, met her on the street, and she showed him her house.* Shukansi *lasted three nights. No* yarad *was paid and they divorced after two months. He was introduced to his third wife (also from a different "family") by a colleague in 1986.* Shukansi *continued five months before they married. There was no* yarad, *and they divorced after one year. The day he divorced this third wife he proposed to his neighbor, who was from a different "family." He and his fourth wife had no children and divorced after six months. In 1988 he married his fifth wife, who was a* boyessa *in the house where he worked as a watchman.* Shukansi *lasted three months, there was no* yarad, *and they divorced after eight months.*

For four of the wives he said he had to buy furniture. The gorob *came with her own. And while he never had to pay* yarad *he says, "without money there is no* shukansi *these days."*

Many wives opposed their husbands taking second wives. Taking a second wife in and of itself led to a great number of divorces or, at best, the perpetual potential for divorce. This potential was often actualized in *masayr* [jealousy]. *Masayr* is not only the feeling of jealousy but jealousy as it is acted out; it may be the quarrel or discussion or fight with a husband when a wife suspects or finds out he is already married to another woman, or intends to marry again, or it may be what the woman feels but does not display. Indeed, citing *masayr,* many men professed dismay at how difficult it was for them to manage two wives. This universal recognition of *masayr* suggests how well some women were able to manipulate and stage-manage a situation that they purported to dislike.

The practical ideal number of wives from the male perspective was either one wife or more than two. Nor should it be so surprising that once a man went beyond one wife he often went way beyond two—compatibility was difficult to ensure. The reasons *why* a man would marry more than one wife could also determine how well he could manage them. Polygyny in the pastoral setting was often compartmentalized, with each wife responsible for a different herd in a separate area, or as Abdullahi managed, with one wife in the village and another in the bush.

Having multiple wives in the same urban area made self-sufficiency far more difficult to achieve. Without the guarantee of an independent source of livelihood, women and children were much more dependent on men. Also, living within permanent, and not just seasonal, proximity of one another, wives were better able to compare conditions, although this is also just the sort of knowledge other women, specifically relatives and neighbors, could exploit for their own ends by stretching (or manipulating) the truth. Children, too, became daily conduits for this type of information as they innocently traveled between households.

To overcome some of these difficulties, namely the outlay for a second wife and jealousy from the first wife over the second wife's (potentially) younger age and fresher looks, many men very consciously sought *gorobs* [widows and divorcees] as second wives. Not only did this prove less costly for them in terms of *yarad* and *sorio,* but many *gorobs* owned their own homes and furniture or other forms of property (tea shops or small businesses). Perhaps more significantly, *gorobs* who had already given birth had also proven their fertility; for men seeking as many offspring as possible, one clear strategy to guaranteeing progeny would thus be to incorporate a *gorob* into their growing family.

Thus, divorce, as Lewis notes (1962) and our cases would indicate, remained extremely common. There appeared to be little shame attached to divorcees, although most men sought "girls" (virgins) as first wives. At the same time, a noticeable percentage of middle-class (middle-aged) women, once having been divorced—and as long as they had children and could support themselves—made little effort to remarry, taking advantage of their freedom to further themselves in business instead. This was evidenced by many of the wealthier merchant women who were either divorced, or had husbands who had married younger women. These women had little use for men as connubial partners, although those who remained married clearly used their husbands' connections for their own financial gain. Again, the girth of many of these women suggests where their interests, literally, tended to lie.

There were also stories afloat that some merchant-women had multiple husbands. This is particularly interesting in the light of historical accounts. Major H. Rayne (1921b) heard cases in which women left behind by men working outside Somalia during the early 1900s tended to remarry without first divorcing. More than eighty years later it was women who traveled who were accused of this. Like their male counterparts, female merchants who traveled must have found it advantageous to have spouses in more than one location. However, this was also illegal; supposedly most of the women in Mogadishu's prison were there because they had been found guilty of having two or more husbands. Whether this was indeed accurate or not I do not know. If so it suggests female success at a male strategy. If untrue, it suggests male fear of successful women, since it is men who believed and repeated these assertions.

Although it is men who were responsible for achieving divorce, by uttering "I divorce you" three times according to Islamic law, women considered themselves (and were considered) perfectly capable of initiating divorces as well. For instance, they might "suddenly" cook badly or become untidy and not keep a clean house. Alternatively, the best way (according to one woman) for a woman to rid herself of a husband was to be caught with another man. Then, according to this popular version of Koranic law, her husband was not allowed to sleep with her and had to divorce her.

Even children, and not just the lack of children, could become an appropriate catalyst/excuse/device (depending on one's perspective) for divorce.

Ahmed's father is between 65 and 67 years of age and is a small-time merchant who got his start smuggling qat *and cigarettes between Ethiopia and Djibouti. He married his first wife, Ahmed's mother, in 1956. Two years later he married a second wife who was a* gorob. *Although Ahmed's mother produced three girls and four boys (one of whom died), her co-wife produced none. Eventually Ahmed's mother left the village and moved to town where she, her children, and the second wife all shared the same house.*

In 1986, Ahmed's father married his third wife. At the time he would have been at least 62 years old and she was 25 or 26 (and Ahmed 24). This third wife was given to Ahmed's father by her father (an elder) after Ahmed's father had helped solve a dispute in her town. She had been given no choice in the matter—she was a "semi-nomad" and old for having never been married before.

Ahmed and one of his brothers lived with her in her house in town. One night Ahmed came home, as usual, and asked her for his supper. She refused to serve him any. So he went to eat elsewhere. In the meantime his brother came home and said, "I need supper." Again she refused, but this time words were exchanged. She became angry, Ahmed's brother was angry and at some point he hit her. She then went to another house to stay.

Because Ahmed's father was out of town he was unaware of this incident until one of his cousins wrote telling him that his wife was no longer residing at home and that she had been involved in a conflict with her stepsons. This news summoned Ahmed's father home and he subsequently divorced her. Perhaps it was not a coincidence that this third wife had only managed to produce one child, who had not survived.

What is unclear in this case is whether Ahmed's stepmother purposely provoked the incident in order to regain her freedom or whether Ahmed's father used the incident as an excuse to divorce a troublesome wife. What this case does demonstrate (in addition to suggesting the expectations placed on stepmothers in regard to stepchildren) is that although tensions might exist, relationships between stepfamily members are expected to be close and to be genial. In many situations they were.

Mahdi (31) is a government employee in Mogadishu. His father, also a government employee, was also born in Mogadishu, as was Mahdi's mother. Mahdi's mother and father divorced when Mahdi, their only child, was five. Both parents remarried.

Mahdi's mother remarried someone she worked with on an agricultural farm and bore one son. She subsequently died and this son now stays with Mahdi in Mogadishu, where he is training to become a mechanic.

As for this son's father, he (too) remarried. He has a small farm and four sons. Mahdi visits them every five or six months—only "as tourism" since this man has enough money to support himself and his family.

Situations that in other societies might spur separation due to divorce and not just death were often also disregarded and reworked into new relationships. Despite divorce, these partial relationships often remained quite close, customarily determined by the husband/father and how he chose to assert his claims on the children born to his lineage.

In 1939 Hassan's father moved from Beled Weyn to Sakow in order to become a farmer and merchant and trade with Kenya from there. In 1945 he married his first wife, Hassan's mother—who came from Beled Weyn (the only one of his four wives from his same "family"). She produced five sons and three daughters. In 1965 Hassan's father married a second wife in Sakow, who bore one son and two daughters.

Hassan's father met his third wife in a different district around 1971. So far, she has given birth to one son and three daughters. Hassan's father married his fourth wife in Sakow in 1982. She died in 1987 leaving three sons.

The oldest of these three "motherless" sons lives with Hassan's oldest brother (offspring of their father's first wife). A second of Hassan's brothers supports the third son, and the second son from this fourth wife lives with the third wife.

Fatuma's parents were first cousins from Las Qoray. They married around 1965. Fatuma was their only child since Fatuma's mother refused to go abroad with her husband when he went to Aden for two years. She demanded a divorce and subsequently remarried.

Fatuma's mother's second husband came from Erigavo. They divorced after one year and one son—whom Fatuma has never seen, as his father (not Fatuma's mother) raised him.

Fatuma's mother met her third husband in Afgoi, where he was working for the government. They married in 1986 and have one son.

Fatuma's father married a second wife from his same "family," and had two daughters with her. One, who is sick, stays with his fourth wife, in Mogadishu, which is where Fatuma also lives. The second daughter, who for a time also stayed there, now stays with her mother's brother in Belgium. Fatuma's father and this second wife meanwhile divorced.

Fatuma's father's third wife produced five daughters and one son. In 1983 he married his fourth wife, who has borne two daughters and a son. It is in this household that Fatuma and the one daughter from Fatuma's father's second wife live—which means children from Fatuma's father's first wife, his second wife, and fourth wife all live under the same roof.

FAMILY SPREAD

Somalis in general participated in remarkable family spread. The extent of this spread was most apparent in terms of geographical location (witness Fatuma's mother finding husbands in Erigavo and Afgoi as well as Fatuma's half sister being able to live in Belgium). However, socioeconomics and education as well as generational time away from pastoralism tended to dictate certain broad patterns about where family members wound up.

For example, most government employees who had a university degree could also boast at least one relative abroad in either the Persian Gulf or the West. Most of those who had relatives in the West (whether as students, refugees, or dependents of diplomats) also had relatives in the Persian Gulf, although the obverse was not usually the case. Clearly the Persian Gulf was easier to reach, and travel and tenure there also served a different purpose than residence in the West. As simply a source for income the Persian Gulf could keep people from having to move any further afield. But in other cases, most often when individuals had education to go on, the Persian Gulf served as a stepping stone to the West.

Abdulla (39) is a government employee whose father was a military officer. In addition to Abdulla (who shuttles between Mogadishu and Bulo Burte and has a wife in each town), Abdulla's father had four other sons (one of whom died) and one daughter. Of the sons, one was a POW (former air force pilot) shot down over Ethiopia, a second (who is also a military officer) married his Somali wife in Egypt, a third works for a Danish construction company in Somalia, and a fourth lives in Italy.

The son in Italy worked first in Saudi Arabia for three years as a driver. His current hope is to emigrate to Canada as a refugee. In Saudi Arabia this son stayed with two cousins (his FaSis' *sons) as well as his father's brother who himself went to Saudi Arabia as a driver. This uncle remits money quarterly to his wife who remains in Somalia. Both sisters' sons, meanwhile, send their mother money annually and have each saved enough to buy villas in Mogadishu, which they rent to nonrelatives.*

*Jabril's father is a nomad from the Hargeisa area, as are Jabril's father's two brothers. One of these brothers has two sons working in Abu Dhabi as laborers. They have been working there five years, and one has his wife and children with him. Both of these men support their cousins (*FaBro's *sons) who are currently unemployed in Mogadishu.*

Jabril's mother has no relatives abroad. However, of her eight children (two daughters and six sons), the eldest boy is now a refugee/student in Toronto. He, too, went to Abu Dhabi to work, staying with his two cousins and serving as a policeman from 1981 through 1987. Presumably because of his connections he was able to go from Abu Dhabi directly to Toronto. While he was in Abu Dhabi he was able to send money home to the family whenever it was needed. Now the family speaks to him occasionally by phone but receives no financial assistance from him.

Cases such as these reveal elements of a pattern that was not uncommon: One family member worked in the Persian Gulf, others joined him (including wives and children when possible), money was earned, saved, and sent home, where it was either invested in real estate, such as villas (which were then rented out to earn further income), or used directly to support the wider family. Whereas levels of education attained often made a difference in where the family spread, the pursuit of education itself also made for patterning.

First, schools were not nomadic. Therefore, pastoralists who sought an education for their children had no choice but to deposit them in one place, with kin they knew they could rely on. Second, as has been noted elsewhere, Somalis did not escape socioeconomic differentiation; advantages accrued to those with (at the colonial outset) at least a modicum of education and these advantages were visible to all Somalis. Third, as education was increasingly identified with advancement it increasingly drew attention as a means to further diversify—diversification being a time-honored pastoralist goal and, in this case, spelling access to all sorts of new (non-livestock-related) resources.

What is particularly intriguing about the increased interest in education is that those who had access to it realized that educating at least some of their relatives, who did not, could benefit them in the long run. In other words, by providing their nomadic relatives with the appropriate means for success, town dwellers could reduce the size of the net of relatives toward whom they had to feel responsible. Once the newly educated could stand on their own two legs they could then be counted on to help support their own parents and siblings, freeing the urbanites to invest more narrowly.

In a certain sense this is not unrelated to the "business" of Somalis in the Persian Gulf trying to find their relatives jobs there. Even if it required effort to bring these relatives over and support them until they found employment, securing their employment freed up those who had been doing the assisting to (if possible) invest more heavily in their own futures.

Nor were these strategies necessarily implicit and covert. Rather, they appear to have been openly acknowledged and accepted. As one Somali academic described his entry into academics: His parents were nomads with relatives in towns. It was these relatives and not his parents who, realizing the value of education, urged his parents to send him and his two brothers to school. Significantly, each brother was taken under the wing of a different relative, so that they were raised by three different families in three different towns: Hargeisa, Jigjiga and Dire Dawa. The only reason these three boys happened to be so fortunate was that they were the youngest of many children and so could be spared from the labor of herding. Thus they managed to gain an education that none of their older siblings had been positioned to receive (and being a Somali in Hargeisa and not in Ethiopian Jigjiga or Dire Dawa helped propel this particular son the furthest).

Having returned to Somalia with a U.S. doctoral degree in hand it was now this academic who was being sent sons by bush relatives. As he summarized it, the situation had reversed itself and *reer miyi* no longer had to be persuaded by urbanites that education was a commodity worth having. They recognized this themselves and voluntarily sent the children they could spare into the towns, at times placing an undue burden on their more "sophisticated" town dwelling relatives.

Ahmed (31), a government worker today, was born in an aqal. *His parents—despite his father's three wives and nine children—were poor. Because they continually asked Ahmed's father's brother (a merchant) for assistance, he eventually got fed up with supplying them with money that never seemed to make a significant enough difference and said to his brother, "I will do you a favor. Bring me the oldest boy and I will teach him." Ahmed, the fourth child but first son (which in and of itself may explain some of the family's "poverty"), was the one to receive the proffered education. Of all his siblings, only one other has attended school and that was Koranic school; Ahmed is a university graduate.*

The choice about which sons (and daughters) would be fortunate enough to attend school was as complex and varied as the choice any other parents might have to make. In some instances it was simply a function of birth spacing, which determined which children were no longer needed to help with the herds. Sometimes the sons who had shown a penchant for learning and were considered clever might be those most easily singled out for school. Alternatively, some fathers chose to rid themselves of their troublesome or inattentive offspring by sending them off to learn rather than risk allowing them to guard the family herds.

In contrast, in the urban setting it was not unusual for at least one daughter to be held back from school so that she could help around the house or with the younger children. In these cases it was usually the daughter who showed the least inclination for learning who "got" to stay home and it was not uncommon to find families in which daughters had been able to shirk school if they found classwork onerous. Little pressure was brought to bear. One reason for this may be that it remained unclear in popular ideology whether it was better to marry an educated woman who "might help you write your reports if you are sick," or an uneducated woman, since marrying an educated one some young men were warned would "be like having two men in the house when both husband and wife have to go to the office in the morning." However, it should also be noted that in many cases every effort was made to educate daughters as well as sons although, invariably, within families more males than females attained higher levels of education.

Because of the uses made of affinal ties it was not necessarily a woman's education that would be of most assistance to her family anyway. Rather, who she married could be more significant and of far greater long-term value.

The irony in this—that who a woman married could contribute more to her parents' and family's welfare and stature in the urban setting than it could in the recent past or pastoral setting—is that such potential emerged at the same time parents and families were losing control over managing their daughters' matches. Thus, it was becoming increasingly a matter of individual taste as to whom one married (and why) and, increasingly, this choice determined how one would live and whose relatives would have to be relied on—his or hers.

Indeed, perhaps that is why marriage, in many young peoples' view, was so confusing: What *was* its point? For instance, as evanescent as love might be, marrying for love could prove safer than marrying for wealth and comfort. Clearly, undreamed-of hypergamy was possible, but since political good fortune could not be guaranteed, a hypergamous situation might not last. At the same time, with so many outside sources of money in the form of remittances and/or foreign bank accounts to draw from, betting on wealth alone may have seemed safe. Still, wealth attracted supplicants and as long as one remained "Somali" one was compelled to take care of relatives. After all, that is the rubric under which a woman marrying for wealth herself would operate, aware that her family would be able to make certain claims on her husband, and she and her husband would pursue certain claims on his family.

Despite patrilineality, a sister's husband (although rarely his family) could be of tremendous assistance to her natal family, just as it was mother's brothers who sometimes had to be called upon. In some instances, it was sisters themselves, generally divorced, more middle-aged merchant women, who supported not only siblings but also their parents. Nor did this seem to be the least bit astonishing to Somalis no matter how handily lineage might be traced through males or how dominant men may have persisted to appear in the public eye. If one was positioned to be called upon to help, one either helped or was asked to help. In recounting how financial assistance was arranged no one denied, downplayed, or discounted affinal ties or the role of women. Nor were women (in these cases) regarded as mere links to other men. Rather, they were given full credit as the lifelines they were.

Fawzia's mother is Fawzia's father's third wife. Of Fawzia's six sisters and three brothers, her oldest sister (33 or 34) is married to a man who works for Somali Airlines. She and their five children are currently in Germany as "refugees" although he continues to work for Somali Airlines, seeing them on fly-throughs to Frankfurt. A second sister married and divorced a commercant and is herself currently in Jidda. She sends home gold and money whenever possible.

One of Fawzia's brothers, who has finished secondary school and national service, is about to go to London to live with their mother's brother; the ticket has been arranged and paid for by his oldest sister's husband (the brother-in-law working for Somali Airlines) and a younger brother, who has also finished secondary school, is about to go to Germany to live with this same sister and her children.

Abdi's father worked in Aden, financially supporting his family back in Somalia. Of seven children, only one is currently married—Abdi's sister.

Abdi's sister met her husband in a cinema in Mogadishu. Shukansi *lasted one and a half years. At the time she was still a student in secondary school and he was studying engineering at the university. Upon his graduation his father gave him money with which to buy and then sell sheep and goats in the Persian Gulf. With his profits from the livestock sales he built a house in Berbera and then asked her to marry him (in 1980). Because he comes from a wealthy family* yarad *and* sorio *were considerable.*

Because her husband comes from a wealthy family, too, Abdi's sister is able to send her family money. Abdi says that receiving money from relatives is not common—just when his mother or father write letters talking about problems, "then relatives will send money. But my sister will send money in any condition."

It is not hard, given these examples, to detect the value of the remittance diaspora. In Chapter Fourteen we set forth the context and the mechanics of remittances. Here it is important to note what remittances meant, not only in terms of what they allowed family members to achieve—marriage (by financing *yarad, sorio,* and furniture), income from rental property, access to higher education, and a direct supplement to local incomes—but also in terms of what they permitted family members both abroad and in Somalia *not* to have to do.

On the most fundamental level, remittances, by keeping families afloat, also afforded family members who were employable but unemployed a cushion. Of course, many young men who did not hold jobs still did "work." They helped tend to family investments (made possible by remittances). Also, although it is clear that there was a dearth of structured job opportunities, having enough money coming in to the family so that these young men could afford to take *caasis* [buses] to their favorite tea shops or "bars," and then drink tea, had to forestall feeling anything more than existential frustration; they themselves were not materially wanting. On a populist level, then, remittances helped subvert the need to seriously protest.

At the same time, having just enough money also fed the individualist tendencies already implicit in opportunism as practiced in Mogadishu. To reconsider tea shop visits: One purpose in tea shop sociability was to find out what others knew in order to use that knowledge to one's own (and one's family's) advantage. This sort of sharing of information on the one hand, and secreting of its meaning on the other, hardly promoted the sort of complicity that would have led to the gainfully unemployed joining forces with those who had no access to remittances (or other informal sources of income). Or, put more succinctly, class alliances became unlikely.

That those who were university graduates were also those who were most likely to have relatives abroad only further splintered the frustrations of a "homogeneous" society that, on the one hand, lauded individualism and, on the other, was so dependent on the corporateness of families.

• 16 •

Meanings in Mobility

Upward mobility was a clear, virtually universal goal. This was evident not only in conversation but also in family trajectories, as we have seen. But also, we cannot forget that the success of some (like Roble) only ensured the failure of others. This is not to suggest that Somalis operated in a zero-sum society, but rather to point out that the more successful some were at operating lucrative networks, the more this led everyone to defensively better their own. And no matter how much some individuals may have sought to catch their networks up, they were unable to do so. Certain advantages could not be beaten. Indeed, as the following case demonstrates, the history of relationship weighed more and more heavily all the time.

THE SONS OF SHEIKHS

Bashir, 30, comes from a long and famous line of central Somali sheikhs. His grandfather and father were both sheikhs, and in total, Bashir's father married six women publicly and three secretly—these last when they were well beyond childbearing age, apparently for humanitarian reasons. Bashir's mother was the last of the "official" wives and he married her in 1952.

Bashir's father married his first wife when he was in his 20s. She had been his uncle's wife. Upon his uncle's death she, her child, and a significant camel herd were left unprotected. Purportedly in order to preserve the family herds Bashir's father married her. However, she died giving birth to their first child.

Upon her death, Bashir's father traveled to Mogadishu to study the Koran and theology, then on to Afgoi and then to the Bakool region, where his father's mother's family was from. He met his second wife there, a relative on his mother's side. He married her (without paying yarad*) and* *they moved to Mogadishu for a time. She gave birth to a son and they subsequently moved back to central Somalia.*

When one of his brothers died, Bashir's father married this brother's wife (as his third wife), again in order "to protect her two children." He had two sons and a daughter with her.

His fourth wife was another full cousin on his mother's side. He reportedly saw her in a dream before ever meeting her. Bashir explains that because his father was a respected sheikh there was probably no yarad. *Two sons and two daughters emerged from this union (although one daughter died). Of these children, one son is currently a regional governor and member of the ruling party's central committee.*

The second son, Bashir says, was considered to be the most educated member of their "tribe"—possessing an engineering degree, a degree in military mechanics, a master's degree in political science, and fluency in seven languages. Having attained his first degree in Germany, he also married a German wife. Then thanks to his degree in military mechanics he was sent to the front in the 1977 Ogaden War. He subsequently took part in the unsuccessful 1978 coup attempt, was caught, and was one of the Somali officers publicly hung. (His wife then returned to Germany where she became a professor of chemistry and married a U.S. citizen.)

Bashir's father met his fifth wife "as a sheikh always meets people." Together they had one son, who is a naval officer today, but Bashir's father did not stay married to this woman. Rather, it was she (his fifth wife) who asked him for a divorce, which he refused to grant on the grounds that "Allah hates divorce." However, she told him that "if you are a good Muslim, I am a good Christian"—her strategy for achieving freedom. As a result of this new tack he did divorce her, telling her that if she remained a Christian she could not remain his wife. She subsequently did marry a Christian Somali and gave birth to two sons.

Bashir's mother was in her mid-20s and lame with polio when she approached Bashir's father in his role as sheikh and implored him to intercede with God to secure her a husband. He told her he would.

Although Bashir's mother was clever, apparently no one in the town or among the region's nomads wanted to marry her. However, Bashir's father had seen her, too, in a dream—one in which he also foresaw her bearing him four children. Thus, he married her himself. His brothers and cousins told him that if he married her she would give them trouble when he died since she did not have her full strength. Nevertheless, as a sheikh he felt he had to give her protection and assurance—and pay two camels as yarad.

She gave birth to three daughters and one son (Bashir) before Bashir's father died. Then, contrary to her in-laws' fears, numerous men sought to marry her. She picked a wealthy suitor (one who had had seven wives previously), with whom she had two more sons and a daughter.

Of Bashir's three full sisters, the eldest married a Garowe sheikh who owns herds, berkeds *[waterholes], and shops, and gave a* yarad *(which the family is still collecting) of three camels, fifteen sheep and fifteen goats in 1972.*

Bashir's second sister married an insurance accountant whom she met at the bank. She reluctantly became his second wife. When she initially refused his advances Bashir reproached her with, "your mother was a sixth wife, what is wrong with us?" The house, furniture, wedding, and sorio *cost 5 million shillings and her husband also bestowed 1 million shillings worth of jewelry on her in 1987. Bashir's mother refused the offer of a 50,000-shilling* yarad.

Bashir's third sister is a nurse working in Jidda, married to a Somali whom she knew from "a long time ago." Yarad *in 1986 was 8,000 shillings.*

Bashir himself only recently married. He had a girlfriend whom he met in 1982 in central Somalia (where he was working) and whom he sought to marry after three years of shukansi. *However, she rejected him. She apparently didn't trust him when he said he had no other girlfriends. Then, by the time he had finally persuaded her to become his wife he decided he shouldn't marry her after all; she wasn't from his "tribe" and he knew his family wouldn't support him. At the same time he received a scholarship to study in Australia. Once he reached Australia he wrote her and told her not to wait for him.*

In Australia, where he was receiving postgraduate range management training, he met a Papua/New Guinean girl whom he decided to marry; he thought that he would settle in Australia. But then, once he completed his course of study and the scheduled date for his return to Somalia approached, he decided Somalia was best and told her that she was welcome to come to Somalia with him, but that he could not stay in Australia with her.

Back in central Somalia Bashir discovered that his former girlfriend had a new boyfriend. He told her that he no longer felt tied to her any way. He decided, instead, to definitely marry someone "whom our family can appreciate, not from a far distant tribe, someone a little bit educated, and young."

He consulted a friend of his, someone who was from a related "family" and with whom he'd previously worked in a nearby town. The two of them discussed marriage prospects and this friend suggested a young woman who "at this moment is ready. She is very conservative." Bashir, aware of her family's standing, secretly investigated Saara and found out that she had not yet "flirted" with anyone. Consequently he went to her and proposed. Taken aback, Saara told him that his proposal was too rushed. Bashir explained that he was serious and that he didn't want to wait a long time. He returned to Saara within a month to propose again, which is when she told him that she would agree if he saw her father.

Bashir solicited a regional governor (a friend of his half brother's) and an important family friend who had known Bashir since he was 10 to visit Saara's father on his behalf. Yarad *(40,000 shillings) was negotiated and the marriage set.*

Bashir bought jewelry (worth 80,000 shillings) and clothes (worth 20,000 shillings) and paid for the wedding celebrations (which cost 60,000 shillings). His sister sent curtains from Saudi Arabia and his half brother along with the general manager of CRDP and other coworkers contributed additional money to defray his expenses. His wife's family supplied subaq *and* oodka.

A number of significant things jump out from this case: All the (full or half-) siblings Bashir knew about married extremely well; the males were all well educated; and they also reached government positions of considerable responsibility, including Bashir himself. Recalling our earlier review of what sheikhs could achieve for their families, this suggests several possibilities. Even from the sketchy details of Bashir's father's life it is clear that, as a well-respected and well-recognized sheikh, certain advantages accrued to him, which he was shrewd enough to make good use of. That his sons could then use this capital, accumulated not only in his good name but in the favors and respect owed him, had to have played some role in their good fortune. In addition, the combination of Bashir's brothers' positions as well as the remarriage of his mother to a wealthy (and thus himself well-positioned) man had to have influenced the trajectory of Bashir's own career—in which, by a relatively young age, he had already received a scholarship to study abroad and semiautonomy as a district-level manager.

Indeed, Bashir himself parlayed the time he spent in Australia (achieved, we don't know how, but can only assume in "some way" beyond his scholastic ability alone) into increased capital for himself. He was able to save enough money there so that he could return home and marry within a reasonably short period of time, and his skill in speaking English (as a direct result of time spent in an English-speaking country) was as effective in his advancement within CRDP as any of the technical range management–related skills he was sent to Australia to learn. In fact, it was precisely the combination of his having learned to speak English so well and his fluency in range management jargon that helped him "convince" the general manager and other coworkers to contribute such a substantial sum (80,000 shillings) to his wedding/marriage. As he explained to me, his district's location was always the first on anyone's tour of the Central Rangelands, therefore he was the person in the field the general manager relied on most to convey the sense and spirit of the project to donors and other foreign visitors.

Here I must add that no doubt there is also a clannist element to this story of which I am largely unaware. Although I know what clan Bashir belongs to, I also know that the general manager was not a member of this clan, although a significant number of CRDP employees were. What is interesting in this regard is how well Bashir's one half brother did, considering where his other half brother wound up (i.e., dead) and that Bashir, likewise, seemed untainted by the association.

In another sense, too, I am limited in the information I can present; I do not know enough details about either Bashir's father's following or Bashir's own claims to religious knowledge. My guess is that Bashir purposely maintained a degree of mystique about his religiosity and that this lack of knowledge on my part was, at least in part, orchestrated.

Like many young Somalis, and particularly young Somalis who spent time abroad where many followed the (colonially fitting) maxim: "when in Rome do as the Romans do," Bashir, by his own admission, became far more religious as a married man than he ever had been when single. Not surprisingly he was also very cognizant of the fact that his father was a famous sheikh. Bashir's father was famed, if not famous in central Somalia; Bashir was working in central Somalia. Doubtless this connection lent Bashir the ability to project a certain kind of conscientiousness, if not *baraka* [charisma], which was very difficult to pin down.

Knowing Bashir in his western guise it was hard to judge how deep this religious vein really ran and whether it wasn't sometimes mined when Bashir was in a certain type of public and then quickly buried when he was with a different public. In a sense, this vicissitude would only stand to reason: He was expected by both groups to behave differently with village elders and political notables than he was with his peer group, and he had different things to gain from both. Giving Bashir the benefit of the doubt—that he was not following any set plan for the future, which he argued would have been impossible to map anyway, given the impending dissolution he (correctly) foresaw—his reactive "maneuvers" were exceptionally shrewd. For instance, he dallied with women whom he knew he shouldn't marry and when he did marry, he married well and (quite pointedly) according to custom. Not only did he have his elders, and quite impressive elders at that, approach his perspective wife's father but he had them offer a respectful *yarad*. The wedding was traditional (down to the *subaq* and *uodka*) despite his wearing an Australian suit, and so was the couple's confinement afterwards.

Although this combining of tradition with unmistakable markers of educated prosperity and modern promise might make Bashir's entire marriage seem calculated when analyzed from without, it is just as likely that Bashir merely did what he knew to be "right" all along—such as marrying a "good" "girl" from his clan. And he continued to do what was, according to him, the Somali (and thus the correct) thing to do. For instance, he was helping support a niece, who, by living with him, also "happened" to assist his wife as a servant-cum-companion.

He also did what he could to stay in good standing within the larger communities outside his "family"—that of CRDP, the district seat where he was located, the villages and other areas he was responsible to, and the political leadership that (in the district) directly oversaw him and, in Mogadishu, directly oversaw the project. Although I must assume from what I saw that Bashir juggled these different interests in part by selectively hiring certain local residents, by making financial arrangements with other people, and by bargaining away some of the material he received from headquarters to satisfy others' immediate needs (which he could later remind them of), he clearly augmented his position by the direct or indirect dispersal of project funds. In this way he had enough people beholden to him that he could deal from a position of strength in order to help those whose interests he regarded as integral to his own.

One small example of this was his allowing one of his drivers to drive the project's water truck after hours. This was clearly illegal. Nevertheless, Bashir's allowing his driver to hire himself and the truck out to other people ensured that the driver could make ends meet and perhaps do even better than that. And although this might have cost the project—in wear and tear on the vehicle, in fuel costs, and perhaps image—it freed Bashir from having to carry an employee who would otherwise have posed a financial burden. At the same time it made the driver beholden to Bashir, and with other people grateful to the driver, gave Bashir a potential and predisposed network to tap into should he ever have to.

This and many other acts won Bashir a measure of respect that belied his years. Nevertheless, it is hard to know whether these acts were a result of his judgment or were made likely (and not just possible) by the position he had "achieved" at the top of the local hierarchy of CRDP. Certainly it is not hard to imagine how he was appointed the position in the first place—ultimately because of who his father and brother were. How he knew how to play that position, though, is much more difficult to ascertain unless one remembers that ideals for *being* Somali still existed.

They existed because the form and even the means of person-to-person assistance had not really changed. Despite institutional trappings of a modern nation-state, the fact that it was individuals within the government and not the government itself that provided people with security meant relations in Somalia stayed grounded in person-to-person contact. Nor, given the tentacles of genealogy, could anyone remain kin-neutral.

This is in stark contrast to a system in which there had been sanctuaries of neutrality, previously embodied in sheikhs. Prior to colonialism, even up through the late 1970s according to some Somalis, it was sheikhs who had been *the* men of respect, who could mediate between lineages, between men and God, and between right and wrong. Half of what was not sitting well with many Somalis in 1989 was that they still would have preferred paying respect to sheikhs who would have done them spiritual good at the very least, rather than men with power or money who only did themselves good, and Somalia badly.

This leads directly to the other half of what disturbed many people: Competition and favoritism over resources was corroding the ideal of a coherent workable Somalia, which Somalia would never be so long as favoritism proved more profitable. Such a tautology meant that it was also becoming increasingly, even inescapably impossible to do good for any such thing *as* Somalia when people had to do good for people they knew and either favored or needed favors from first—who were never *just* other Somalis.

RECONSIDERING THE CONNECTIONS

Caught in such circles, was Bashir the victim, beneficiary, or collaborator of a failing state? After all, he managed to marry, to profit by the system, help others, and further himself at the same time. Like his father, the sheikh, he was respected in the central rangelands town where he lived although he actually had little respect for the government he represented. But perhaps his father felt no differently when confronted by the petty quarrels and jealousies of those whom he succored in order to achieve renown.

What Bashir predicted about Somalia's turmoil, given what he did and what he purported to believe (there *would* be a future—why else did he get married?) is confusing. On a number of fronts he, like Roble, presents consistency in the face of rampant contradictions and tolerance in the face of glaring inequities. We might wonder how. He might answer, "by living."

Moving beyond the level of the individual, though, I have presented two other frames in this book: On the one hand, there is marriage, kinship, and money. On the other, is supra-local level intrusion, war, and dictatorship. Both created frustrations. Both also fed expectation: that enough money would secure a good marriage, that a good marriage could override kinship, that kin relations would supply money. Money was a sticking point thanks to Siad Barre's behavior. Siad Barre was a dictator thanks to others not handling money well, although among those who condemned all this the most (non-Somalis) were some of Siad Barre's most generous backers. But money is not all. There is another way to hook the frames together.

Taking the longer view: It was supra-local level interest in Somalia that created a Somali consciousness, which, forged in war, led to other wars over whom this consciousness applied to—Kenyan Somalis in the *shifta* war, Ethiopian Somalis in the Ogaden War, all or only some Somalis in the civil war between the SNM (? the north, the Isaq) and the government (? the center, the Darood).

Perhaps no one could have done anything to contain such a—not necessarily volatile, but certainly elastic—sense of consciousness. Still, the parallels are striking and perhaps too transparent. A Somali consciousness that can expand or contract must be related to the fission and fusion described by segmentary lineage opposition, which itself emerges out of nomadic principles, designed to best the worst Somalia's ecology can throw at people. Somalia's climate and landscape have long demanded flexibility. But so too has the social environment if we reconsider the flux over the past 100 years of who has been interested, involved, and in Somalia: the British, Italians, Soviets, the United States, Libyans, Saudis, Germans, even the Chinese (to cite some); or if we consider the assortment of governing arrangements—colonial, wartime, mandate, representative, dictatorial, socialist, free market. The only consistency here is change—on the one hand.

On the other hand, if we examine certain institutions, like marriage, there has been some, but perhaps not all that much change. For instance, there remain clear continuities—in *yarad, sorio, masafo.* Assistance, like *qaaran,* still roots itself in genealogy. Even the link between marriage as a union between two sets of people (and not just two individuals) and kinship persists. Why?

Either such continuities represent primordial threads, or they allude to situational consistencies, or they reveal something more cyclical still: namely, the fact that so long as flux is both the constraint and opportunity people have to cope with, the same pastorally grounded principles for determining trust and securing survival can be applied, now as then, here as there.

PART SIX

Conclusions

A Rigorous Ending

If we return to the idea of analogy in the Introduction, we can now see what undid Somalia: regroupment.

Key to the vicious cycle was this: Nationalism was unable to keep state resources from being abused so long as state institutions were incapable of delivering them. Although from the start, state institutions may have been disabled by policies well beyond Somali control, it still remains unclear which *should* have shored up the other. All that is evident now is that functioning state and functional nation were never coexistent for long enough (despite moments of political optimism and promise in the pre-Independence 1950s, democratic early 1960s, and benevolently ruled early 1970s). As a consequence, it is perhaps we who study people who should now also regroup and ask more pointed questions. To students of state, society, and nation, what can Somalia explain?

BROADER GENERALITIES AND THE QUESTION OF THE NATION-STATE

Although the body of literature on the state is as old as the concept of the state, there is a growing movement to analyze how African states, as structure(s), no longer work to capture society (Chazan et al. 1988; Rothchild and Chazan 1988; Migdal 1988). This new focus presents a rough parallel to the surfeit of literature on the projected breakdown of nationalism (Breuilly 1982; Smith 1983, 1986; Hobsbawm 1990; Davidson 1992).[1] However, the two perspectives have not yet been fully synthesized. In part this must result from the divide between the interests of political science and the interests of social history. Nevertheless, even the slightest shift in emphasis—over which comes first, state or nation, organization or sentiment—means that many works do not engage in dialogue across causal divides despite their disputing the content of the same terms. For instance, although ethnic mobilization is often described as an instrumentalist development for attaining state resources (Young 1976; Horowitz 1985), the state as a source of resources tends to be ignored by those who describe nationalism as a political tool for acquiring state power (e.g., Breuilly 1982). Meanwhile, what is state power over?

Power itself may be the most slippery of the elements at issue in this literature, although it is rarely directly addressed (e.g., Mann 1986, 6). Rather, it seems assumed, but what should it be assumed for/as/to do? Should we regard it as an end in itself, a means, or an incidental? Does it thrust, causing people to seek command (via hierarchy)? Or does it parry, causing them to avoid command (through autonomy)? Does it have cultural content such that power in the United States is different in representation, efficacy, purpose than it is, say, in Somalia—in which case, how should we (can we even) cross-culturally discuss it? Alternatively, is any explanation necessary when all cross-cultural contacts involve a power differential (i.e., both colonizer and colonized recognize colonial power despite their cultural differences)?

In other words, power, as an explanatory device, may explain far less than we assume. At the same time, however, it is projected as something awesome and great: as the motor behind formation of the state, with monarchs seeking to consolidate and project their power from within their container/fortress/states (Hobsbawm 1990), or as the desire around which both nationalism and ethnic mobilization cohere as people seek to offensively or defensively project their power vis-à-vis one another, either from the top-down/inside-out or from the bottom-up/outside-in (Horowitz 1985). However, we still do not know whether it is something primordial people possess (like they possess charisma, or *baraka*) or something they charismatically manufacture (like the symbols with which they make it manifest) (Kertzer 1988).

Clearly, power's success as concept, tool, or goal may well reside in its ambiguity (Balandier 1970). For instance, whoever captures it (however it may be conceived) and then captivates others with it as a result, not only tends to worship the force of—or the force that is—power (as do we) but sees and wants to see it refracted everywhere. Illusory, elusive, ineluctable, expandable, contractable, mercurial. What else but power enlivens state, nationalism, and ethnic mobilization, granting each a lifelike beginning (*The Birth of the Modern*) and end (*The Rise and Fall of the Great Powers* just to cite a few random but popular titles).

However, we should recognize anthropomorphism when we see it. We should also know by now not to trust neatness. It is too simplistic to suggest that the nation-state fades in as the empire fades out; was the Soviet Union only an empire in action, but not by definition? Neither should we suggest that the nation-state is fading out as ethnic groups fade in, since it is statehood many stateless nationalisms have sought (i.e., the Kurds, Palestinians, Eritreans—even now the Isaq).

Also, anthropologists in particular should know better. We have a history of investment in our own difficult terms: tribe and tribalism. Perhaps a taste of the stickiness of these terms could help clarify how *state, nationalism,* and *ethnic mobilization* could better be defined in terms of both sentiment *and* organization (*social* history *and* political *science*) if they are to be used for cross-cultural, space-time travel.

A tremendous amount of ink has been spilled on the topic of tribalism, which has seemed to mean all things to all Africanists. However, despite a resurgence of interest in the topic today it was perhaps most rigorously debated more than two decades ago, as members of the Manchester School (many of whom were also associated with the Rhodes-Livingstone Institute) strove to cope with issues of social change in the face of rural/urban, traditional/modern transformations primarily in southern Africa but elsewhere too (see Hannerz 1980).

For instance, in a seminal article on tribalism, Max Gluckman distinguished between two types: a working political system among individuals in rural areas, and a means of classification used by town dwellers (Gluckman 1960, 55). He found a radical disjuncture between the two, with rural tribalism referring to a "highly organized system of social relations" (68) in contrast to informally organized affinities struck among migrants in towns (65). In other words, read through our lens, although it was organization that defined tribalism in the rural setting, associative sentiment defined tribalism in the urban context.

Interestingly, Aidan Southall also found tribe to be a very specific type of society: a "political entity with political autonomy" (Southall 1970, 29). Tribalism was the carrying over of certain features from this setting into a different system (30). Following Gluckman, Southall alluded to the breakdown of rural autonomy but did not specify whether it was vestiges of political structure or political sentiment that were carried into the broader urbanized environment.

Taking a different tack, J. Clyde Mitchell who, like Southall found the cross-cultural use of both *tribe* and *tribalism* troublesome, focused on tribal behavior and distinguished between manifestations. There was *categorical interaction*: individuals identified one another according to ethnic indicators, which then forecast expected behaviors. Alternatively, there were enduring personal relationships that led people to share norms and values, which then imparted a particular form and content to behavior (Mitchell 1970, 85).

What is significant about this latter distinction is that although, like the others, it implies a rural/urban, old/new split it also hints at more: First, that the sharing of norms and values, particularly for dislocated individuals in new settings (i.e., towns, factories, armies, etc.) could build affiliations that seemed to be, and acted as if they were, tribal. And second, that affiliation via sentiment may have created new structures that still *felt* tribal.

Unexpectedly and from a very different (French marxist) quarter Maurice Godelier intimates the same possibility. He, too, finds fault with empirical conceptions of *tribe,* citing two definitions: *tribe* as a type of society and also as a stage of evolution (Godelier 1977, 70). This is in line with the neo-evolutionist view that tribes can be defined according to a series of characteristics that places them between bands and chiefdoms (see Service 1968/1962). However, Godelier pointedly criticizes this approach for only examining the surface structure and appearance of social relations, without getting at distinctions in essence or internal meanings (94).

Considered from my perspective, and bearing in mind the recent Africanist literature that overwhelmingly emphasizes either an instrumental imperative in the conscious culture brokerage of tribal ties (e.g., Vail 1991) or the significance of tribal routines and habits as a form of discourse with, and resistance to, state structure (Comaroff and Comaroff 1992), sentiment still appears to be the critical missing link for getting from tribe to tribalism both literally (from countryside to city) and figuratively (from model to practice).

Indeed, if we rethink Victor Turner's apposition of structure to *communitas* (1969), it may well be that both conditions are operative but with mutually constructive—and not just opposing—effects. By this I mean that it cannot be enough for people to merely know where they stand in relation to one another structurally (whether as literal or figurative brothers); they also have to be able to *feel* that they can trust one another and that their linkages (whether accidentally or intentionally formulated) are, in fact, inviolable. Or to turn this around, although erection of a national arena may obliterate tribal or parochial autonomies it does not necessarily destroy formerly tribal or parochial bonds between people.[2]

So how can we reintegrate state or nation *as* structure and nationalism/tribalism/ethnic mobilization *as* sentiment? On the one hand, we could regard the state as a structured container (pace Giddens 1987). Following Benedict Anderson (1983), nationalism is then what is imagined to fill or create the bounds of statehood, lending sentiment to sovereignty and linking (if not locking) all people within the container. Meanwhile, given that it is colonial structures that remained in place to form secondary states in Africa (Anderson 1983; Smith 1983; Service 1968/1962), new people manning these old structures found themselves in new positions, able to harbor new interests for old relationships. Given kinship obligations, competition over political representation doubled as economic competition over what amounted to scarce rewards of state (Davidson 1992). Subsequently, the jostling to control levers and resources became as much a matter of consolidating *for* as consolidating *against* (Cohen 1969, 1981; Maybury-Lewis 1984), or even of consolidating against being consolidated against (Horowitz 1985)—and the struggle over control, via violence, ensued.

Of course, many other syntheses also seem possible. For instance, there appears to be general agreement that modern states emerged to tie people into more efficient structures of organization as trade expanded zones for economic *and* military influence (Breuilly 1982), although whether out of the city-state (Braudel 1981, 1982, 1984) or the empire (Hobsbawm 1990) remains in dispute. Regardless, there is still the matter of whether quotidian ties among people were ever really severed in the effort to link individuals directly to the state via nationalism. That seems a far more contentious issue. For example, Clifford Geertz argues that primordial sentiments (by definition) are inescapable although they may not always be mobilized (Geertz 1963). David Maybury-Lewis points out that people have always associated parochially (Maybury-Lewis 1984, 227–228).

Nevertheless, despite disagreements over whether ethnicity is a universal human attribute (Kellas 1991), whether ethnic mobilization is a product of modernism and an offshoot of nationalism (Gellner 1983; Guidieri and Pellizzi 1988), whether African tribalism is a colonial creation (Southall 1970; Vail 1991), or whether it emerges from the confluence of precolonial responses to slavery and postcolonial reactions to failures of the state (Ekeh 1990), most disquisitions on ethnic mobilization or tribalism describe a condition that they do not directly address: namely, solidarity.

Durkheimian notions of solidarity divide societies into two ideal types: those with mechanical solidarity, in which the division of labor is minimal, people share most life experiences and know one another directly, and societies with organic solidarity in which there is a complex division of labor and a great deal of functional interdependence between large numbers of people (Durkheim 1933/1984). Meanwhile, societies with organic solidarity are necessarily composed of mechanically solidary sub-units (Durkheim 1933/1984, 242, 293). Or to come at this slightly differently: When pluralism exists in any organized form it is because something like organic solidarity holds its mechanically solidary components together (M. G. Smith 1984).

Read through a Durkheimian lens, then, the question looms large: What is the glue for keeping mechanically solidary segments (whether new or old, manufactured or primordial) *voluntarily* together under the organic umbrella? Ernest Gellner suggests that for the state it is mass education and the promulgation of high culture (Gellner 1983), Benedict Anderson heavily weights the printed word, which transcends localisms (Anderson 1983), and E. J. Hobsbawm emphasizes the consolidation of language uniformity over dialect differences (using both Gellner's and Anderson's positions to strengthen his own) (Hobsbawm 1990). Ultimately, however, these are quibbles over the attempted institutionalization of nationalism. It is nationalism that is, often intentionally, meant to be the organic solidarity glue. Arguably, then, tribalism may be the sentiment that exists within the mechanical segments, subsumed and absorbed but not quite dissolved in the organic medium—reemergent as ethnic mobilization under the state. In fact, this is what Peter Worsley suggests in his discussion of nationalisms: National identity emerges from the direct relationship between individual and state (Worsley 1984, 186), whereas ethnicity *mediates* between individuals and the state (192).

Although it may well be confusion over definitions that has led to so many different theories, too many causal arrows still point at cross purposes. Beneath the schools of thought, which are often divided into perennialist and modernist (Smith 1986), there would appear to be an equally significant divide over relevant diagnostics: that between Weberian considerations of *political* economy and Marxist consideration for political *economy*.[3] Curiously, Durkheimian references to morality remain glaringly missing. The state as a container for moral order beyond coercion and surveillance (Giddens 1987) is not well described.

There would appear to be several related reasons for this. Since one purpose in focusing on the roots of nationalism, ethnic mobilization, and tribalism has been to understand cohesion in the face of intergroup conflict (either within or among states), how groups distinguish the "them" from the "us" has led to obsession over issues of group definition and boundedness. Consequently, etic characteristics have been unduly emphasized not only because it is assumed that these are the obssession of those being studied, but because they are critical to describing who *is* being studied. Hence, motivation to preserve and further the group vis-à-vis the outside world has received far more attention than sentiments that exist among group members for any other reason—that is to say, as ideology: to make for moral order, to fulfill ritual and religious demands, to preserve harmony, to model good behavior, to be true to faith or belief, and so on. Likewise, given the overriding assumption that solidarity forms in opposition (i.e., it is impossible to have an "us" without a "them," allies without enemies, the Nuer without the Dinka), coherence has tended to be regarded as a means to an end and never the goal itself. Again, such an intellectualized approach (agreed to even by native-born academics who have themselves thought their way out of tribalism) suggests persistent disregard for sentiment.

Certainly emotion and feeling seem critical to the formation and maintenance of solidarity at any level. It seems more than doubtful that bonds of obligation are uninvested with emotion and feeling. Yet the essence of solidarity has long gone understudied. Even more ironic, this is precisely what much of the literature on nationalism, ethnic mobilization, and tribalism suggests—that people have to feel bonds linking them (whether common ancestry, language, custom, etc.) to belong. However, how these bonds feel and what is shared by *sharing* language, common ancestry, custom, and so on, is what has not been adequately considered. Thus, from this angle as well, we can suggest the need to readdress the question: Is it simply by virtue of scale or by virtue of content that we do better distinguishing nationalism from ethnic mobilization from tribalism? Meanwhile, it seems clear that when examined from within these frames there may be new ways to construct not only our definitions of these distinctions but the very idea of distinction and how it feels.

For instance, if we accept the view that the "nation" in Africa tends to be a colonially imposed territorial shell granted structures of state (i.e., bureaucratic and military capabilities), we can see why Somalia, as a new nation, would have been so enthusiastically welcomed into the world fold of nations: with national form permitting access to international levels of association, nations being the unit of account, and so on. Or so the rhetoric, from the "United Nations" to the Inter*nation*al Monetary Fund implies. However, what if we reconsider this imagined international community from within Somalia-the-nation looking out: How national *has* its discourse with the world really been? For example, is the IMF a national entity? Or how often was it specific elements within governments that formulated contrasting policies (e.g., the State Department and USAID)? Or what about the U.S.-USSR rivalry, a rivalry between empires and not just nations? Plus, what kinds of nations would Somalia's neighbors have seemed to be? Djibouti: a city-state (replete with French soldiers and sailors standing guard—or guarding?). Ethiopia: an aggressive, land-hungry imperial power. Kenya: Kikuyu or Kalenjin? legitimately or illegitimately in possession of Somali-occupied grazing grounds?

In other words, even if we could regard Somalia itself as a monolith, as something live with a view, we would be fooled if we did not look beyond our view of it as a nation to see what *nation,* from the inside-out, means. Even now. In fact, particularly now. Given the catastrophic events of 1989 through the present it seems clear that although for thirty years Somalia may have been treated as a *nation*-state by the outside world because it occupied geographical space, Somalia as "an" entity may never have existed for most Somalis, *except* as an ideal, floating in the imaginations of some.

SOMALI PARTICULARS

Consequently, it should come as no surprise that what makes Somalia's recent history so difficult to present tidily is that a coherent national sentiment was never practicably there.[4] Parochial and patrimonial moralities instead held sway, reinforced by pastoralist ideology tailored to seek opportunities in unpredictable environments. Thus, in some regards the beginnings of the state's dissolution can be analyzed as concomitant with its founding in 1960 (a somewhat different approach from that suggested by Laitin and Samatar, who entitled their history of Somalia *A **Nation** in Search of a State* [emphasis mine, 1987]).

According to the dominant prevailing view, Somali culture writ large has always been essentially pastoralist.[5] Even in 1988–1989 it was commonly asserted in Mogadishu that well over half of the population was still nomadic and that Somalia contained the world's largest camel herds. However, urban Somalis, while perhaps adhering to an idealized pastoralist ideology for want of a substitute, no longer practiced nomadic pastoralism. Rather, commercialization, sedentarization, and the pull of urban employment were just three of the accelerations that had hastened increasingly divisive socioeconomic practices. Also, colonial and postcolonial policies consistently introduced change from without. Taken together, all of these factors helped constitute what David Parkin has elsewhere called "a variable environment of opportunity" (Parkin 1978, 314).

This as much as anything is what made for consistency in people's lives: the persistence of unpredictability. Nor did this environment ever really fade. Rather, while Siad Barre's twenty-one years in power (1969–1990/1991) should have allowed certain political and economic patterns to become well-established and entrenched, the arbitrariness of his patrimonialism actually promoted unpredictability throughout the urban landscape, embodied most significantly in incessant personnel shifts. As a result of such turmoil, one could assume that knowledge of who was in control of which office and for how long would have seemed unnecessary for the average Somali to possess *except that* this same pattern of arbitrariness afforded everyone the hope that someone they knew might be among the chosen (or among those with access to the chosen) one day. Consequently, there existed a very real "horizon of expectations" in Somalia, which, while not millenarian on the national scale, did incorporate elements of millenarianism read through a Muslim lexicon at the individual level; Allah was easily invoked as the ultimate arbiter of all fortunes.[6] Although not vouchsafing forgiveness, this still allowed Siad Barre to carry on.

Such interaction between expectation and reality, reality and the reading of events, and events and personal fortune, can be scanned differently as well. Although perhaps rhetorically attributable to Allah, all government actions and reactions had real-world roots. As Sally Falk Moore has written, behind the "foreground preoccupation" of actors looms the "background conditions" informing their situation (Moore 1987, 127). Supralocal influences were multiplex. And they were not all visible. Rather, those that were most important to the running of the state were often kept purposely obscure from Somalis in Somalia. Ironically, conflicting rumors about diplomatic efforts, the ambiguous actions of various foreign entities (the IMF, World Bank, USAID, UN), and the secretive nature of ruling party politics left people little choice but to explain events according to the partial knowledge they did possess: of who was related to whom and why *they* had access to state resources.

Indeed, if anything it was the too-successful fit between this thinking and how government seemed to work that ensured crisis. That the ruling clique appeared family and lineage-based in a society that reckoned its history in terms of lineages and lineage interrelationships only reassured people that the smoking gun *was* in tribal hands.

However, tribal lines of fissure still do not present us with a cause for dissolution. Rather, as in instances elsewhere (Zaire [Young and Turner 1985; MacGaffey 1987, 1991], Liberia [Harden 1990]), cause would seem to have emerged from competition over the control of resources in Somalia—resources that were never quite controllable enough (see Goody 1971). Porous borders with Djibouti, Kenya, and Ethiopia, interfamily links across these borders, Africa's second longest coastline, and historic trade connections to the Persian Gulf helped make smuggling easy and lucrative. At the same time, a national economy flooded with aid money on the one hand, yet under the thumb of a government that restricted access to foreign exchange and foreign exchange-earning businesses on the other, encouraged unlicensed activities and subversion of the law. Likewise, there was an ongoing struggle between government and citizenry over a situation everyone knew the government could not afford to control if the man in the street was to survive. And so too there was competition among moralities and over who morality pertained to.

For two reasons, then, the literature does not exactly fit in this regard either. Despite recent rereadings of local culture as resistance (Scott 1985; Comaroff 1985), few Somalis could behave as passive, everyday resistors. Not only was the public not a peasantry, it was also not monolithic across classes. Rather, alliances were vertical, through families (Hoben 1983). Indeed, members of the public had relatives or sought to have relatives in the government in order to better position themselves *to* subvert or avoid the law.[7] Also, it would be wrong to interpret individual misdeeds as symbolic acts of conscious resistance; for most people, their own welfare came first. If earning money required evading the authorities avoidance was certainly intentional, but not as protest. Rather, the aim was far more elemental: to get away with the crime in order to further one's own (and one's family's) ends, and to be able to do so again and again.

On the broader scale, the lack of a unified resistance might well be held as one factor accountable in dissolution, with simple revolution or government takeover never really possible. This inability of the armed insurgent groups to unite has generally been attributed to factionalism within the individual movements and tribalism among them, since they were generally perceived to be clan- or clan-family-based. However, it may rather be that resistance was actually significantly different from within the opposition groups than it appeared to those without. For instance, the argument was made in Chapter Six that many of the opposition movements emerged to protect members' interests and that they only emerged once success of other, already-established groups looked likely. Achieving specific goals (rather than broad policy) thus came to represent the thin edge of the wedge, distinguishing groups from one another and marking them as potential rivals. On the one hand, such fission can be explained according to classic segmentary lineage opposition principles. On the other hand, it may also be an instance of mechanical solidarities seeking to remain autonomous *yet* in control.

For instance, there is the example of the role of July 14, 1989—somewhat clearer now than it was in 1989. The violence that day and on those to follow opened Mogadishu up to increased criminal violence, and its aftermath (of arrests but not reform by the government) suggested to people that something else beyond demonstrations would be needed to oust Siad Barre *and* the Marehan. Because so many Marehan had been made conspicuously wealthy through their connections to members of the regime, all Marehan were villified. Indeed, despite internal dissension among the Marehan, all Marehan were condemned. Meanwhile, the more Marehan individuals were lumped together and their safety threatened, the more they found themselves having to react defensively *as* Marehan.

At the same time, the shootings in general brought terror home to all sorts of people who had previously not had to worry about their immediate safety. In a sense, then, it bonded Mogadishu residents to Somalis in the north and south who had already been experiencing violence. At the same time, although there was general acknowledgment that it was this disintegration in the peripheries that was threatening to finally destabilize the center, it was these bonds—people's loyalties to their points of origin—that were directly tested by the need for response to July 14, a response that was not forthcoming in Mogadishu.

As street violence did not continue after July 14 one Somali reassured me that war itself could not come to the capital. After all, Somalis from every part of the country had invested in Mogadishu, owned property in Mogadishu, needed Mogadishu; there was too much at stake; if Somalis destroyed Mogadishu (after having already destroyed Hargeisa) they would have nothing left. But, as events since have demonstrated, it may be precisely because so much was at stake in Mogadishu that Mogadishu became the target, not only because Siad Barre and the Marehan beckoned removal, but because anyone who controlled Mogadishu would prevent Others from controlling it: the past would not be foisted on them, although they could ignore, mystify, or vengefully pursue making history for (or of) Others.

However, opposition groups were not acting in a vacuum (and, at least initially, they were not based on Somali soil). Again we must consider the supra-local subscript, this time from without. Where was support for oppositions and for the government coming from, and what was it meant to achieve? One thing it did inadvertently purchase was paralysis at the national level, with Somalia caught between partisan Somali machinations at the local level and strategic maneuvers by non-Somalis at the supra-local, international level. Meanwhile, the international contribution to national disarray, although documentable in the record (of UN, U.S., and other foreign government policies), was lived out on a daily basis by expatriates in Somalia.

Unfortunately, anthropology has largely ignored the expatriate experience and the expatriate role (although R. O'Brien 1972; van der Bor 1983; Putnam 1984; and Hansen 1989 offer some insights and Hancock (a nonanthropologist) delivers a scathing attack [1989]).[8] This is surprising given the impact of expatriates on local economies. For example, in 1984 it was estimated that 5,000 Somalis were directly employed by expatriates and expatriate agencies, paid at rates often five times as high as those attainable from the Somali government for similar work (Somali Ministry of Planning 1984). Not only did such employment set up a dynamic of pursuit within the Somali community but it also made plain, on the smallest scale, the expatriate capacity to deal from a position of largesse, if not strength.

At the same time, whereas Somalis were relying on the welfare and insurance provided through tribal solidarities and not the state, most expatriates were accorded all sorts of welfare-related privileges by their state agencies: free housing and utilities, appliances, furniture, access to duty-free shopping and diplomatic pouch privileges, cheap liquor, and a variety of other subsidized allowances. Indeed, although aid agencies and embassies ostensibly hired individuals who sought foreign immersion, the incentives to work abroad enabled most expatriates to live as if they were at home, but in bigger houses and with servants. As a result, "the provision of such perquisites" made it possible for expatriates to stay at "arm's length from the local culture" (Putnam 1984, 322).

More than evident in Mogadishu, such distance in turn fostered the perfect atmosphere for conceit of knowledge without understanding. As Marshall Sahlins points out in *Islands of History* (1985), people from different cultures with different histories can mix signals as well as misunderstandings. Whereas on one level the Somali situation (prior to 1992) did not devolve into the kind of cultural warfare Sahlins documents for the Pacific, the interplay was fraught nonetheless. Danger was always imminent as far as most expatriates were concerned, revealing as a sentiment in and of itself, since there was also a taint of hubris in this expatriate assumption that however limited their view of Somalis, it was accurate and sufficient enough for them to have to justifiably worry.

In fact, one reason I began my analysis with the expatriate gaze was to view dissolution from this intuitively accurate yet analytically incorrect angle. For instance, how July 14 affected expatriates was very different from what it signified to Somalis. Although the unleashing of violence was frightening to both communities and signaled impending chaos across the spectrum, the expatriate response of alternately hunkering down and then dragging out a partial withdrawal impacted Somalis in a variety of ways. On the one hand, for project counterparts, now left on their own, it was disastrous. For servants about to lose their jobs, on the other hand, the goods that many suddenly inherited from their now-departing employers proved an unprecedented boon. In fact, for all Somalis any opportunities that presented themselves in the form of items or last-minute favors to be asked for *were* seized for whatever potential they seemed to possess—confirming the long-standing expatriate reading of Somalis *as* grasping opportunists, unable to think ahead or plan for the future (which to expatriates looked increasingly doomed thanks to the pervasiveness of this very behavior).

At the same time, from within the Somali frame, whenever individuals were able to successfully gain goods that could be turned into money (or more goods or favors), such windfalls renewed hope and reaffirmed the importance of being able, even staying poised to take advantage of opportunity; expectations could pay off—"look, in this case and this case and this case they did." On the larger scale this was echoed in assumptions that the Soviets (or someone else, i.e., the Libyans) would come to Somalia's rescue if the United States withdrew. After all, quotidian as well as regional history had long proved the efficacy of this logic.

With such expectations and frustrations often amounting to flip sides of the same coin, it was almost impossible for someone in my position *not* to see the manufacture of self-fulfilling prophecy in both opposed, interdependent, wary camps. What made this tragedy all the worse, though, was that neither camp was interested in scrutinizing itself as if it was the other, in sharp contrast to more self-reflexive encounters reported elsewhere (Comaroff and Comaroff 1992).

As a result, without constructive mutual interest, spheres of communication continued to stay partial, channeling the flow and availability of information such that two relatively impermeable logics persisted. Nor did it help that, on the one hand much local-level information was not available to expatriates, and much supra-local level information was not available to Somalis.

Consequently, when the crisis finally progressed to the point of being beamed into U.S. living rooms in late 1992, non-Somali Somalia "specialists" could use their cumulative "knowledge" to advantage to analyze shifting patterns of daily life at levels that had never borne much relationship to what Somalis alone experienced. Similarly, what Somalis could learn on a daily basis proffered little clue as to what the rest of the world actually understood (or didn't understand) about them. Hence, Operation Restore Hope was virtually guaranteed to confirm Somalis' inflated sense of Somalia's importance for all the wrong (but historically correct) reasons, at the same time need for such a mission only reaffirmed Western convictions: that Somalis were not capable of reason or self-help, or even sentiment. Why else were they killing each other? How else explain how one group of Somalis could let another group of Somalis starve?

Epilogue: No Ending

As I write this, Rwanda has replaced Somalia on the front pages. Literally. In fact, as morning newspapers headline President Clinton's decision to initiate a massive U.S. relief effort to Rwanda a small story about Somalia is buried on the inside pages of the *New York Times*. Wedged between stories about the U.S. Navy and Haiti, and Argentinians protesting a terrorist attack aimed at Argentinian Jews, the *New York Times* captions: "U.S. Weighs Pulling Out Troops and Diplomats from Somalia." The first paragraph reads, "Spurred by a rise in violence, the Clinton Administration may decide as early as Friday [July 22, 1994] to withdraw the last American diplomats and marines in Somalia, even as United Nations peacekeepers are questioning their own usefulness there" (*New York Times*, July 22, 1994).

So much for Operation Restore Hope, the much heralded U.S./UN effort to save starving Somalis and put Humpty Dumpty back together again. On the bright side the United States and the UN did save some Somalis. But saving Humpty Dumpty, as the nursery rhyme suggests, was impossible. Plus, as the new Africanist rhetoric keeps reiterating, only Humpty Dumpty can really save himself. Somalis have to solve Somalia's problems.

There is so much irony in all of this that it is hard to know where to begin. First, we should remember that the United States has withdrawn from Somalia twice before: in the early 1970s, when the United States and the USSR could not coexist as Somalia's patrons, and then in 1991 when Mogadishu was overrun by antigovernment forces. Both times the United States returned. It is likely we are not abandoning Somalia for good now.

I say this because we do not seem to have a very good institutional memory. Emotions often get the better of us. In fact, it would seem that reason has actually been lost between U.S. comings and goings to and from Somalia. Certainly this is the case if we remember expatriates' prescriptions for Somalia in 1989: Somalis should be left to themselves for twenty years, then once they had sorted out their problems, westerners could return and perhaps be of some credible assistance. The span between 1989 and 1992 is not twenty years. Had Somalis truly sorted out their problems before the United States (among others) returned? Of course not, which is one of the rationales the U.S. government used *for* returning.

Who then were the government's advisers for all of this? Certainly not the expatriates who had been in Somalia in 1989, which raises a whole slew of further questions. If few U.S. citizens working in Somalia prior to collapse had seemed to really appreciate what most Somalis were up against, would people with less experience be able to understand more?

Months before the full humanitarian invasion was launched, when the State Department was just beginning to coordinate the first U.S.-sponsored food shipments into Somalia I called to speak to someone on the Somalia desk. I was curious to know who *was* advising the government, not because I thought I should but because I knew how few Somaliists there were in this country and how fractured even their sense of Somalia might be. I was really only curious, and a little worried. Already it seemed likely that without people who did know something admitting that they only knew some things, the same old conceit of knowledge would cause the United States to do things all of us might later regret.

Revealingly I was told by two different government officials that they were essentially only talking to people who had up-to-the-minute information on the political situation in Somalia and knew who the key Somali players might be. They needed information. They needed facts. This is when I knew U.S. initiatives were doomed.

Of course, from the perspective of policymakers knowledge without understanding would make sense. One definition of chaos is senselessness. There was chaos in Somalia. What more did one need to understand?

But although it may have looked on the surface as though there was confusion—and anarchy—that did not mean there was no structure to what was occurring. Traditionally Somalis had never had a social structure outsiders could see. For instance, pastoral nomadism does not produce government buildings or permanent edifices. Yet nomads can very quickly tell where they stand vis-à-vis one another, depending on who they happen to be standing with at the time. In this book I have attempted to explain how pastoralist ideology, and many pastoralist principles proved useful in Mogadishu and "modern" life. On numerous counts, then, not only were Somalis working with a social structure outsiders were unfamiliar with and unused to, but Somalis were also adept at reworking this structure, situationally.

These were the facts that all outside judgments should have been based on, not who was allied with whom at the moment. Without context what could such associations mean anyway? After all, who was allied with whom today in Mogadishu could not predict how fallings-out might occur tomorrow, or new alliances be put together the day after. Thinking in terms of how and why segmentation works, it is the past, even more than the present, that predicts the future and how former ties, former enmities, former suspicions, former jealousies, former favors, yield groups that will or will not throw in together.

On the one hand, although segmentation and recognizing the lines of fissure can structurally explain much—the fighting in Mogadishu, for instance, between Abgal and Habr Gedir Hawiye—Somalia's unraveling was actually far more complex than just the Hawiye opposing one another when no one opposed them *in* Mogadishu, yet coalescing whenever they faced opposition from Darood without. Even understanding structure can't explain everything.

What about Hawiye former ministers who had shared prison cells with Darood former ministers? What about school ties, or connections made through the workplace? Without question (or compunction) someone's tribal connection could serve as a convenient excuse for killing him. But former ties could just as easily save his life, broker a deal, divert the most hostile of intentions.

I am not sure policymakers understood either Somalis' social structure or how sentiment tempered this. For instance, as a catchphrase "ancient ethnic hatreds" seemed perfectly designed for making deeper understanding seem all the more superfluous. Once it was uttered history was outlined: What more did anyone need to know except that Darood and Hawiye were not getting along, Hawiye were fighting among themselves, and Raxahnweyn farmers were starving. The content of those relationships was immaterial, even though content and meaning was at least a portion of what Somalis were fighting over in their contests to see who would control whom.

But it may not have been policymakers' responsibility to have to delve this deeply. That is what desk officers, whether at the State Department, Department of Defense, USAID, or elsewhere, are for. They are the ones who are supposed to know what should be known. My suspicion is that they did not when it came to Somalia, and that all sorts of wrong assumptions were made beginning with them. But perhaps this is also less their fault than bureaucracy's.

After all, what can a desk officer do: admit that he or she does not fully know what is going on—or understand what has been going on—in the country he or she is responsible for being able to analyze? At the same time, government requires simplification. All the way up and down the chain of command, whether this is in the military, State Department, or White House, complicated situations must continually be boiled down. By the time descriptions reach key policymakers they must more often than not fit onto a single page, and this page, in turn, must be devoted more to recommendations for action than allusions to complication.

Nor was it just government officials simplifying. Others simplified for them. After all, where did most information have to come from? Ultimately all of it came (whether directly or second hand) from Somalis. And what were Somalis busy doing? Being as fluid as possible—in who they said what to, when, how, and why, whether they were in this country speaking with Senators or in Kenya responding to humanitarian relief consultants. Audiences were situational; so was what was worth supplying them. Plus, every Somali only represented a single perspective. Even if someone's report was objective, one would do well to remember that no Somali could be in complete command of all relevant information. If there had been no centralized, credible news or information source in July 1989, there was surely none in December 1992. Essentially, so long as fluidity is what the situation created fluidity was what was called for in Somalis' reactions. Flexibility—this is how one survived uncertainty *as* a "Somali."

Meanwhile, what about what had helped create this uncertainty? What of Somalia's—never mind just Somalis'—relationships? Policymakers also turned a blind eye to what had helped bring on dissolution in the first place: namely, aid. Worse, they acted even less aware when it came to what aid was achieving all over again, as the humanitarian assistance organizations paid pirates' ransoms to hired guns, bribed well-fed people in order to be able to deliver food to the starving, and otherwise created new inequities based on who they employed, elevated, and had to secure protection from.

There are eerie parallels to how the relief organizations descended on Somalia in 1978 and how they returned in 1992.[1] Relief is now an industry; it seeks business. Perhaps I would not be quite this cynical had heads of two different NGOs not admitted to me that the only reason their organizations were still in Somalia (despite impossible levels of corruption) in 1989 was because they expected there to be a major disaster or crisis in the near future; they needed to keep one foot in the door.

This is neither the time nor the place to question the motivations of individual relief volunteers (who deserve study in a book all their own). Rather, I merely want to point to a further set of parallels: between the role of relief agencies in drawing the United States/UN in to assist them in the 1990s and the role of European missionaries in Africa prior to colonialism (before the turn of the last century). In fact, in a number of cases missionaries were directly responsible for colonial takeovers by the countries they hailed from. Intervention came in response to their passionate pleas, as they fervently argued that they needed to be protected in order to save souls—not too dissimilar from the needs of new humanitarian missionaries to save bodies. Another parallel resides in the use of numbers. However, at least one difference should have loomed larger: Africa was remote then. Given the speed with which the medium becomes the message these days, Africa should no longer be so remote, which brings us to the dubious role of the media in Operation Restore Hope, and their witting or unwitting (?) collusion with the relief organizations.

One of the problems journalists faced as the Somali "story" broke was that reporters had not been in Somalia in years. Thus, there was very little institutional memory among members of the Fourth Estate. Journalists found themselves having to rely on others for background. Conveniently, the humanitarian assistance organizations were already in Somalia; they were eager for the story to get out. In fact, they proved critical in getting the story out, not only logistically, but by supplying the local expertise reporters lacked. Unfortunately, though, this expertise was also informed by an agenda: Relief organizations do not just assist, they need assistance to do so. The relief agencies had to solicit donor dollars and, given the anarchic situation, serious armed protection as well. Journalists provided them with the perfect vehicle for heralding their cause.

The U.S. government then responded much as France and Britain had to missionaries in the past. The cavalry was assembled, and Operation Restore Hope launched.

Doubtless there are many reasons for President Bush's decision to initiate Operation Restore Hope, some of which I have surmised about elsewhere.[2] However, what they were is almost immaterial. Operation Restore Hope satisfied a number of micro-agendas—the marines would get an amphibious landing, the army real world training, news anchormen a dramatic backdrop, relief organizations new infusions of money, the public would get to eat dinner again without having to watch Somali children starve in their television screens, and politicians could breathe easier without members of the public clamoring over this distant famine.

Together these separate agendas happened to converge. Sadly, this was not because anyone put them together in a big picture or any one among the proponents of intervention was wholly informed. Each was only partially informed, looking through their own particular window of opportunity. For instance, so long as the mission was just feeding people Somalia looked doable. So long as it was just keeping people from firing weapons it looked feasible. So long as achieving food security was the only goal it could be done. From within these separate windows, Somalia seemed eminently salvageable. Between agendas, however, were monumental walls. Or to break away from the metaphor, there were disconnects—in the knowledge, information, *and* understanding each party interested in intervention bore. This, as much as anything, undid Operation Restore Hope.

Thanks in part to the disconnects between what people actually knew, thought they knew, and didn't know, an accurate big picture never got painted for top policymakers. Nor could one have been, which is basically my point. Dissolution does not have *a* storyline.

Meanwhile, there was also a fundamental series of disconnects at yet another level. I do not know exactly how to characterize this level, but it emerged as politicians (especially) talked as if they knew nothing about politics in the aftermath of the U.S. Army Ranger tragedy in early October 1993, which then precipitated U.S. troop withdrawal by March 1994.

While dust from this final attempt to capture General Mohamed Farah Aideed was still settling, congressmen were lining up on the floor of Congress to shake their fists from the podium. Suddenly, more U.S. soldiers than usual had died in Operation Restore Hope; clearly the mission must have changed. It was not meant to be bloody, but humanitarian. Obviously, the politicians bellowed, the United States had become politically embroiled. There must have been mission drift; this was outrageous.

Nonsense. The soldiers had not strayed, nor had anyone jerked the rug out from under congressmen. Being generous, it was they who had been caught sleeping. Worse, they had deluded themselves from the outset.

There is no such thing as purely humanitarian assistance. From the moment the United States intervened (and arguably before that) U.S. citizens were involved in local Somali politics. As soon as the first official U.S. citizen was back on Somali soil the United States government had enmeshed itself—by who U.S. citizens were talking to first, second, third, in which part of Mogadishu, under whose control, and so on. And that is only for starters. There was also the issue of famine relief. Congress had voted appropriations for famine relief numerous times before. It has been clear for more than a decade that famine, unlike drought, is a political problem. From the outset the rhetoric stated that U.S. soldiers were intervening in Somalia to save Somalis from famine. There is no way the United States could alleviate Somalia's famine without intevening in Somali politics. Who made for the disconnect here?

All of this, however, is to not even delve into the past. Clearly no one paid much attention to the fact that, given the United States's history of assistance to Somalia, Somalis would have certain expectations of the United States, the very thing that had so turned U.S. expatriates off before.

Expectation almost brings us full circle, but not quite. Even if policymakers did not realize how much of what they were doing in 1992–1993 fit old patterns of what others had done, Somalis were well aware. In fact, the mission name—Operation Restore Hope—perhaps best epitomizes just how miscalculated U.S. intentions were. On the one hand it revived expectations. On the other hand it promised restoration. But of what? For whom? At the same time, what was delivered did indeed line certain pockets, accord select individuals power, create new inequities, and breed all sorts of suspicions. That is on the small scale.

On the larger scale the purpose behind the mission was never very clear. Was it just to feed starving Somalis *or* to restore some semblance of order; Somalis certainly knew to what extent one would be impossible without the other, which raised a far larger question: Why? Why Somalia?—and not Angola, Liberia, the Sudan, or any one of a number of other places? People were in dire straits all over the world. Obviously Somalia had to have something the United States and the rest of the world wanted. Otherwise, why did the world suddenly profess so much interest in a country it had abandoned a mere three years before? The rhetoric of humanitarianism had to be a smokescreen. There had to be some hidden purpose. Why else would the United States return?

Did policymakers understand that this is what many Somalis had to be thinking? It seems not. But then, Somalia is hardly the only place where misunderstandings seem to know no end. Logics have been growing increasingly impermeable elsewhere too.

Notes

Chapter 1

1. At the time it was acknowledged that the American embassy in Mogadishu was the second most expensive facility in sub-Saharan Africa, the first being the embassy in Gabarone, Botswana.

2. This is the hotel owned by Ali Mahdi Mohamed.

3. Of course, many of the expatriates' assumptions about Islam came from the wider world and were assumptions they had brought with them to Somalia either from their own direct experience in other Muslim countries or from general knowledge about world events. I do not think it would be inaccurate to suggest that much of what informed the expatriate attitude toward Islam in Somalia stemmed from a general (and generalizable) fear that something like the fundamentalist revolution in Iran could occur in any Muslim country, and U.S. citizens in particular (given the fact that it had been U.S. hostages taken from the American Mission in Tehran) would be most vulnerable. This suspicion and wariness, coupled with a genuine lack of curiosity about Muslim beliefs (as opposed to practices) or Islam-as-practiced *in* Somalia, allowed expatriates to further convince themselves that Islam opposed them. Logically, then, they also viewed themselves as being in opposition to Islam, only lending further credibility to their already besieged mentality.

4. None of what I describe can be applied to Italians. The Italian expatriate community, composed of many part-time permanent residents, was decidedly different, in large part because it was grounded in a different, more long-term interest in, and commitment to, Somalia.

Chapter 2

1. These generalizations are based on close readings of Burton 1894/1987 (whose travels preceded James's); James 1888; Swayne 1900; Hamilton 1911/1970; Drake-Brockman 1912; Rayne 1921a; Jardine 1926/1969; Collins 1960; Hanley 1971/1987. A fuller analysis appears in Simons 1992.

2. For all intents and purposes, USAID, GTZ, the WFP, and the World Bank played the largest roles in the project. This is because USAID and GTZ expatriates were most visible, the WFP rations served as coinage in the field, and World Bank officials occasionally visited on supervisory trips.

3. South Asians were often cast in a dishonest light. Perhaps because many were members of Somalia's merchant class. Alternatively, more recently many South

Asians had worked as accountants in a good number of the multinational (particularly UN) agencies.

4. Revealingly, his actions never ceased to suggest that he was far more interested in pursuing plants than in furthering any long-term project goals, although having said that, there was not a single one of his Somali counterparts who did not admire the sheer intensity with which he attacked his work. Most of the other expatriates did not even come near earning the kind of respect his counterparts paid him.

Chapter 3

1. For northern/pastoralist trade patterns see Pankhurst 1965a, 1965b; Lewis 1969b; Hersi 1977; Abir 1980; A. I. Samatar 1989; and A. Y. Farah 1988. For southern patterns see Lewis 1969a; Luling 1971; Puzo 1972; Lewis 1980; Cassanelli 1982; Alpers 1983; and Helander 1988.

2. New work is being done by Francesca Declich on these questions, and I am grateful to her for broadening my sense of the range of possibilities..

3. Renderings of the region's history vary considerably depending on the primary sources used by historians as well as their regional slant. In addition to sources directly focused on the history of Somalia (i.e., Kaplan 1960; Touval 1963; Hess 1966; Lewis 1980; A. I. Samatar 1988) the following are my primary sources: Seton-Watson 1967 and Smith 1977 (on Italian involvement); Thompson and Adloff 1968 (on Djibouti and the French role); Gavin 1975 (on the British and Aden); Rubenson 1976 (on Ethiopia and the European powers); Kinross 1977 (on the Ottoman Empire and the European powers); Laitin 1977 (on Somalia and the European powers); Sanderson 1985 (on Egypt, the Horn, and the European powers).

4. Again, there may be foreshadowing here. During Operation Restore Hope, Muslim fundamentalists were also in Somalia providing humanitarian assistance in rural areas.

5. One of Siad Barre's tactics in prosecuting his government's war against the SNM (Somali National Movement) was to arm Ogadeni refugees in UNHCR (United Nations High Commission for Refugees) camps in northern Somalia and encourage them to help him in fighting the Isaq.

6. Three things should be noted about this control. First, the British dismantled virtually all Italian industry in Somalia, shipping locomotives, railroad track, electric generating plants, and even tractors to theaters of operation elsewhere. This stripped Italian Somaliland (and as a result the country) of what little manufacturing capability it possessed. Second, the British, in their ongoing attempts to pacify the tribes, disarmed the Ogaden, while allowing northern clans to remain armed. Thus, whether or not the British actually favored other clans, the Ogaden felt persecuted. Similarly, British actions (such as closure of the salt works at Ras Hafun) created hardships for select other groups (i.e., the Majertein). Third, this sudden enforced territorial union of the Ogaden and both Somalilands suggested national, regional, and ethnic Somali unity and set the stage for formation of the Somali Youth Club (later the Somali Youth League), a protonationalist organization (Pankhurst 1951).

7. Because liberated Ethiopia had (belatedly) been a World War II ally, the British government was accused (by Haile Selassie) of having made certain promises

including the return of the Haud and the Ogaden. Also, powerful U.S. oil interests wanted to see Ethiopia rewarded and enhanced. At the same time, Britain was more interested in retaining control in Libya than in Somalia, while the Western powers were eager to keep Italy in the Western non-Communist fold. Thus, a compromise effort was made to placate the Italians.

Chapter 4

1. Also, there is no agreement yet on what clans coalesce for, whether they are ancient or modern, or whether clanship should even be regarded as the most salient organizing principle among Somalis (see Chapter Twelve for further discussion of this).

2. It would certainly seem that Somali politics is best explained genealogically. For instance, Touval (1963) describes the five main political groupings active at Independence in 1960 according to clan-family or clan affiliations. However, not every lineage or branch within the same clan or clan-family joined the same party. Two of the clan-families—Hawiye and Darood—were both split between at least two parties. How can we account for this?

Simply put, geography would dictate at least one rationale for otherwise illogical-seeming splits within clan-families. This is because in some situations geographical proximity may well outweigh genealogy as a determinant of allegiance. Also, although lineages may have been the structural building blocks (into clans and clan-families), the ground is more cluttered than neat. For instance, a stable democratically elected government has to rely on a balance at the national level, which often contravenes the balance (or lack of balance) that exists at the local level. Balance achieved nationally, with one Hawiye carefully placed in this position and a Darood in that position, will not necessarily translate outside of Mogadishu, where in any given area most people would be *either* Darood *or* Hawiye (or Isaq, Raxanweyn, etc.), and more specifically still from X or Y lineages and not A or B clans. Hence, there is constant potential for friction at the national level over what is taking place locally, which can't be translated nationally. At the same time, what is being posited nationally has the potential for alienating local power blocks.

3. This coup came only six days after the "legally" elected president was assassinated. Although this assassination clearly paved the way for Siad Barre's takeover, the president-elect's death was not necessarily the trigger for the coup. Supposedly corruption was. However, it is worth dwelling on the president-elect's assassination for a different reason. According to I. M. Lewis (who has long favored examining the national government according to the grammar of clan and lineage), the assassin was a policeman who "belonged to a lineage which had been persistently ill-treated by the President, and sought revenge rather than revolution." (1972, 400). By contrast, Ahmed Samatar, a Somali Somaliist of a more recent generation, merely describes the assassin as "a member of his [the president's] own police force" (1988, 75).

Although such a difference in these two Somaliists' approaches might seem minor and merely academic, it becomes pointedly apropos here precisely because it highlights the difficulties in reading the Somali situation (or any particular Somali event) any one way. At the same time it serves as a further reminder that the legitimacy of clans, as units of political analysis, is under advisement by some (Ahmed and Abdi Samatar, in particular, have demonstrated how else events in Somalia can be interpreted focusing on political economy instead). Nor is this "forgetting" the assassin's clan (or lineage) affiliation unusual. Rather, it is symptomatic of a much broader lived Somali history in which being able to forget clanship has often proved more useful than having to remember.

4. Interestingly, it should be pointed out, this deferral was made in alignment with Ethiopian desires; Ethiopia wanted no territorial adjustments in the Horn of Africa.

5. As with the supra-local history prior to independence, there are multiple views concerning the superpower interplay in the Horn of Africa. In addition to the histories of Somalia (i.e., Lewis 1980; Laitin and Samatar 1987; A. I. Samatar 1988) primary sources for this section are: Mehemet 1971; Farer 1976; Selassie 1980; Gorman 1981; Ottaway 1982; Shepherd 1985; and Patman 1990. Concerning the Ogaden War and its aftermath also see Laitin 1979, 1983; and Ododa 1985.

6. Socialism held all sorts of other appeals—particularly to Marxist intellectuals who were hardly marginal in Africa during this period.

7. Among a number of pressures: Somalia had what was said to be the most powerful army in sub-Saharan black Africa. And the government, although having publicly disavowed the Western Somali Liberation Front (whose raison d'être was freeing the Ogaden), had not banned it outright. This meant the movement was still in place, making it all the easier for it to wrest at least tacit government support in 1974, which elements in the army also sought.

8. Although the ultimate reason probably lay in geography—exacerbated by the Somalis' lack of accountability (and loyalty) from the Soviets' point of view—there were lesser reasons, too, for this Horn of Africa flip-flop, having to do with internal Soviet power plays as well as U.S. domestic politics (i.e., the paralysis of the new Carter administration) and Soviet and U.S. engagements elsewhere in the Third World (e.g., Angola).

9. One of the surviving officers involved in the coup indicated that the coup emerged from genuine discontent. He claimed that after three years in the Soviet army he was detained shortly after his return to Somalia in 1969, together with other officers opposed to Siad Barre. He was released from detention only once the Ogaden War broke out and he was sent to the front "where he could be 'conveniently eliminated'" (ARB May 1–31, 1978: 4853). Indeed, I heard similar embittered accounts of the "conscription" of former officers (out of detention) for participation in the Ogaden War—see Roble's life history in Chapter Five.

Chapter 5

1. Indeed, this has become more and more evident as time has gone by. With the initial violence in Mogadishu it was the Marehan who were cast as villains by all other groups. But as Mogadishu and then Somalia fell apart (after December 1990) and the clan-family-based opposition groups began to exert regional control, it was members of the president's clan-family—all the Darood—who were targeted by the Hawiye and no longer just the Marehan.

2. Interestingly, by 1986 the government's official refugee figures, long heralded by relief agencies and the press alike, were in dispute:

> The whole question of the number of refugees present in Somalia has become a sensitive political issue. The UNHCR, hampered by cuts in its own budget, has reduced its contribution to Somalia over the years. The Somali authorities are accused of inflating the figures in order to keep up the flow of foreign aid. The findings of a census taken in 1981 were disputed and disregarded in favor of a compromise planning figure of 700,000, which has remained the official estimate ever since. (ACR 1986–1987: B412).

Of course, the timing of the discovery of this error was motivated by more than just UNHCR budget cuts (since surely it did not take five years to realize that a reproductively active population had shrunk by half)—raising questions of complicity in corruption.

3. Initiated in 1970, or 1976 according to *Africa Confidential.*

4. In subsequent studies it has been demonstrated that *franco valuta* was not inflationary but deflationary (Hoben 1983).

5. According to AC the SNM was founded in 1980 although other sources indicate it was founded in 1981.

6. This was a predominantly Majerteini movement founded in response to (or in conjunction with) Siad Barre's 1978 execution of six Majertein officers. Three things are worth nothing: It has gone through a number of transformations over the years, was not always only Majerteini, and never represented all Majertein (some of whom continued to support the regime).

Part 3

1. I examine the significance of this in more detail and consider how July 14 may yet be canonized as a watershed period in (Simons forthcoming).

2. Sources for this section chiefly comprise *Africa Confidential* (AC), *Africa Diary* (AD), *Africa Research Bulletin* (ARB), and the *Indian Ocean Newsletter* (ION). Here it may also be worth noting that both *Africa Confidential* and the *Indian Ocean Newsletter,* the two most comprehensive sources, very often shared the same wording about the same events.

Chapter 6

1. For some years the DSSF had received arms and funding from Libya, but with the 1985 rapprochement between Siad Barre and Gadhafi, Libya as a source dried up and the DSSF became moribund, only lately reviving as the SSDF (ION Oct. 8, 1988; Dec. 24, 1988).

2. In addition, there is always the very real possibility that Saudi Arabia was being held for "ransom" by Siad Barre in terms of Somalia's potential in oil. With the apparent discovery of oil fields in North Yemen, oil companies were expressing a great deal of interest in Somalia (ION Oct. 22, 1988). If the common Somali conjecture is correct—that there *is* oil, but the Saudis and other Persian Gulf Arabs have been bribing those in power to pretend there is no oil to minimize competition—then Siad Barre's ability to hold something over the Saudis' head would stand to reason.

Alternatively, Saudi Arabia and Egypt alike may have willingly done favors for Siad Barre in return for his not giving Islamic fundamentalists safe haven. According to rumors, Abu Nidal (among other terrorists) had been sighted in Mogadishu, suggesting that Somalia was a relatively easy country in which to hide out.

3. Interestingly, neither journal cites the 1975 demonstrations led primarily by Muslim leaders opposed to promulgation of scientific socialism's Family Law, and almost immediately after which ten Muslim clerics were executed, having been arrested for preaching against the law in their mosques (Nelson 1982).

Chapter 7

1. "Official Americans" were all those working for the United States government, either directly, at the embassy, USAID, USOMC (United States Office for Military Cooperation), or under contract. "Unofficial Americans" were PVO and NGO workers as well as U.S. citizens employed by multilateral agencies, such as the World Bank or United Nations. For example, CRDP expatriates were "official Americans" because they were being paid for with USAID funding, through LBI. "Unofficial Americans" had no privileges at any U.S. embassy facility, were not on the U.S. embassy walkie-talkie net, and for all intents and purposes did not exist as far as U.S. officialdom in Mogadishu was concerned. I, luckily, was in an "official" house when the shooting began.

2. A deeper meaning was put on the German pullout by several German aid workers: The German government had been eager to scale back its commitments to Somalia for some time (GTZ was no longer as flush as it once was); this offered the perfect opportunity.

3. Some people actually looked forward to a Soviet return, since they felt there had been much less corruption and tribalism under the Soviets.

4. Although it is possible the shortage was a real one related to the massive expenditures paid to nomads for livestock transshipped to Saudi Arabia for the hajj in early July.

Part 4

1. These Somalis fall into a number of categories: principally educated civil servants whom expatriates worked with and domestic workers (*boyessas* and drivers) who worked for them. I describe these categories in greater depth elsewhere (Simons 1992), but should add here that expatriates held many misconceptions about these Somalis who tended to be the only Somalis they interacted with on a more than superficial basis. For instance, many *boyessas* (most of whom had to speak English in order to work for English-speaking expatriates) were from middle-class backgrounds and were socially mobile; they were hardly illiterate or poor.

2. Unfortunately, although the commercialization of herds has had numerous critical impacts on Somalia's rural economy, close consideration of changes in actual pastoral practices is beyond my scope here. Clearly, changing pastoral principles have impacted urban as well as rural Somalis. I do not want to suggest otherwise. However, my emphasis is on broad principles of what I call pastoral ideology and how these have infiltrated the urban setting as part of change.

3. This figure was widely cited in conversation in Mogadishu, as was the fact that 60 percent of Somalis were still nomadic.

4. I would suggest that traders on the Benaadir coast and those who mixed with them were similarly dismissable as foreign, before they were swamped by the post-colonial influx of pastoralists.

5. Although many towns could be found throughout Somalia I did not consider them urban. Population was not concentrated in them, they had no industry, and so on. They were essentially commercial and administrative centers that acted as way stations, serving as places people could come to from out of the bush, gain a sedentarized foothold, and if successful move on from—to Mogadishu (or, presumably, Hargeisa).

Chapter 8

1. Of course, some people did purchase herds, but they themselves did not return to the bush. Instead, they farmed the herds out to relatives or hired herders to manage their investments; they not only did not return to the subsistence economy themselves, they purchased livestock for the purposes of marketing them; the animals *were* an investment.

Chapter 9

1. My comments on the nature and changing nature of pastoralism are informed by theoretical outlines provided in Dahl and Hjort 1976, 1979; Horowitz 1979; Salzman 1980; Galaty 1981; Western 1982; Anderson and Johnson 1988; and Smith 1992 among others.

2. This is not to assume that many of these same criteria do not apply in other settings as well, or that they are not universal, to a certain extent, in the developing world. Perhaps it is merely another fortunate confluence that pastoralism is "designed" to cope with uncertainties, and developing countries are full of economic and resource-related uncertainties as far as their citizens are concerned; it therefore appears that Somalis' reactions are pastoralist reactions when, in fact they simply epitomize what would be most salient under such circumstances—although I would suggest that (as expatriates well realized) Somalis were unusally adept at making opportunities out of scarcity, hardship, and uncertainty.

3. Although these are often elided through intermarriage, intermarriages are not common enough to blur the distinctions or merge two groups—except in rare cases, such as that of the Ariaal (Fratkin 1986) and the Ilgira Samburu (Hjort 1981) in northern Kenya. Boundaries have always been permeable by individuals (Wolf 1982). However, many neighboring tribes in East Africa are detectably different from one another linguistically and physiognomically (either structurally or because of scarification), particularly when they raise similar stock in similar ways: that is to say the Nuer and Dinka, Dinka and Shilluk, Rendille and Gabra, Rendille and Somali, and so on. One could speculate at great length about why this might be the case among these groups but not among Somali pastoralists and about what this says about tribal definitions and the use of "Somali" *as* a tribal definition. However, although I cannot address this issue in the fullness that it deserves, I have hinted at Somalis' convenient self-definition and in Chapter Twelve I will address the need for

Somalis to determine "in" groups and "out" groups without relying on the kinds of distinctions that tribes elsewhere normally display. Again, although the "why" and "for" behind these determinations are intriguing, they are beyond the scope of this work.

Chapter 10

1. I must point out here that there were many residents of Mogadishu for whom the following descriptions won't hold true. These were the small artisans and shopkeepers who sold their services and goods directly to other Somalis and did not rely on the government either for employment or "business" opportunities. The Somalis I am concerned with remain the same Somalis expatriates were likeliest to run into—either in offices, in the few Somali-run shops expatriates patronized, in airports, or other settings where expatriates and Somalis would be likely to meet. I am grateful to Lee Cassanelli for reminding me how misleading generalizations can be.

2. Of course, this is precisely why marriage could prove so difficult to attain. Money *was* the hurdle there, suggesting a breaking point between being able to survive and being able to reproduce. And not just at the individual level; so long as this was true for individuals it was true for society.

3. Davies (1988) concentrates a chapter of his study of poverty in Mogadishu on assistance and loans, since these were what allowed so many of his survey subjects to subsist. However, he does not address *qaaraan* per se.

4. "The dia-paying group are pledged to support each other in collective political and jural responsibility, and in particular, in the payment and receipt of compensation in respect of actions committed by or against their group" (Lewis 1961: 6). Or, as it can be more concretely explained: To resolve feuds in particular, *dia* was collected to compensate the relatives of victims for the loss of the victim's life.

5. Although in the urban setting it could also subsume *dia*.

6. In some instances *dia* was also calculated according to the number of male sons a household head had.

7. Doubtless there were elements of honor at stake as well, and preventable failure reflected on family honor and family standing and was thus something that devolved on the family to mitigate and ward off.

8. I assume there were also other means received through the mosques and the religious community and methods for providing assistance to the destitute, down-and-out, and abandoned who had suffered more than just temporary setbacks.

9. Again—this across-the-board solicitation also hinted at the common knowledge that even the lowliest civil servant might have extraordinarily important or lucrative connections, thus resulting in the generalized attitude that every relationship was worth nurturing. Also, one never knew who may suddenly have received a windfall.

Chapter 11

1. Again, I must note that not all Somalis in Mogadishu were similarly employed. Clearly, artisans and small shopkeepers would have had very different interests, strategies, and tactics for coping with economic conditions than members

of the government-employed middle class. Also, numerous Mogadishu residents had ties to the rural South, to agriculture, and to Italy, and not to central, northern, or northeastern Somalia, pastoralism, or the Persian Gulf as do many of the Somalis I describe.

2. For a further comparison, see Parker Shipton's elucidations about "bitter money" for the Luo (Shipton 1989) and Sharon Hutchinson's distinctions between cattle *for* and cattle *from* bridewealth among the Nuer (1992).

3. Virtually all members of Mogadishu's middle and educated class that I spoke with had at least one close relative they defined as being a merchant or otherwise involved in commerce.

4. Figures of 200,000–300,000 Somalis abroad in the Persian Gulf have often been bandied about, but no one has put very much faith in these figures and no accurate count has ever been made.

Chapter 12

1. What is intriguing about the contradictions in the ethnographic literature is that most ethnographers note cross-cutting ties, whether age-set (Spencer 1973; Evans-Pritchard 1940/1978), religious (Lewis 1961, 1965), stock associate (Gulliver 1955) or affinal (Marx 1967). Generally, these are the very types of tie that pastoralism would seem to require, since they guarantee individuals nets of assistance beyond the immediate genealogy; all eggs are not put in the kinship basket, just as all animals are not left in one herd. With fluidity a necessity given uncertainties in the environment, and movement one of the few constants, cross-cutting ties also provide a method for fixing the identity of nonrelated strangers. These ties allow for this without being fixed themselves. Thus, non-kin connections exist and are purposely not invested with permanency, which could undermine genealogy—the primordial but certainly not the only (or necessarily most useful) identifier.

Nevertheless, it *was* genealogy that appeared to be central—and genealogical ties to be the central ties—to the first generation of ethnographers who concentrated on pastoralists.

2. From 1990 through 1994 one way for armed groups to decide whether someone was friend or foe was to get them to speak and give away the region they hailed from.

3. Segmentary lineage opposition is most easily described by the saying, "I against my brother, my brother and I against my cousin, my cousins and I against the world." In other words, whether conflict is contained or expanded depends (1) on the situation and (2) on who is involved.

4. The conditions for the time when Evans-Pritchard was studying the Nuer are well documented by Johnson and suggest Nuer unity in the face of encroaching slave and ivory frontiers (Johnson 1981). As for Somalia prior to Independence, documented large-scale unities seem only to have emerged in the face of external threats by Ethiopian and European colonial forces (Cassanelli 1982; A. I. Samatar 1988). Intriguingly, these appear to be the only instances when there has been large enough scale unity to prove that opposition steadily mounts and escalates (see Boehm [1984] for a Mediterranean twist on this). This issue is something I intend to address in greater detail in a future publication.

Of course, the popularity of the segmentary lineage model has declined for other, anthro-historical reasons. Nevertheless, the structural principles on which it is based are still quite evident in our conceptualizations of how ethnic groups mobilize. Indeed, the Us/Them dichotomy that we now wring our hands over reflects the same old binary problem.

At bottom the problem with any binary approach is that it attempts to describe all behavior—individual, lineage, clan, tribe—as a matter of balanced oppositions. However, this cannot be accurate. In such a system there could never be long-term winners or losers. Yet, history indicates that some lineages, clans, and tribes have disappeared (if not wholly, through decimation, then by being subsumed into others) (Schlee 1989). At the same time, some individuals have clearly done better than others and have been able to pass on their successes (whether substantively through large herds, or reflectively through honor). More to the point, the model, by being so structurally binary, results in a mechanically binary depiction of action: Either people are mobilized to confront one another or they are not; they are turned "on" or they are not, just as alliances are turned on or off and, writ much larger, tribalism itself is made to seem an either on-again, off-again phenomenon.

Meanwhile, there is no explanation beyond self-interest proffered for why individuals might suddenly feel mobilized or why different events might elicit different responses at different times and how these, rather than lineage rules, evoke allegiance to group. I would suggest that group-interest may be something quite separate and different from the sum total of individual interests such that there can be ideologically based acts of altruism as well as genuine sentiment for pursuance of solidarity.

I would also suggest that on closer examination our (human) ability to think in terms of the group goes a long way toward explaining many social anthropologists' discomfort with sociobiological and inclusive fitness theorizing. Or alternatively, this may well explain the feeling among many people that humans *are* different from other animals: "We" (the singular, royal, or collective "we") *can* act for the good of the group, implying automatically that we also do think in terms of "we" different from an aggregate of "I"s.

5. And I would include in this category Western-educated native-born academics who, for a wide variety of reasons, tend to be detribalized.

6. Clearly this is also the basis for Rosaldo's critique of anthropology in "Grief and a Headhunter's Rage" (*Culture and Truth,* 1989).

7. And here I am not referring to class groups or gender divisions. Most Somalis, in everyday discourse, euphemistically discussed clans/tribes and although all Somalis were aware of socioeconomic differences as well as differences in gender roles, these were not the divisions which dominated most non-intellectuals' conversation. However, it is crucial to note that the strong correlations between socio-economic differentiation and clan affiliation were widely recognized. But it was not wealth or class per se that people condemned; instead, it was the privileged position of certain clans and their monopolistic access to the resources of government that angered people most, and caused their own *reactively* "tribal" hackles to rise.

Thus, although differential access to controllable wealth did create and exacerbate intertribal tensions I think few Somalis would deny that incipient lines of fracture existed. This is what tribalism was about. Positioning by some members of some tribes is why so many Somalis regarded Somalia as divided by tribe.

8. As John Davis has written, "Wunis [who did not believe in tribalism] was saying that although you can opt out among friends, your enemies will never believe your non-combatant status to be anything but a ruse. It would be rational for them to assume the worst possible case from their point of view, and so they imposed solidarities on you by their expectations of how you ought to behave" (Davis 1987, 103–104).

9. See Meyer Fortes' description of the axiom of amity (Fortes 1969) and Walker Connor (1994: 105).

10. Iran and Afghanistan would offer an interesting contrast. Tapper (1983, 66), too, recognizes the significance of shared morality within the tribe. However, he pursues a different direction and arrives at a conclusion for Iran and Afghanistan that the Somali case would seem to counter, but that is beyond the scope of our concern here.

11. This view may be historically substantiated if we consider the sources of most interclan (or tribal) fighting: grazing grounds and water sources. In most cases, there was probably nothing particular that differentiated one grazing ground or watering hole from another except the presence, at that particular moment in time, of good grazing or good water.

I should make one other suggestion: Historically there may have been more than just a productive practicality motivating intergroup conflict. Indeed, water and grazing may often have been used as an excuse for provocation. Fighting and raiding may well have been activities of social relief and release for young men in particular. Other possibilities, which have not yet been sufficiently discounted in the literature, include fighting as a way to recoup livestock losses and as an avenue to enhanced prestige (Turney-High 1949/1991). Disregarding the motivation behind conflict, in order for it to have served any purpose, "in" groups and "out" groups had to have existed. This would have required recognizable markers of easily (sensibly) distinguishable difference.

12. I believe this is also why lineage politics are beginning to break down in settled settings (Lewis 1969a; Luling 1971; Helander 1986, 1988). Permanence in villages and settlements allows for different measures of trust than fluid situations require, where quick judgments often carry sentences of life or death.

13. An important work suggesting how slippage has occurred historically among proto-Somali groups in Northern Kenya is Gunther Schlee's *Identities on the Move* (1989). Schlee questions the value of using the term "tribe" and documents numerous instances of "whole" clans switching alliances, and traditions. It seems clear from his work that larger umbrella groups existed (such as the Borana), which through their strength, were able to command allegiance. Depending on fluctuations in the strength of these dominant groups, individuals and individual clans at various points had to decide who they felt most affinity for or safest by joining. The fact that slippage and switches were relatively easy indicates the potential for momentary ambiguity as well as the potential that the existence of cross-cutting ties provides.

Part 5

1. This has also been cited as a *pastoralist* strategy in the face of changes to pastoralism, whereby pastoralists are purposely sloughed off by the system as intentional diversification (Dahl and Hjort 1979; Horowitz 1979; Salzman 1980;

Anderson and Johnson 1988)—and has been specifically documented for Kenyan Somalis (in Merryman 1984).

2. One note: there are many segments drawn from life histories in the following chapters. I consider my interpretations of them to be suggestive, but not conclusive; my sample is not broad enough to be definitive or to squeeze rates or percentages from. However, I should add that even if I could work with numbers I am not sure I would. Too often the crux of pastoralist existence—variability—goes unaccounted for, with statistics belying the pastoralist requirement that herd compositions and structures vary widely pastoralist to pastoralist depending on household size, structure, age, and proximity to others. Consequently I also believe aggregate figures would only obviate and hide why two individuals marry or are married, how negotiations are conducted, and why they then result in what they do. Ditto for considerations of bridewealth. Bridewealth has perhaps been the most studied aspect of marriage in livestock-producing societies. And again, most often it is the numbers (of animals, animals converted to money, money representing animals) that count in trying to understand meanings of bridewealth. However, here too comparions based on numbers gloss variability and are too divorced from the reality I am interested in: why youth regard bridewealth as *the* bottleneck to marriage.

Chapter 13

1. Under Islam polygyny is generally regarded as allowed. Men may have up to four wives simultaneously, although many men who marry more than once marry more than four times and shed wives through divorce. It is widely acknowledged that, as the Koran dictates, every woman must be treated equally, which means every woman must receive equivalent support (and similar gifts). The Koran also prescribes rules of inheritance: There is no preference accorded children of one wife over children of another, or older children over younger children. As a result, jealousy appears to be muted between wives in regard to their children. Indeed, children of different wives often grow up with strong bonds. Nevertheless, there is jealousy between wives, over the apportionment of a husband's time, affection, and attentiveness toward his other wives.

2. Among my interviewees, *recent* means one or two generations ago (although some people even report their siblings having offered livestock *yarad*). I am referring to Mogadishu residents who are not Benaadiris, but immigrants from the bush. The problem with trying to map their historic differences is that although I know regional and sometimes clan origins I do not know individuals' lineages. People used the potentially expansive word "*family*" (*jamaa*) in their discussions with me. Thus, I use this term—rather than lineage, clan, clan-family, or tribe—to designate *a* difference, and because I do not know the magnitude, extent, depth, or actual significance of difference for all cases. Nevertheless, it was abundantly clear that "families" at some, if not all levels, did behave differently and adhered to different customs.

3. Sometimes the size and cost of the feast was taken into account in negotiating *yarad*.

Chapter 14

1. In the first instance the purpose for elopement was identical to that described by (or for) pastoralists, who certainly made use of this option whenever there was fear that one or both sets of parents would oppose a match. In the second instance *masafo* may indeed have received a new spin, since the likelihood of a nomad being able to manage a secret second marriage (hidden not only from his wife but from his new wife's parents) seems improbable.

A Rigorous Ending

1. I cannot possibly review the entire literature on nationalism or the potential collapse of nation-states. Hence, this is meant to be selective yet representative of a set of theorists who cross-reference one another within the loose bounds of social history.

2. Alternatively, if tribes are old (or even colonially-engineered) autonomous political units, and ethnic groups are new formations that result when tribes are engulfed by larger forces, then tribalism and ethnic mobilization resemble one another and can be confused in large part because solidarity within the ethnic group develops as if the ethnic group were a tribe (seeking political satisfaction); the fact of sentiment does not alter. However, one major distinction does call for closer scrutiny: It may be that sentiment expressing solidarity within the tribe holds different moral implications than that pursued through ethnic mobilization, such that there is an instrumental, even opportunistic nature to ethnic groupings, which bonds of tribal obligation subsume but also surpass.

Under colonialism, tribes were parochial collectivities allowed indirect rule and, in this sense, were granted semi-autonomous political powers (witness customary law, etc.). In the broadened postcolonial landscape, ethnic groups have emerged in order to seek, make or increase their stake in control over state resources that the state has proven incapable of protecting or pursuing for all of its citizens. With the scope of the setting having shifted, then, the goals and the gaze *have* changed. Under this rubric, tribalism and ethnic mobilization may even be said to exist in two quite different sets of historical conditions. However, given the penchant for recasting history and inventing tradition to create sentiment (Hobsbawm and Ranger 1983) such a distinction may still not be quite so discernible in the minds of those who feel bound.

3. Indeed, Richard Fardon—who sees the "invention" of ethnic identities making "an isolable type of difference which was not distinguished in a pre-colonial context"—(Fardon 1987, 179) makes this point for me: "I have emphasized the political conditions under which ethnicity crystallized as an autonomous form, and most especially the role of the State in this; some other writers have given prominence to the economic conditions associated with the spread of capitalist organization of production and marketing."

4. Although Laitin seems to set out to prove the opposite, there is plenty of proof in his 1983 article, particularly in the context of current conditions, to suggest that Somali identities have both broadened and narrowed over time, determining different uses for the concept of *a* Somali nationality.

5. During the late 1980s, and again in the aftermath of anarchy in the 1990s, a number of Somaliists and new students of Somalia (including a number of graduate students) turned increasing attention to the history, culture, and political economy of inter-riverine Somali populations. Whether defined as southerners, agriculturalists, Bantu Somalis, and the like, one aim of this new focus on these peoples has been to counter the portrayal of Somalis as nomadic pastoralists. Also implied in these revived studies (since seminal work on these same issues had been undertaken by Luling, among others, in the late 1960s) is a pointed, yet accurate criticism that those without a voice in Somalia have been too long marginalized not only by the Somali-powers-that-be, but by students of Somalia as well.

Indeed, after the 1993 Somali Studies Congress held in Boston numerous participants commented on the seriousness with which inter-riverine peoples were being considered, and reconsidered. Of course, in no small measure such interest also grew out of recent media attention about the famine and devastation in the Southwestern Triangle. But also there was a grassroots, even organized effort by many inter-riverine and coastal Somalis to approach scholars *in order* to set their record straight, and secure some sort of future in Somalia.

Still, no matter how significant and overdue this new interest and self-interest by/about/in nonpastoralists, this demand for recognition actually only makes my larger point for me. Pastoralist ideology *has* been dominant—therefore this reaction to it.

6. "Horizon of expectations" is a phrase I borrow from Peter Worsley (1968).

7. Sara Berry documents a similar situation and similar strivings in *Fathers Work for Their Sons* (1985).

8. Another notable exception to the overwhelming silence is Rene Lemarchand, who refers to expatriates as foreign "accomplices" who contribute to the "corruption syndrome" on multiple levels: as accomplices, exemplars, *and* silencers of criticism (Lemarchand 1988, 160).

Epilogue

1. And of course there are also parallels to how Burton had to purchase protection, prior to there being *a* Somalia.

2. *The Boston Globe,* November 22, 1992; *Washington Post,* December 6, 1992; *Africa News,* December 21, 1992–January 3, 1993; *Washington Post,* August 15, 1993.

Bibliography

Abir, M. "Ethiopia and the Horn of Africa," in Richard Gray (ed.), *The Cambridge History of Africa IV (c. 1600 to c. 1790)*. Cambridge: Cambridge University Press, 1975

———. *Ethiopia and the Red Sea: The Rise and Decline of the Solomonic Dynasty and Muslim-European Rivalry in the Region*. London: Frank Cass, 1980.

Abokor, Axmed Cali. *The Camel in Somali Oral Traditions*. Sweden: Motala Grafiska, 1987.

Abu-Lughod, Lila. "Zones of theory in the anthropology of the Arab world," *Annual Review of Anthropology* (1989).

Africa Confidential, 1981–1990.

Africa Contemporary Record, 1968/1969–1986/1987.

Africa Diary, 1973–1984.

Africa Events, 1985–1990.

Africa Report, 1982–1989.

Africa Research Bulletin, 1977–1990.

Alpers, Edward. "Muqdisho in the nineteenth century: A regional perspective," *Journal of African History* 24 (1983).

Anderson, Benedict. *Imagined Communities*. London: Verso, 1983/1991 (revised edition).

Anderson, David M., and D. H. Johnson, "Introduction: Ecology and society in northeast African history," in David M. Anderson and D. H. Johnson (eds.), *The Ecology of Survival: Case Studies from North African History*. Boulder: Westview Press, 1988.

Aronson, Dan. "Kinsmen and comrades: Towards a class analysis of the Somali pastoral sector," *Nomadic Peoples*, no. 7 (1980).

Balandier, Georges. *Political Anthropology*. New York: Pantheon Books, 1970.

Behnke, Roy Jr., and C. Kerven. "Herd management strategies among agro-pastoralists in the Bay Region, Somalia." Unpublished report, 1984.

Berry, Sara. "The food crisis and agrarian change in Africa: A review essay," *African Studies Review*, 27, no. 2, (1984).

———. *Fathers Work for their Sons: Accumulation, Mobility and Class Formation in an Extended Yoruba Community*. Berkeley: University of California Press, 1985.

———. "Social institutions and access to resources," *Africa* 59 (1989).

Black-Michaud, Jacob. *Cohesive Force: Feud in the Mediterranean and the Middle East*. New York: St. Martin's Press, 1975.

Boehm, Christopher. *Blood Revenge: The Anthropology of Feuding in Montenegro and Other Tribal Societies*. Lawrence: University of Kansas Press, 1984.

Bourdieu, Pierre. *Outline of a Theory of Practice*. Cambridge: Cambridge University Press, 1977.

Braudel, Fernand. *Civilization and Capitalism,* vols. 1–3. New York: Harper and Row, 1981, 1982, 1984.

Breuilly, John. *Nationalism and the State*. New York: St Martin's Press, 1982.

British Broadcasting Corporation (BBC), "Somalia Disturbances in Mogadishu," July 17, 1989.

Brunken, Heiko, and Wolfgang Haupt. "The importance of the Juba Valley for the development of agriculture in Somalia," in Peter Conze and Thomas Labahn (eds.), *Agriculture in the Winds of Change*. Germany: Saarbrucken-Schafbrucke, 1986.

Burton, John. "Ethnicity on the hoof: Economics of Nuer identity," *Ethnology* 20 (1981).

Burton, Richard. *First Footsteps in East Africa*. New York: Dover Publications, 1894/1987.

Cassam, Mohamed. "International market for Somali livestock, final report," RONCO. Unpublished report, 1987.

Cassanelli, Lee. *The Shaping of Somali Society: Reconstructing the History of a Pastoral People, 1600–1900*. Philadelphia: University of Pennsylvania Press, 1982.

Central Rangelands Development Project. Future range/livestock development strategies for the Central Rangelands of Somalia, proceedings of the seminar and workshop held in Mogadishu, Somalia, on March 24–27, 1986.

Chazan, Naomi, R. Mortimer, J. Ravenhill, and D. Rothchild (eds.), *Politics and Society in Contemporary Africa*. Boulder: Lynne Rienner Publishers, 1988.

Clark University. "Rural-urban exchange in the Kismayo region of Somalia." Unpublished report, 1988.

Cohen, Abner. *Custom and Politics in Urban Africa: A Study of Hausa Migrants in Yoruba Towns*. Berkeley: University of California Press, 1969.

———. *The Politics of Elite Culture: Explorations in the Dramaturgy of Power in a Modern African Society.* Berkeley: University of California Press, 1981.

Collins, Douglas. *A Tear for Somalia*. London: Jarrolds, 1960.

Comaroff, Jean. *Body of Power, Spirit of Resistance: The Culture and History of a South African People*. Chicago: University of Chicago Press, 1985.

Comaroff, John, and Jean Comaroff. *Ethnography and the Historical Imagination*. Boulder: Westview Press, 1992.

Connor, Walker. *Ethnonationalism*. Princeton: Princeton University Press, 1994.

Dahl, Gudrun, and Anders Hjort. *Having Herds: Pastoral Herd Growth and Household Economy.* Stockholm Studies in Anthropology vol. 2 (1976).

———. Pastoral Change and the Role of Drought. SAREC report R2, 1979.

Davidson, Basil. *The Black Man's Burden: Africa and the Curse of the Nation-State*. New York: Times Books, 1992.

Davies, Rick. *Xaafadda, Suuqa iyo Jidka: A Study of Disadvantaged Areas and Groups in Muqdisho, Somalia*. Mogadishu: UNICEF, 1988.

Davis, John. *Libyan Politics: Tribe and Revolution*. London: I. B. Taurus and Co., 1987.

Drake-Brockman, Ralph. *British Somaliland.* London: Hurst & Blackett, Ltd., 1912.
Dresch, Paul. *Tribes, Government, and History in Yemen.* Oxford: Clarendon Press, 1989.
Drysdale, John. *The Somali Dispute.* New York: Praeger, 1964.
Dualeh Abdalla, Raquiya Hagi. *Sisters in Affliction: Circumcision and Infibulation of Women in Africa.* London: Zed Press, 1982.
Durkheim, Emile. *The Division of Labor in Society.* New York: The Free Press, 1933/1984.
Ekeh, Peter. "Social anthropology and two contrasting uses of tribalism in Africa," *Comparative Studies in Society and History* 32 (1990).
Elmi, Ahmed. Management, foraging behavior, diet composition and forage quality of free-ranging but herded camels in CeelDheer District, Central Somalia. Ph.D. diss., Utah State University, 1989.
Evans-Pritchard, E. E. *The Nuer.* New York: Oxford University Press, 1940/1978.
———. *The Sanusi of Cyrenaica.* Oxford: Clarendon Press, 1949.
Farah, Ahmed Yusuf. The milk of the Boswellia forests: Frankincense production among pastoral Somali. Ph.D. diss., London School of Economics, 1988.
Fardon, Richard. "'African ethnogenesis': Limits to the comparability of ethnic phenomena," in Ladislav Holy (ed.), *Comparative Anthropology.* Oxford: Basil Blackwell, 1987.
Farer, Tom J. *War Clouds on the Horn of Africa: A Crisis for Detente.* New York: Carnegie Endowment for International Peace, 1976.
Ferguson, James. "The bovine mystique," *Man* 20, no. 4 (1985).
Fortes, Meyer. *Kinship and the Social Order.* Chicago: Aldine Publishing, 1969.
Fratkin, Elliot. "Stability and resilience in East African pastoralism: The Rendille and the Ariaal of Northern Kenya," *Human Ecology* 14, no. 3 (1986).
Freeman-Grenville, G.S.P. *The East African Coast: Selected Documents from the First to the Earlier Nineteenth Century.* London: Rex Collins, 1975.
Galaty, John. "Introduction: Nomadic pastoralists and social change—processes and perspectives," in John Galaty and P. Salzman (eds.), *Change and Development in Nomadic and Pastoral Societies.* Leiden, the Netherlands: E. J. Brill, 1981.
Gavin, R. J. *Aden Under British Rule, 1839–1967.* London: C. Hurst & Co., 1975.
Geertz, Clifford. "The integrative revolution," in Clifford Geertz (ed.), *Old Societies and New States: The Quest for Modernity in Asia and Africa.* London: Free Press, 1963.
Gellner, Ernest. *Saints of the Atlas.* Chicago: University of Chicago Press, 1969.
———. *Muslim Society.* Cambridge: Cambridge University Press, 1981.
———. *Nations and Nationalism.* Ithaca: Cornell University Press, 1983.
Geshekter, Charles. "Entrepreneurs, livestock and politics: British Somaliland, 1920–1950," presented at International Colloquium "Enterprises et entrepreneurs en Afrique, XIX et XX siecles," Universite Paris, VII, 1981.
Giddens, Anthony. *The Nation-State and Violence.* Berkeley: University of California Press, 1987.

Gluckman, Max. "Tribalism in modern British Central Africa," *Cahiers D'Etudes Africaines,* vol. 1, 1960.

Godelier, Maurice. *Perspectives in Marxist Anthropology.* Cambridge: Cambridge University Press, 1977.

Goldschmidt, Walter. "Independence as an element in pastoral social systems," *Anthropological Quarterly* 44, no. 3 (1971).

———. "A general model for pastoral social systems," in *Pastoral Production and Society.* Cambridge: Cambridge University Press, 1979.

Goody, Jack. *Technology, Tradition and the State in Africa.* London: Oxford University Press, 1971.

Gorman, Robert F. *Political Conflict on the Horn of Africa.* New York: Praeger, 1981.

Greenfield, Richard. "An Embattled Barre," *Africa Report.* May–June 1987, pp. 26–29.

Guidieri, Remo, and Francesco Pelizzi. "Introduction: 'Smoking mirrors'—modern polity and ethnicity," in R. Guidieri, F. Pellizzi, and S. Tambiah (eds.), *Ethnicities and Nations: Processes of Interethnic Relations in Latin America, Southeast Asia, and the Pacific.* Austin: University of Texas Press, 1988.

Gulliver, P. H. *The Family Herds: A Study of Two Pastoral Tribes in East Africa, the Jie and Turkana.* London: Routledge and Kegan, 1955.

Hamilton, Angus. *Somaliland.* Westport, Conn.: Negro Universities Press, 1911/1970.

Hancock, Graham. *Lords of Poverty: The Power, Prestige, and Corruption of the International Aid Business.* New York: Atlantic Monthly Press, 1989.

Hanley, Gerald. *Warriors and Strangers.* London: Hamish Hamilton Ltd., 1971/1987.

Hannerz, Ulf. *Exploring the City: Inquiries Toward an Urban Anthropology.* New York: Columbia University Press, 1980.

Hansen, Karen Tranberg. *Distant Companions: Servants and Employers in Zambia, 1900–1985.* Ithaca: Cornell University Press, 1989.

Harden, Blaine. *Africa: Dispatches from a Fragile Continent.* Boston: Houghton Mifflin Co, 1990.

Hart, Keith, and Louise Sperling. "Cattle as capital," *Ethnos* 52, nos. 3–4 (1987).

Helander, Bernhard. "The social dynamics of southern Somalia agro- pastoralism: A regional approach," *Working Papers in African Studies,* 25 (1986).

———. The slaughtered camel: Coping with fictitious descent among the Hubeer of southern Somalia. Ph.D. diss., Uppsala University, 1988.

Helm, June (ed.). *Essays on the Problem of the Tribe.* Seattle: American Ethnological Society, 1968.

Hersi, Ali A. The Arab factor in Somali history: The origins and development of Arab enterprise and cultural influence in the Somali peninsula. Ph.D. diss., UCLA, 1977.

Hess, Robert L. *Italian Colonialism in Somalia.* Chicago: University of Chicago Press, 1966.

Hjort, Anders. "Ethnic transformation, dependency and change: the Ilgira Samburu of Northern Kenya," in John Galaty and P. Salzman (eds.), *Change and*

Development in Nomadic and Pastoral Societies. Leiden, the Netherlands: E. J. Brill, 1981.

Hoben, Allan. *Somalia: A Social and Institutional Profile*. Working paper SP-1, African Studies Center, Boston University, 1983.

———. "The political economy of land tenure in Somalia," in R. E. Downs and S. P. Reyna (eds.), *Land and Society in Contemporary Africa*. Hanover: University of New Hampshire Press, 1988.

Hobsbawm, E. J. *Nations and Nationalism Since 1780: Programme, Myth, Reality*. Cambridge: University of Cambridge Press, 1990.

Hobsbawm, E. J., and T. Ranger (eds.), *The Invention of Tradition*. Cambridge: Cambridge University Press, 1983.

Holt, Richard. "Agropastoralism and desertification in Ceel Dheer district: Preliminary investigation and trial results." CRDP technical report no. 3, 1985.

Holy, Ladislav. (ed.),. *Segmentary Lineage Systems Reconsidered*. Belfast: The Queen's University of Belfast, 1979.

Horowitz, Donald. *Ethnic Groups in Conflict*. Berkeley: University of California Press, 1985.

Horowitz, Michael. "The sociology of pastoralism and African livestock projects," *AID Program Evaluation Discussion Paper* no. 6, May 1979.

Hussein, Mohamed Ali. "Emic notes on camel breeds in Somalia," *Working Paper 17*, Somali Academy of Sciences and Arts, 1987a.

———. "Traditional practices of camel husbandry and management in Somalia," *Working Paper 19*, Somali Academy of Sciences and Arts, 1987b.

Hutchinson, Sharon. "Changing concepts of incest among the Nuer," *American Ethnologist* 12 (1985).

———. "The cattle of money and the cattle of girls among the Nuer, 1930–1983," *American Ethnologist*, 19 (1992).

Hyden, Goran. *No Shortcuts to Progress: African Development Management in Perspective*. Berkeley: University of California Press, 1983.

Indian Ocean Newsletter, 1981–1990.

Ingold, Tim. *Hunters, Pastoralists and Ranchers: Reindeer Economies and their Transformations*. Cambridge: Cambridge University Press, 1980.

Jamal, Vali. "Somalia: Survival in a 'doomed' economy," *International Labor Review* 127, no. 6 (1988).

James, F. L. *The Unknown Horn of Africa*. London: George Philip & Son, 1888.

Janzen, Jorg. "Economic relations between Somalia and Saudi Arabia: Livestock exports, labor migration, and the consequences for Somalia's development," *Northeast African Studies* 8, nos. 2–3 (1986).

Jardine, Douglas. *The Mad Mullah of Somaliland*. New York: Negro Universities Press, 1926/1969.

Johnson, Douglas. "The fighting Nuer: primary sources and the origins of a stereotype," *Africa* 51 (1981).

Johnson, John. *Heellooy, Heelleellooy: The Development of the Genre "Heello" in Modern Somali Poetry*. Bloomington: University of Indiana Press, 1974.

Kaplan, Mark. *The Economics of Trusteeship in Somalia*. Boston: Boston University Press, 1960.

Kellas, James. *The Politics of Nationalism and Ethnicity.* New York: St. Martin's Press, 1991.

Kelly, Raymond. *The Nuer Conquest: The Structure and Development of an Expansionist System.* Ann Arbor: University of Michigan Press, 1985.

Kertzer, David. *Ritual, Politics and Power.* New Haven: Yale University Press, 1988.

Kinross, Lord. *The Ottoman Centuries: The Rise and Fall of the Turkish Empire.* New York: First Morrow Quill, 1977.

Kuper, Adam. "Lineage theory: A critical retrospect," *Annual Review of Anthropology* (1982).

Laitin, David. "The political economy of military rule in Somalia," *Journal of Modern African Studies* 14, no. 3 (1976).

———. *Politics, Language, and Thought: The Somali Experience.* Chicago: University of Chicago Press, 1977.

———. "The war in the Ogaden: Implications for Siyaad's role in Somali history," *The Journal of Modern African Studies* 17, no. 1 (March 1979).

———. "The political crisis in Somalia," *Horn of Africa* 5, no. 2 (1982).

———. "The Ogaadeen question and changes in Somali identity," in D. Rothchild and V. A. Olorunsola (eds.), *State Versus Ethnic Claims: African Policy Dilemmas.* Boulder: Westview Press, 1983.

Laitin, David, and S. Samatar. *Somalia: Nation in Search of a State.* Boulder: Westview Press, 1987.

Lemarchand, Rene. "The state, the parallel economy, and the changing structure of patronage systems," in D. Rothchild and N. Chazan (eds.), *The Precarious Balance.* Boulder: Westview Press, 1988.

Lewis, Herbert. "The origin of the Gala and Somali." *Journal of African History* 1 (1966).

Lewis, I. M. *A Pastoral Democracy.* London: Oxford University Press, 1961.

———. *Marriage and the Family in Northern Somaliland.* Kampala, Uganda: East African Institute of Social Research, 1962.

———. "The problem of the NFD of Kenya," *Race* 5 (1963).

———. "Shaikhs and warriors in Somaliland," in M. Fortes and G. Dieterlen (eds.), *African Systems of Thought.* London: Oxford University Press, 1965.

———. "Conformity and contrast in Somali Islam," in I. M. Lewis (ed.), *Islam in Tropical Africa.* London: Oxford University Press, 1966.

———. "Integration in the Somali Republic," in Arthur Hazelwood (ed.), *African Integration and Disintegration: Case Studies in Economic and Political Union.* London: Oxford University Press, 1967.

———. "From nomadism to cultivation: the expansion of political solidarity in southern Somalia" in Mary Douglas and P. M. Kaberry (ed.), *Man in Africa.* London: Tavistock Publications, 1969a.

———. "Lineage continuity and modern commerce in northern Somaliland," in Paul Bohannan and G. Dalton (ed.), *Markets in Africa.* Chicago: Northwestern University Press, 1969b.

———. "Nationalism and particularism in Somalia," in P. H. Gulliver (ed.), *Tradition and Transition in East Africa: Studies of the Tribal Element in the Modern Era.* Berkeley: University of California Press, 1969c.

———. "The tribal factor in contemporary Africa," *Africa Contemporary Record* 2 (1969–1970).

———. "The politics of the 1969 Somali coup," *Journal of Modern African Studies,* 10, no. 3 (October 1972).

———. "Confessions of a government anthropologist," *Anthropological Forum* 4, no. 2 (1977).

———. "Kim Il-Sung in Somalia: the end of tribalism?" in William A. Shack and P. S. Cohen (eds.), *Politics in Leadership*. Oxford: Clarendon Press, 1979.

———. *A Modern History of Somalia: Nation and State in the Horn of Africa.* London: Longman, 1980.

———. *Social Anthropology in Perspective (Second Edition).* Cambridge: Cambridge University Press, 1976/1988.

———. *Somali Culture, History and Social Institutions: An Introductory Guide to the Somali Democratic Republic.* The London School of Economics and Political Science, 1978/1981.

———. "The Ogaden and the fragility of Somali segmentary nationalism," *African Affairs* 88 (1989).

Lewis, I. M., (ed.), *Nationalism and Self Determination in the Horn of Africa.* London: Ithaca Press, 1983.

Luling, Virginia. The social structure of southern Somali tribes. Ph.D. diss., University of London, 1971.

———. *Somali-English Dictionary.* Wheaton, MD: Dunwoody Press, 1987.

Lytton, Earl of. *The Stolen Desert.* London: Macdonald, 1966.

MacGaffey, Janet. *Entrepreneurs and Parasites: The Struggle for Indigenous Capitalism in Zaire.* Cambridge: Cambridge University Press, 1987.

———. *The Real Economy of Zaire.* Philadelphia: University of Pennsylvania Press, 1991.

Mann, Michael. *The Sources of Social Power.* Cambridge: Cambridge University, 1986.

Marlowe, David. The Galjaal Barsana of central Somalia: A lineage political system in a changing world. Ph.D. diss., Harvard University, 1963.

Marx, Emmanuel. *Bedouin of the Negev.* Manchester: Manchester University Press, 1967.

Mascott, Ltd. A study of the future of the Central Rangelands of Somalia: Final report, February 1986.

Mauss, Marcel. *The Gift.* New York: W. W. Norton & Co., 1967.

Maybury-Lewis, David. "Conclusion," in David Maybury-Lewis (ed.), *The Prospects for Plural Societies.* Washington, D.C.: The American Ethnological Society, 1984.

Mehemet, Ozay. "The effectiveness of foreign aid—the case of Somalia," *Journal of Modern African Studies* 9, no. 1 (1971).

Merryman, Nancy. Economic and ecological stress: Household strategies of transitional Somali pastoralists in Northern Kenya. Ph.D. diss., Northwestern University, 1984.

Migdal, Joel. *Strong Societies and Weak States: State-Society Relations and State Capabilities in the Third World.* Princeton: Princeton University Press, 1988.

Miller, Norman. "The other Somalia," *Horn of Africa* 5, no. 3 (1982).

Mitchell, J. Clyde. "Tribe and social change in South Central Africa: A situational approach," *Journal of Asian and African Studies* 5 (1970).

Moore, Sally Falk. "Explaining the present: Theoretical dilemmas in processual ethnography," *American Ethnologist* 14, no. 4 (1987).

Nelson, Harold D. (ed.),. *Somalia: A Country Study.* Washington, D.C.: Department of the Army, 1982.

News from Africa Watch, July 25, 1989; July 21, 1989.

O'Brien, Donal Cruise. *Saints and Politicians: Essays in the Organization of a Senegalese Peasant Society.* Cambridge: Cambridge University Press, 1975.

O'Brien, Rita Cruise. *White Society in Black Africa: The French of Senegal.* London: Faber and Faber, 1972.

Ododa, Harry. "Somalia's domestic politics and foreign relations since the Ogaden War of 1977–78," *Middle Eastern Studies* 21, no. 3 (1985).

Ottaway, Marina. *Soviet and American Influence in the Horn of Africa.* New York: Praeger, 1982.

Paine, Robert. "Animals as capital: Comparisons among northern nomadic herders and hunters," *Anthropological Quarterly* 44, no. 3 (1971).

Pankhurst, Richard. "The trade of the Gulf of Aden ports of Africa in the 19th and early 20th centuries," *Journal of Ethiopian Studies* 3, no. 1 (1965a).

———. "The trade of southern and western Ethiopia and the Indian Ocean ports in the 19th and early 20th centuries," *Journal of Ethiopian Studies* 3, no. 2 (1965b).

Pankhurst, Sylvia. *Ex-Italian Somaliland.* London: Watts and Co., 1951.

Parkin, David. *The Cultural Definition of Political Response: Lineal Descent Among the Luo.* New York: Academic Press, 1978.

Parry, J., and M. Bloch (eds.). *Money and the Morality of Exchange.* Cambridge: Cambridge University Press, 1989.

Patman, Robert. *The Soviet Union in the Horn of Africa.* Cambridge: Cambridge University Press, 1990.

Putnam, Diana. A cultural interpretation of development: Developers, values, and agricultural change in the Somali context. Ph.D. diss., Bryn Mawr College, 1984.

Puzo, William. Mogadishu, Somalia: Geographic assets of its evolution, population, functions, and morphology. Ph.D. diss., UCLA, 1972.

Ragsdale, Tod, and A. S. Ali. "A case study of the resettlement of nomads in Somalia," in A. S. Oberai (ed.), *Land Settlement Policies and Population Redistribution in Developing Countries.* New York: Praeger, 1988.

Rayne, Major H. *Sun, Sand and Somalis: Leaves from the Notebook of a District Commissioner in British Somaliland.* London: H. F. & G Witherby, 1921a.

———. "Somal marriage," *Journal of the Africa Society* 21, no. 81 (1921b).

Rosaldo, Renato. *Culture and Truth.* Boston: Beacon Press, 1989.

Rothchild, Donald, and Naomi Chazan (eds.). *The Precarious Balance: State and Society in Africa.* Boulder: Westview Press, 1988.

Rubenson, Sven. "Ethiopia and the Horn," in John Flint (ed.), *The Cambridge History of Africa, V (from c. 1790 to c. 1870).* Cambridge: Cambridge University Press, 1976.

Sahlins, Marshall. *Islands of History.* Chicago: University of Chicago Press, 1985.

Salzman, Philip (ed.), *When Nomads Settle: Processes of Sedentarization as Adaptation and Response.* New York: Praeger, 1980.

Samatar, Abdi I. "The state, agrarian change and crisis of hegemony in Somalia," *Review of African Political Economy* 43 (1988).

———. *The State and Rural Transformation in Northern Somalia, 1884–1986.* Madison: University of Wisconsin Press, 1989.

Samatar, Abdi I., and Ahmed I. Samatar. "The material roots of the suspended African state: Arguments from Somalia," *Journal of Modern African Studies* 24, no. 4 (1987).

Samatar, Ahmed I. *Socialist Somalia: Rhetoric and Reality.* London: Zed Books, 1988.

Samatar, Said. *Oral Poetry and Somali Nationalism: the Case of Sayyid Mahammad Abdille Hasan.* Cambridge: Cambridge University Press, 1982.

Sanderson, G. N. "The Nile Basin and the Eastern Horn, 1870–1908," in R. Oliver and G. N. Sanderson (eds.), *The Cambridge History of Africa, vol. 6, 1870–1905.* Cambridge: Cambridge University Press, 1985.

Schancle, Didrikke. "Executions, Arrests Follow Religious Riots in Somalia," Associated Press, July 21, 1989.

Schlee, Gunther. *Identities on the Move: Clanship and Pastoralism in Northern Kenya.* Manchester: Manchester University Press, 1989.

Schneider, David. *Livestock and Equality in East Africa.* Bloomington: University of Indiana Press, 1979.

Scott, James. *The Moral Economy of the Peasant: Subsistence and Rebellion in Southeast Asia.* New Haven: Yale University Press, 1976.

———. *Weapons of the Weak: Everyday Forms of Peasant Resistance.* New Haven: Yale University Press, 1985.

Selassie, Bereket Habte. *Conflict and Intervention in the Horn of Africa.* New York: Monthly Review Press, 1980.

Service, Elman. *Primitive Social Organization.* New York: Random House, 1968/1962.

Seton-Watson, Christopher. *Italy from Liberalism to Fascism 1870–1925.* London: Methuen & Co., 1967.

Sheikh-Abdi, Abdi. "Ideology and leadership in Somalia," *Journal of Modern African Studies* 19, no. 1 (March 1981).

Shepherd, George W. Jr., "Dominance and conflict on the Horn: Notes of United States-Soviet rivalry," *Africa Today* 32, no. 3 (1985).

Sheriff, A.M.H. "The slave mode of production along the East African Coast, 1810–1873," in John R. Willis (ed.), *Slaves and Slavery in Muslim Africa.* London: Frank Cass, 1985.

Shipton, Parker. *Bitter Money: Cultural Economy and Some African Meanings of Forbidden Economies.* American Ethnological Society monograph series, 1, 1989.

Simons, Anna. Networks of dissolution in Somalia. Ph.D. diss., Harvard University, 1992.

———. "The Beginning of the End," in C. Nordstrom and A. Robbens, *Fieldwork Under Fire*. Berkeley: University of California press, forthcoming.

Smith, Andrew. *Pastoralism in Africa: Origins and Development Ecology.* London: Hurst & Company, 1992.

Smith, Anthony. *State and Nation in the Third World: the Western State and African Nationalism.* New York: St. Martin's Press, 1983.

———. *The Ethnic Origins of Nations.* Oxford: Blackwell, 1986.

Smith, Dennis Mack. *Mussolini's Roman Empire.* London: Penguin Books, 1976/1977.

Smith, M. G. "The nature and variety of plural unity," in David Maybury-Lewis (ed.), *The Prospects for Plural Societies.* Washington, D.C.: The American Ethnological Society, 1984.

Somali Ministry of Planning. "Somali civil service study," 1984.

Southall, Aidan. "The illusion of tribe," *Journal of Asian and African Studies,* vol. 5, 1970.

Spear, Thomas, and Richard Waller (eds.). *Being Maasai.* London: James Currey, 1993.

Spencer, Paul. *Nomads in Alliance: Symbiosis and Growth Among the Rendille and Samburu of Kenya.* Oxford: Clarendon Press, 1973.

Swayne, Major H.G.C. *Seventeen Trips Through Somaliland and a Visit to Abyssinia.* London: Rowland Ward, Ltd., 1900.

Swift, Jeremy. "The development of livestock trading in a nomad pastoral economy: The Somali case," in *Pastoral Production and Society.* Cambridge: Cambridge University Press, 1979.

Tapper, Richard. "Introduction," in R. Tapper (ed.), *The Conflict of Tribe and State in Iran and Afghanistan.* New York: St. Martin's Press, 1983.

Thompson, Virginia, and Richard Adloff. *Djibouti and the Horn of Africa.* Stanford: Stanford University Press, 1968.

Touval, Saadia. *Somali Nationalism: International Politics and the Drive for Unity in the Horn of Africa.* Cambridge: Harvard University Press, 1963.

Tucker, Jonathan. "The politics of refugees in Somalia," *Horn of Africa* 5, no. 3 (1982).

Turner, Victor. *Schism and Continuity in an African Society.* Manchester: Manchester University Press, 1957.

———. *The Ritual Process: Structure and Anti-Structure.* Ithaca: Cornell University Press, 1969.

Turney-High, Harry H. *Primitive War: Its Practice and Concepts.* Columbia: University of South Carolina Press, 1949/1991.

Vail, Leroy (ed.). *The Creation of Tribalism in Southern Africa.* Berkeley: University of California Press, 1991.

van der Bor, Wout (ed.). *The Art of Beginning: First Experiences and Problems of Western Expatriates in Developing countries with Special Emphasis on Rural Development and Rural Education.* Netherlands: Pudoc Wageningen, 1983.

Verdon, Michael. "Where have all their lineages gone? Cattle and descent among the Nuer," *American Anthropologist* 84, nos. 3–4 (1982).

Western, David. "The environment and ecology of pastoralists in arid savannas," *Development and Change* 13, no. 2 (April 1982).

Wolf, Eric. *Europe and the People without History.* Berkeley: University of California Press, 1982.

World Bank. "Somalia: Towards economic recovery and growth," report no. 5584-SO, 1985.

———. "Somalia agricultural sector survey main report and strategy," report no. 6131-SO, 1987a.

———. "Somalia: Recent economic developments and medium-term prospects," Report no. 6542-SO, 1987b.

Worsley, Peter. *The Trumpet Shall Sound.* New York: Shocken Books, 1968.

———. "The three modes of nationalism," in David Maybury-Lewis (ed.), *The Prospects for Plural Societies.* Washington, D.C.: The American Ethnological Society, 1984.

Young, Crawford. *The Politics of Cultural Pluralism.* Madison: University of Wisconsin Press, 1976.

——— (ed.). *The Rising Tide of Cultural Pluralism: The Nation-State at Bay?* Madison: University of Wisconsin Press, 1993.

Young, Crawford, and Thomas Turner. *The Rise and Decline of the Zairian State.* Madison: University of Wisconsin Press, 1985.

About the Book and Author

In this penetrating and timely book, Anna Simons documents Somalia's impending slide toward anarchy. How do people react to a failing yet still repressive government? What do they do when the banks run out of cash? How do they cope with unprecedented uncertainty? These are some of the questions Simons addresses as she introduces the reader to Somalia's descent into dissolution from within the Somali capital of Mogadishu.

Exploring the volatile mix of external interest in Somalia, internal politicking, and enduring social structure, she shows how cross-cultural misunderstanding and regroupment are key to explaining Somalia's breakdown at the national level. One aim of this book is to challenge broadly held assumptions about the content of nationalism, tribalism, and the state, as defined and debated by academics and as experienced by individuals. Another is to analyze the making of a pivotal moment in Somali history. Simons charts new ground in the study of the dissolution of a state at all levels, shuttling back and forth between micro and macro frames, historical and everyday practices, and expatriate and Somali experiences.

Anna Simons is assistant professor of anthropology at the University of California at Los Angeles.

Index